Social Theory and the Crisis of State Socialism

STUDIES OF COMMUNISM IN TRANSITION

General Editor: Ronald J. Hill
*Professor of Comparative Government
and Fellow of Trinity College
Dublin, Ireland*

Studies of Communism in Transition is an important series which applies academic analysis and clarity of thought to the recent traumatic events in Eastern and Central Europe. As many of the preconceptions of the past half century are cast aside, newly independent and autonomous sovereign states are being forced to address long-term, organic problems which had been suppressed by, or appeased within, the communist system of rule.

The series is edited under the sponsorship of Lorton House, an independent charitable association which exists to promote the academic study of communism and related concepts.

Social Theory and the Crisis of State Socialism

Larry J. Ray

Department of Sociology
Lancaster University, UK

STUDIES OF COMMUNISM IN TRANSITION

Edward Elgar
Cheltenham, UK • Brookfield, US

Published by
Edward Elgar Publishing Limited
8 Lansdown Place
Cheltenham
Glos. GL50 2HU
UK

Edward Elgar Publishing Company
Old Post Road
Brookfield
Vermont 05036
US

British Library Cataloguing in Publication Data

Ray, Larry
  Social theory and the crisis of state socialism. – (Studies of
  communism in transition)
  1. Social sciences – philosophy 2. Post-communism – Europe,
  Eastern 3. Europe, Eastern – Social conditions – 1989–
  I. Title II. Series
  303.4

Library of Congress Cataloguing in Publication Data

  Social theory and the crisis of state socialism / Larry J. Ray.
  (Studies of communism in transition)
  1. Postmodernism—Social aspects. 2. Communism and society.
  3. Communism. 4. Post-communism. I. Title. II. Series.
  HM73.R39 1996
  303.4—dc20   95–42409
                                                  CIP

1 85278 688 4

Electronic typesetting by Lorton Hall

Printed and bound in Great Britain by
Hartnolls Limited, Bodmin, Cornwall

Contents

Figures

Figures

Charts

Acknowledgements

I am grateful for assistance provided in preparation for this work by the British Council, the Gorbachev Foundation, the Friedrich Ebert Stiftung and Lancaster University Research Fund, although the opinions and any errors are my own. Thanks to Ronald Hill for meticulous editing. I gratefully acknowledge the permission granted by Professor Grzegorz Kołodko to reproduce Figure 5.4, which appeared in his Report to the IMF, *From Output Collapse to Sustainable Growth in Transition Economies* (1992). I am indebted to a host of colleagues and friends who, over the past few years, have assisted in different ways with the collection of material for this book. The following merit particular thanks: Reni Avramova, Ferenc Erös, Jerzy Hausner, Bob Jessop, Stoyan Kambourov, the late Lyuben Nikolov, Vasilka Nikolova, Mark Ournov, Sasha Ournov and family, Caroline Schwaller, Ekaterina Squires and Zsuzsa Vajda. Finally to Emma, for patience, support and encouragement, very special thanks.

1. Introduction: Social Theory and Socialism

The theoretical debates that have occupied sociologists most during the 1980s and 1990s are concerned mainly with advanced capitalist societies. Issues surrounding modernity and post-modernity, new social and economic spatial organization, globalization and the risk society, for example, originate in places where the contours of an industrialism familiar to classical sociologists have receded. In their place are the new profiles of consumer and leisure cultures, information technologies, service industries, global media, and new risks such as social disorder, declining welfare and the threat of ecological disaster. In the midst of this rethinking the social terrain, the collapse of communism in Europe and Western Asia further transformed familiar landscapes. Yet there is little agreement as to what its significance is, except perhaps that the world after the fall of the Wall harbours further risks, of westward migration, an uncomfortably close civil war and resurgent nationalism. What is not so clear is how the central debates of sociological theory bear on either the experience of bureaucratic state socialism or its transition to post-communism.

Indeed, sociological theory was the product of US–European modernity and its concepts and frames of analysis have tended to remain tied to the development of late capitalist societies. Thus attempts to account for state socialist social systems have often begun from the premise that they are variants, albeit deviant ones, of familiar forms. This is illustrated in the widely different views of the relationship between communism and modernity. Soviet systems have been understood sometimes as the essence, perhaps the promise, of modernity – the embodiment of instrumental reason and technical progress – and sometimes as a grand failure that was doomed because it lacked the flexibility and diversity of Western, market-oriented social systems. For some Western intellectuals, especially in the 1930s, the Soviet

Union was, as the Webbs said, a New Civilization. The mirror image of this view appears in those for whom Soviet communism represented a culmination of the Enlightenment's 'tyranny of reason' (Bauman 1992). This point of view draws on Weber's 'iron cage' thesis, and to some extent on Adorno and Horkheimer's denunciation of instrumental reason in *Dialectics of Enlightenment* (1944/1973). It appears for example in Arendt's concept of totalitarianism and in Václav Havel's (1988) claim that the Soviet systems represented 'the inevitable consequences of rationalism', of the break with *Naturwelt* and an immediate pre-rational empathy with nature.

Zigmunt Bauman further links this critique to the claim that the collapse of communism signals the exhaustion of the project of modernity. He sees Soviet societies, with their giant steel mills, grandiose irrigation schemes, mass mobilization and new Soviet men and women, as archetypes of modernist productivism. Bauman argues that

> Like socialism ... communism was thoroughly modern in its passionate conviction that a good society can only be a carefully designed, managed and thoroughly industrialized society. ... Communism was modernity in its most determined mood and most decisive posture ... purified of the last shred of the chaotic, the irrational, the spontaneous, the unpredictable ... (1992:166–7)

Confronted by a post-modern consumer society in the West, the obsolete steel-per-head philosophy proved no match for the lure of the narcissistic culture of self-enhancement, self-enjoyment, instant gratification. Similarly, Paul Piccone (1989) claims that the collapse of communism signals the end of the Enlightenment vision of social reconstruction through scientific planning. On the other hand, writers such as Fehér, Heller and Márkus (1984), Janos (1991), Kopstein (1994) and Sztompka (1993) regard communism as a failed modernity, a faked copy that having unsuccessfully attempted to reform in the 1960s, retreated into conservative stagnation prior to its eventual demise. This argument can be developed, as it has been by Habermas (1990) and Holmes (1993) for example, into a defence of the as yet unfulfilled potential of modernity, rather than its exhaustion.

Yet this raises the question of what form of modernity, what terrible beauty, is being born. Both these views imply a core model of 'modernity' which the Soviets either fulfilled, or from which they deviated. Debates about the existence of such a model go to the core of sociological understandings of the contemporary world, debates that have become all the more poignant in the light of the post-communist transformation. Western admirers projected on to the Soviet Union (and later Eastern Europe and China) fantasies of a type of modernity – rationally planned, socially just and harmonious – that has not existed anywhere. This being so, the reverse side of the argument, Bauman's vision of communism as a demonic modernity, is surely fantasy too. An alternative and more nuanced view, developed for example by Arnason (1993), suggests that 'modernity' is an ambiguous field of tensions that admits 'counter-paradigms', fusions of modernism and traditionalism that simultaneously claim to be morally superior to Western modernity and to prefigure its future. This will be considered in Chapter 3.

However, this still leaves unanswered the question why, after decades of crisis management, did Soviet systems disintegrate so rapidly and decisively? In accounting for the fate of Soviet-type societies one encounters central sociological questions about how societies cohere and reproduce themselves over time, despite severe social strains and periodic crises. What are the limits of systemic adaptation that precipitate the transition from one type of society into another? Addressing the integrating dynamics of societies, sociologists have paid attention to cultural traditions, values or normative consensus; concepts of territory, ethnicity and religion; the institutional system, hegemony, legitimacy or social control systems; and even (as with Niklas Luhmann) the integrating properties of complexity itself. Disintegrative forces, on the other hand, typically tend to include mass organized opposition; class, status or intra-élite conflict; systemic crisis and multiple dysfunctions; legitimation crises; and externally-induced destabilization. The analysis here will examine these issues, while drawing on the recent work of writers such as Luhmann, Offe, Arato, and Habermas, in ways which have been explored to some extent in Ray (1993).

A central theme here will be how the crisis of socialism arose in such a way that significant sections of its élite came to the view that fundamental change was desirable, which in part accounts both for the speed of the collapse and for the direction taken by post-communist

developments. In Autumn 1985 I interviewed the Director of the Institute of Marxism–Leninism at the Medical University of Szeged, a
medium-sized city in south-eastern Hungary. In the light of events in
the following few years, what he had to say was of considerable
importance. As we sat in his well-appointed office, in leather-
upholstered furniture, under a huge portrait of Lenin, he explained, in a
cautious but matter-of-fact way, how the Institute, which had formerly
exercised ideological surveillance within the Medical School, was re-
defining its role in common with similar bodies elsewhere in Hungary.
Having abandoned teaching Marxism–Leninism, the Institute now
offered a forum for discussion of sociological, historical and
philosophical issues, which included studies of the potential relevance
of Western multi-party systems for Eastern European societies. He
went further, to describe how the one-party system, along with the
centrally-directed economy in Hungary were now redundant, and the
Institute was formulating models for a multi-party, competitive system
in which the ruling Hungarian Socialist Workers' Party (HSWP), his
party, would contest elections in the not-so-distant future. He was not
an opposition intellectual, but a voice from within the heart of the
system, and he was not merely expressing his own opinion, but the
policy of (perhaps one faction of) the ruling Party. In the course of
other interviews, such as those at the Institute of Social Sciences in
Budapest (then the research bureau of the Party's Central Committee)
similar views to those of the Director were expressed. The Party's own
research bureau was engaged in work, among other things, on
legitimation problems in socialist systems, social inequalities in
Hungary, the 'second economy' and, again, the relevance of the
experience of the Western democracies for socialist systems.

It is true that Hungary had periodically been experimenting with
reform communism since the New Economic Mechanism of the early
1970s, which had created the basis for a kind of market socialism, and
it is further true that by the mid-1980s Hungarians enjoyed more freedom of expression than people elsewhere in the communist bloc. So
one might not be surprised to find radical and experimental ideas there,
even from a Director of a Marxism–Leninism Institute, or from the
Party's research bureau. However, others, especially those outside the
Party, were far more sceptical about the prospects for political
pluralization or economic restructuring in the foreseeable future, and

remained so a few years later, immediately prior to the collapse. This indicated, perhaps, that a change of considerable significance was maturing, not only because of external pressure to improve political and economic relations with the West, although this was certainly a factor, but also because of a movement within the ruling group itself that was in effect preparing for its abdication.

This view was reinforced three years later, in a different context, at a meeting of young researchers at the Academy of Social Sciences of the Central Committee of the Bulgarian Communist Party. Unlike Hungary, Bulgaria in the 1980s was hardly thought of as a place for experiment and innovation within the communist system. Yet at the September meeting of the Social Sciences and Management Academy at the Central Committee of the BCP (AONSU) in Varna, radical criticism of the system was again evident, now encouraged by some visiting Soviet economists who advocated, for example, the joint-stock company as a model for 'socialist property', wage differentials as a stimulus to motivation, along with investment autonomy for banks and enterprises. Whether participants at this meeting favoured Western-style political economic models, or some variant of what was understood as Yugoslavian self-management, or more decentralized council communism, there was a consensus that it was impossible to continue with the existing set of social organizations. The centralized statist system had exhausted its reproductive capacities and would have to yield to something else. Again, from within the heart of the system, from its privileged intellectual milieu, came demands for a radical change.

Of course, these kinds of proposals for pluralization of the system were to become dominant, if highly contested, among the leadership in the Soviet Union in the later years of Gorbachev's rule, and the events described above to some extent merely reflected this. However, these anecdotes are significant in that they illustrate how, in the absence of organized mass opposition (this was not Poland) the impulse for change was articulated from within a ruling group that was experiencing a profound crisis of confidence in its legitimacy and capacity to rule. It was not really surprising then, that in Hungary in 1989 it was Imre Poszgay of the HSWP who initiated the formation of the Democratic Round Table with which the abdication of the government was negotiated. This pattern of abdication, often preceded by a reformist coup within the ruling party (e.g. the ousting of Zhivkov in

Bulgaria, Honecker in the DDR, or Kádár in Hungary) was to be replayed in different ways throughout the bloc between 1989 and 1992.

What is not so clear is how one might explain this remarkable process and its consequences. Although the collapse of communist governments came as a surprise to many in the West, their demise had actually been long expected, if in a rather general way. Nearly forty years ago in *The New Class*, for example, Milovan Djilas predicted that,

> [w]hen the new class leaves the historical scene – and this must happen – there will be less sorrow over its passing than there was for any other class before it. Smothering everything except what suited its ego, it has condemned itself to failure and shameful ruin. (Djilas 1957:69)

The view that a bankrupt system could not indefinitely survive its legitimacy deficit was shared by other commentators such as Ferenc Fehér, Agnes Heller and György Márkus, who predicted that a new global crisis was 'again approaching Eastern European societies [since] the very consequences of the working of this system undermine the social basis on which post-Stalinist stabilization has rested to date' (1984:21–2). Bugajski and Pollack (1989:1) identified a submerged network of social and political fault lines across the communist states, although they cautioned that it was premature to predict an imminent earthquake. An understanding of crisis tendencies, though, needs to be linked to an account of how Soviet societies were able to survive for as long as they did, despite huge dysfunctions, and why the implosion finally occurred.

What was the Soviet system? The answer to this question is far from obvious, and a variety of core features have been proposed that will be discussed in Chapter 4. Broadly speaking though, the system can be understood in terms of the command economy, which was centralized and planned, geared to rapid agro-industrial growth, with a high percentage of GDP accumulated, particularly through sudden spurts of mass mobilization, underpinned by terror or its threat. This ensemble has sometimes been described as 'Soviet Fordism', an application or exaggeration of the organizational forms of capitalist Fordism, such as synchronization of production flows, gigantic scale and product standardization. To what extent this analogy is valid will be discussed in Chapter 3, which considers points of convergence and divergence between the Soviet and capitalist systems. However, the very notion that these were 'planned' societies and economies is open to serious doubt, since central planning agencies could not use the majority of planning information they received, and local enterprise organization and resource management was consequently often ad hoc.

Soviet systems did not offer a unitary model of socialism, but rather a diversity of adaptations subject to national evolution and experiment, as the core Soviet system of militaristic industrialization gave way to reform and routinization, amidst increasing disorganization. By the 1980s the strategy of industrialization based on extensive growth had become inflexible and deeply enmeshed in self-generated limits, in particular its inability to satisfy consumer demand combined with lack of innovation and motivation. These were identified as key problems in the 1960s by Soviet academicians such as Abel Aganbegyan, whose Novosibirsk Economics Institute later developed plans for perestroika. Indeed, the whole post-Stalin period (from 1953) was marked by gradual decentralization, increasing incentives for work brigades, a decline of terror, increased *de*-politicization and a tacit understanding between political leaders and people. By the 1970s this was being described as 'Brezhnevite corporatism', an arrangement often parodied as 'you pretend to work: we pretend to pay you'. How this system underwent critical strains and the implications it had for the motivation and legitimacy resources available to Soviet states will be discussed in Chapters 5 and 6.

Now that the New Class of Party bureaucrats and its privileged élite, the nomenklatura, appears to have left the historical scene (in Europe at least) social scientists have a rare opportunity to examine first-hand the disintegration of a complex form of social integration and its replacement by other, diverse forms of society and economy. However, Western social science did not develop a systematic theory of Soviet-style socialism, which makes it all the more difficult to comprehend the current transition. Many sociologists have analysed Soviet-type systems, such as David Lane, Andrew Arato, Ivan Szelenyi, T.H. Rigby, Agnes Heller, Maria Márkus, György Márkus and Ferenc Fehér. Yet mainstream sociological theory rarely gave detailed consideration to state socialism while, according to Ken

Jowitt (1991), the great failing of communist studies, in contrast to Latin American studies, has been a marked disdain for theory.

On the other hand, sociological theory tended to deal with Soviet societies in an ad hoc way, as deviations from a core model of modernity, while the core concepts of political sociology – social integration, legitimacy, social class, élite/mass, the state, party, and even bureaucratic organization can be applied to Soviet systems only with difficulty.[1] For example, the influential model of totalitarianism in its various guises was informed by the cognitive framework of the Cold War, and produced forms of theorizing which were insufficiently sensitive to the underlying dynamics and diversity within the 'Eastern Bloc'. As a result, sociologists of state socialism tended to work with a polarized model of 'Party–State versus society', in which systemic change could arise only through the triumph of the latter over the former. Two problems with this view were that, first, it underemphasized the extent of disorganization within Soviet administrative systems; and second, it obscured the way in which, adapting to systemic differentiation, key élite groups began to disengage from the very structures upon which they were previously dependent. Further, these conceptual polarities risk mistaking political codes, binary oppositions that enhance the selectivity of the political system (such as state versus society) for analytical categories.

Meanwhile, with the major exception of feminist research, the dominant paradigms of sociological theory – Marxism, Weberianism, systemic functionalism, regulation theory, critical theory – tend to address primarily the social organization of official public spheres, states, civil society, social classes, social structure, parties and organizations. Yet it will be argued that understanding Soviet systems (and contemporary problems of the transition) requires a theory of latent integration through the informal channels of the socio-cultural system that took place in ways that could not be acknowledged by the authorities, because to do so would have undermined their authority. Where such issues are addressed by mainstream sociology, with refer-

---

1 The enigma represented by Soviet-type systems is reflected in the plethora of concepts which appeared at different times, with different degrees of theorization, such as 'totalitarian', 'state capitalist', 'actually existing socialism', 'bureaucratic socialism', 'bureaucratic collectivism', and 'neo-patrimonialism'. The relatively neutral term 'Soviet-type societies' will be used here.

ence to sub-cultures or the micro-dynamics of social interaction, this tends to assume a conflict between institutional and informal goals. In Soviet systems, though, integration was performed through increasing, if largely unacknowledged, symbiosis between public and private systems in a kind of privatization of apparently public political and bureaucratic institutions. This set these systems apart from the formal–rational public culture of (Western) modernity, the implications of which are addressed throughout this book, but especially in Chapters 5 and 7.

This bears on a further issue, the tradition–modernity dichotomy which has been, and arguably remains, central to sociological thinking even where a third phase of late, post, or reflexive modernity is added to the evolutionary schema.[2] In some versions, this approach implies a kind of optimal convergence in which industrial societies tend towards similar core organizational forms. This issue is central to understanding the risks involved in the transition to capitalism in post-communist societies, which is often presented as a problem of modernization, of overcoming archaic cultural and institutional practices. Although the modernization thesis was generally advanced in relation to the developing world, convergence theory (Kerr et al. 1960) suggested that the process of optimal evolution would involve a bi-polar convergence of capitalist and socialist systems, driven by a logic common to industrial societies. Although heavily criticized during the 1970s, the notion of convergence between socialism and capitalism has resurfaced since 1989 in a variety of forms, including Habermas' (1990) notion of the 'rectifying revolutions' of 1989 through which the East 'overcame distance' from the Western world.

An alternative view is that there can be no single model of modernity to which developing regions should aspire, because one country's potential is affected partly by how it is integrated into the global

2 The decline of Marxist theory in Western sociology in the 1980s was attended by a resurgence of interest in the character of 'modernity'. Always an ambiguous notion open to a plurality of interpretations, modernity has been qualified by temporal specifications, such as post-industrial (Bell 1973); post-modernity (e.g. Bauman 1992; Lyotard 1990); reflexive or high modernity (Giddens 1990). Although indicative of real theoretical disagreements, there are common themes here concerning the diminution of bi-polar class conflict, the growth of tertiary sectors, and expansion of cultural, consumption and leisure activities as constitutive features of contemporary society.

system, and anyway no industrial nation exactly recapitulates the experience of another. Thus each nation's developmental path is conditioned by its particular historical experience (e.g. experience of colonialism, absolutism, religious and cultural traditions) and its mode of integration into the world system (e.g. terms of trade, level of debt, relative costs of production and competitive advantage). According to this view, capital accumulation in the world system creates increasing heterogeneity rather than approximation to a single cultural or economic form of organization. If this is so, then the Soviet systems in which Bauman and others see the essence of modernity, might be better understood as peripheral to developed core regions of the world, deploying communism as an ideology of mass mobilization, until this dissipated and became largely ritualistic. If Leninism was a revolt against backwardness (von Laue 1971:3), which produced a substitute for, rather than a variant of, Western institutions (Jowitt 1978), then there is no reason to expect a smooth transition to Western-type social organization so long as the systemic inequalities between the capitalist core and post-socialist regions persist.

Bureaucratic-socialist societies, then, posed dilemmas for sociology on at least three levels. First, there was the problem of identifying the system of stratification and structural contradictions. Second, there was the problem of explaining the rapidity of the system's collapse following decades of more or less successful crisis management and answering the question, why did the systems disintegrate when and how they did? Third, there is the problem of understanding the present trajectory of post-socialism as it manifests in the diverse countries of the former Soviet bloc. This book aims to contribute to these debates by developing a framework of sociological explanation around four central claims, which in due course will be qualified and elaborated.

First, in complex societies forms of co-ordination are developed that enable a large volume of anonymous interactions to occur, tasks accomplished in capitalist societies principally by money and bureaucratic power. If money is to act as a store of value, and political decisions are to be effective, they both require social embedding in ways that generate confidence and legitimacy. Both of these are provisional and depend upon structures for negotiating and mediating diverse interests and identities, as well as a juridical system of rights and redress. According to a long sociological tradition, these in turn tend towards the formalization of society in which procedural claims to authority replace substantive ones (such as religion) and rules of conduct supersede dominant values.

Second, Soviet societies likewise required impersonal co-ordination and compensated for the limited role of money by the politicization of everyday life via the vanguard Party. However, establishing the authority of the Party through terror and its threat was intended to reduce primary group loyalties in favour of commitment to the organization and leader, but had the reverse effect of undermining trust in official agencies, media and institutions, which in turn encouraged retreat into private life. Impersonal, systemic trust is essential for anonymous co-ordination to operate effectively, but impersonal steering was increasingly replaced by informal cultures of reciprocity and clientelism at all levels. These became increasingly important the more reforms attempted to increase innovation by decentralization. In these informal networks, such as the 'second economy', de-bureaucratized social spaces, new forms of opposition and social organization took shape, which were to have considerable significance for the subsequent transformation.

Third, as dysfunctions of Soviet systems became more visible, reform communism, generally involving increased scope for market regulation, often legitimated, and thereby encouraged, the privatization of state resources by members of the political and economic élite. Informal economic activity had placed state property (often regarded as 'nobody's property') in a grey area subject to competing proprietary rights among those who used it. The abdication of communist governments in the European socialist states seems to have permitted the conversion of the political power of a status group, the former nomenklatura, into economic power deriving from ownership of newly privatized resources. This has the capacity to be re-converted into political power through the sponsorship of political parties, evidenced in the recent success of post-communist parties throughout the region. Meanwhile, by disengaging from direct control of the economy, and separating the political and economic systems, new sources of formal legitimation might be released. Certainly this process generates unintended consequences, and it is not being argued that there is a simple continuity between the former nomenklatura and new class formations. However, it is likely that the former nomenklatura will be key players in whatever new alliances of forces emerge.

Finally, despite their attempt to develop an autarkic growth strategy, Soviet states were from the outset coupled with the world economic order upon which they remained dependent in various ways, for example for technology or credit. Indeed, as global integration increased, so the crisis of state socialism worsened. The post-socialist transition is a site of conflict over modes of integration into the global system, in which quite different regional and sub-regional interests come into play. How these are resolved at national and sub-national levels will be crucial for the fate of post-communist transitions. The potential for democratic citizenship, which was after all the principle goal of the anti-communist revolutions, is threatened both by exclusive, nationalist definitions of community and the rapid dislocations of social order arising from rapid marketization. Both of these are caught up with and are responses to a complex local and global nexus.

Chapters 2 and 3 will discuss sociological theory in relation to Soviet systems. The specific sociological features of Soviet-type societies will be described in Chapters 4 and 5. Chapter 6 discusses the particular patterns of conflict arising from this mode of domination. Chapters 7, 8 and 9 discuss the implications of the crisis of state socialism for the new Great Transformation. This study takes account of the specific national and cultural traditions and post-war histories and identifies the major problems of the transition mostly in four countries: Russia, Hungary, Bulgaria and Poland. These countries are selected because they illustrate different phases and models of the transition. In the Soviet Union (most data will relate to Russia), inner-Party conflicts of long gestation – arguably originating in the Stalin period itself – combined with economic crisis to produce a reforming leadership whose actions had unintended (and largely unwanted) consequences. Poland illustrated weak crisis management throughout the post-war period, for historically-specific reasons, and the government eventually confronted a religiously-based mass movement of workers – a process without parallel elsewhere in the bloc. Hungary displayed a long period of reform and experiment with deviations from the Soviet model (market socialism and cultural liberalization) which had its origins in the aftermath of 1956. While exemplifying the ability of bureaucratic socialism to generate mechanisms of crisis-management, Hungarian reform communism ultimately created conditions in the 1980s for the abdication of the Party. Bulgaria, though receiving less attention in Western literature than the other cases, illustrates a divergent route of transition. In December 1989, Bulgaria emerged out of the unreformed neo-Stalinism of Todor Zhivkov, to begin a year of upheaval which left the Communist (latterly Socialist) Party with a parliamentary majority, but with only tenuous legitimacy in the urban areas. This has subsequently been strengthened as the Bulgarian Socialist Party (BSP) returned to power in 1994 with a clear majority but in a polarized society. To understand these differentiated patterns of the crises of state socialism, I will propose a theory of the social dynamics of integration, legitimation and change in bureaucratic-socialist societies which both accounts for the crises in general, and explains their nationally-specific forms.

2. Social Theory, Modernity and Differentiation

This chapter outlines a theory of social development in order to lay the foundations for understanding state socialism and post-socialism with reference to recent debates about modernity and legitimation. This excursus into general sociological theory is necessary in order to develop a framework for analysis in subsequent chapters around the theme of social complexity and structural differentiation. Some of this account is abstract but the ideas will be fleshed out in subsequent discussion. It will be suggested that the central organizational problem of modern societies is that of co-ordinating impersonal and anonymous interactions, which involve the fragmentation of social life into increasingly discrete spheres and the extension of social interaction across space and time, a process Giddens (1990:17ff.) describes as 'time-space distanciation'. Many sociologists have argued that a central problem arising with social differentiation is the loss of normative cohesion, as worldviews that once provided integrated frameworks of meaning are replaced by formal and instrumental patterns of co-ordination. A consequence of this is that modern societies confront new types of legitimation problems, and discussion of this issue in relation to Western modernity will be the basis for subsequent examination of legitimation problems in state socialism.

SOCIOLOGY AND MODERNITY

Since its inception, with Comtean positivism, sociology has been primarily concerned with problems of modernity, to which it offered critical institutional diagnosis (Giddens 1990:15). Indeed, the very concept of 'society' itself was the product of modern organizational forms, in which social processes such as the market and bureaucracies escape everyday understanding and operate 'behind the backs' of social actors (Wellmer 1971) becoming susceptible to the specialist understanding of the social sciences (Habermas 1991). Nineteenth-century theorists tended to identify a dominant tendency that underlay social evolution – such as collective learning through successive worldviews (Comte), contradictions within the mode of production (Marx), forms of moral integration and regulation (Durkheim), and rationalization and systematization (Weber). Classical sociological theory, moreover, tended (with some exceptions and qualifications) to assume that all modern societies were developing towards a core optimal organizational form through successive stages that each society would recapitulate. Classical theory thus lived at least to some extent in the future, since the present could be analysed from the standpoint of an underlying evolutionary tow – towards the positive age, communism, organic integration or, more pessimistically, the iron cage of bureaucracy.

Contemporary sociology, by contrast, tends (though again with exceptions) to emphasize societies' capacities for diversity, and to regard the notion of a single or dominant form of modernity as untenable. This issue is of central concern given the questions arising from the transition from communism towards post-communist socie-ties, regarding both the direction and speed of their transformation. Moreover, Colomy (1990) suggests that as old theoretical alignments dissolve, sociological theory is moving towards an increasingly syn-thetic analysis, drawing together intellectual trends that might have been previously regarded as fundamentally irreconcilable. An out-standing illustration of this trend is the work of Jürgen Habermas (especially 1984 and 1989) who has brought together phenomenology, systems theory, linguistics, classical sociology, Marxism and critical theory.

It is true, though, that there is no consensus as to what is meant by 'modernity' nor its boundaries with other concepts, notably the 'post-modern'. The 'modern' is often used in at least two senses (Sztompka 1993:69–70). The first is chronological, referring to the period in Europe from the end of the seventeenth century and suggests that what is 'modern' is whatever occurs in this time frame (Kumar 1988:5). The second is analytical and, defining modernity according to key traits, differentiates modern from pre-modern or traditional sectors of the world. The latter view was pronounced by classical social theorists such as Comte, Durkheim, Spencer, and Marx and Engels, who were convinced that a specific line of historical development culminated in Western Europe, and who saw the West as the vanguard of a movement that would eventually encompass the whole world. Thus the spatial organization of the world into more and less developed regions coincided with a temporal sequence, through which different societies were situated along a developmental continuum. As a consequence, according to Marx, the more developed country industrially shows to the less developed the image of its own future (Marx 1978:416). This assumption is relevant to the Soviet experience (and to developing countries for which the Soviet system was regarded as exemplary) where the goal was to compress this time difference through accelerated industrialization. In the process, moreover, Soviet communism would not only overcome its temporal distance from the West, but would surpass it, to create a new civilization that prefigured the future of Western societies themselves. More will be said of this in Chapter 3.

In the Enlightenment tradition, 'modernity' connotes societies where the potential for control of the natural environment is such that diffuse dangers are converted via professional-scientific knowledge into calculable risks, which further encourages the belief that social development can be 'reflexively' regulated.[1] In terms of social structural changes, state and economy are differentiated, markets developed, and there is an independent civil society and individualistic ethos, along with cultural pluralism and previously unprecedented levels of organizational complexity. The social structure is sufficiently fluid to permit extensive geographical and social mobility, rapid social change and urbanization. Thus a key feature of modernity is increasing complexity, which presupposes increasing functional differentiation at micro, mezzo and macro levels of the social order. Richard Münch (1990:463) has argued that social differentiation is the only possible answer to the problem of social order under modern conditions. If this is so, then social systems that failed to institutionalize differentiation adequate to the demands placed upon them, such as the Soviet systems, would experience pressure towards crisis and breakdown. In order to

---

1 Reflexivity refers to the application of a process to itself, such as 'thinking about thought' or 'making decisions about decision-making'.

examine this hypothesis, we need to examine the notion of social differentiation in more detail.

Sociological theory conceives of modernity in terms of a rupture with past 'traditional' forms, in the course of which solidaristic communal relations were broken asunder to be replaced with instrumental, impersonal and radically fluid types of action. Thus for Marx, as capitalism revolutionized productive and social relations, traditional ('feudal, patriarchal, idyllic') society was drowned in the icy water of egotistical calculation (Marx 1978:223). Again, Durkheim's typology of mechanical and organic divisions of labour identified traditional society in terms of high levels of fatalism and altruism,[2] a simple occupational system with a low degree of specialization, a single value system, where the individual was subordinate to society, which was illustrated by an extensive criminal or legal code. Organically integrated societies, on the other hand, displayed high levels of egoism and anomie[3] (with correspondingly low levels of fatalism and altruism); a complex occupational structure with a high degree of specialization; diversity of values; separation between work and home; decentred and multiple authorities; the cult of individuality; extensive civil restitutive law (Durkheim 1984).

For Weber, modernity institutionalized secular law, privatized religious belief and differentiated the institutional orders of society, culture and personality. Society enables participants to regulate their membership of social groups, while drawing upon culture (stocks of knowledge and interpretations), and develops competences that permit actors to reach understanding and thereby assert an identity (personality). According to Weber (1976) the Protestant Reformation had the unintended consequence of transposing the salvation ethic into the secular spirit of rational accounting and accumulation as an end in itself. Henceforth personality was oriented to instrumental goals and veneration of the sacred dissolved into privatized individualism, goal-setting rationality, personal responsibility, creating conditions for a

2 Altruism and fatalism were collectivistic forms of moral regulation, the former acknowledging a commitment to a higher order outside the self; the latter to the predictable and inescapable limits to human action.

3 Egoism and anomie refer to individualistic modes of moral regulation, the former emphasizing autonomy and individuality; the latter, uncertainty, ambiguity and change.

decentred self capable of moving among a plurality of roles which serve as the basis for a patchwork of potential collective identifications.[4]

Anonymity, complexity and the disintegration of systematic worldviews is accompanied by a process Max Weber described as *Sinnverlust*, or a loss of all-encompassing meaning. With the decline of tradition and the collapse of old authorities there is a shift of authority from 'without' to 'within', such as Adam Smith's 'spectator', the voice of inner conscience that determines the moral worth of actions (Smith 1966). The decline of a pre-given order where authority was based on natural or supernatural justifications means that subjects are called upon to exercise authority in the face of disorder and contingency, and thus actions become self-authored (Giddens 1991:207). Habermas (1989:47–56) argues that as worldviews that once exercised indisputable sway over action and belief are eroded, they are replaced not so much by a modern worldview as by a set of procedures for evaluating moral validity which, following Kolberg and Piaget, he describes as 'post-conventional'. As the authority of tradition becomes weaker, so the latitude for interpretation and reasoned justification increases, and moral authority is premised on our capacity to offer good reasons for moral claims.

Sociological theory, then, has described modernity variously in terms of commodification and class conflict (Marx), rationalization and formalization of both organizational structures and beliefs (Weber), functional differentiation (Durkheim, Parsons, Luhmann), and the fragmentation of meaning (Weber, Habermas). These tendencies will be manifest to different degrees at different stages of modernization, but one will tend to act upon the other so as to prevent any single inclination deciding modernity's fate. For example the effects of class conflict have been mitigated by functional differentiation of work organization and those of rationalization by collegial associations (Sciulli and Bould 1992; Sciulli 1992). In this way, Sciulli claims, one

---

4 The secularization thesis is often misunderstood to be claiming that religious belief disappears in modern societies, which it clearly does not. However, beliefs, religious or otherwise, do become privatized, while a detraditionalized public sphere is largely concerned with formal–rational questions of policy, the economy, the ordering of goals and balancing of interests. Further, the religious idea of the calling (*Beruf*) passed over into sober economic virtue and careerism as its religious roots faded, giving way to instrumental goals.

avoids 'Weber's dilemma', namely, if a tendency towards an iron cage of control is so powerful, how have Western capitalist societies escaped totalitarianism? By extension one might argue that none of these tendencies alone is likely to drive social development since each checks the other to some degree.

What, then, is post-modernity? The question is relevant because the collapse of communism has been interpreted as indicating the exhaustion of modernist structures in a post-modern age. The concept of post-modernity is contested and confused, and Featherstone (1988) suggests that it purports to illuminate changes in daily experiences and cultural practices, but the evidence for a decisive break with modernity is weak, and there is a danger of simply re-describing familiar experiences that were formerly granted little significance. Moreover there is a difference of emphasis between sociological and cultural–philosophical accounts of post-modernity. Sociologists such as Bauman (1992), Crook et al. (1992) and Smart (1992) tend to regard post-modernity, not unlike the earlier notion of post-industrial society (Bell 1973), as a sequential stage following modernity. On the other hand, Lyotard claims that such distinctions are overly mechanical, since the post-modern signifies not the end, so much as a changed relation to modernism. Thus cultural forms 'must first become post-modern in order to be modern' (1990:79). So, as Kellner (1988) comments, there is nothing like a unified 'post-modern social theory': rather, one is struck by the diversities between theories often lumped together as 'post-modern'.

According to Lash (1988) and Lash and Urry (1994:272) modernity is characterized by vertical and horizontal differentiation, organized capitalism and the development of separate institutional, normative and aesthetic spheres, each with their specific conventions and modes of evaluation. There are multiple separations of high and low culture, science and life, auratic art and popular pleasures. Post-modernity, by contrast, involves de-differentiation, disorganized capitalism, and a breakdown of both the distinctiveness of each sphere, and of the criteria which legislate within each vertical dimension. In addition (following Baudrillard 1983), the relationship between representation and reality is problematic in post-modernity. For Lash and Urry this is illustrated by new consumption patterns which reflect a transition from mass (Fordist) consumption to more individualized (post-Fordist) consumption, in which 'cool' consumers respond to the global array of available images and experiences, with ironic detach-ment. Thus, for example, 'post-tourists' are sufficiently self-reflective to know that travel is part of the popular culture industry, and now offers few authentic experiences, unlike (they suggest) the earlier unsophisticated pleasures of the English seaside (1994:276).[5] However, this depiction of post-modernity as de-differentiation is problematic. It is true that advanced industrial societies do display evidence of de-differentiation, such as the declining significance of class and status positions which follow the expansion of citizenship rights grounded in values of formal equality and individual autonomy (Rueschemeyer 1986:165). Yet such developments are constrained by contrary tendencies of *longue durée* towards increasing social differ-entiation. Schuluchter (1985) points out that social differentiation was not specific even to modernity, but was a feature of traditional societies and emerged as economic contacts grew between communities that did not share a common value system. Traditional economic behaviour was governed by instrumental values and exempt from the code of 'brotherliness' binding on members of one's own community. It was Calvinism that prepared the ground for further differentiation between the economy and cultural values by sanctifying profit maximization. As market economies and universalistic values spread, the differentiation between the instrumental and expressive orientations were restructured around notions of the public versus private.

If post-modernity involves de-differentiation, then it needs to be shown that modern societies experience a collapse of differentiated cultural value spheres and a blurring of the institutional orders of society, culture and personality. Yet such evidence is not forthcoming. On the contrary, for Lyotard (1990) the differentiation of three 'regimes of phrases', science, morality and aesthetics (which are re-markably similar to Weber's cultural value spheres), is precisely part of the condition of *post*-modernity. Further, Lash and Urry themselves refer to what are in effect new kinds of social differentiation in the shape of new consumption cultures, niche markets, role distanciation and so on, as characteristic of the present. So the notion of post-modernity as a process of de-differentiation is not persuasive. More-

5   They further claim that for the post-tourist there is little difference between seeing a
    particular view through the viewfinder of one's camera and through the television
    set (1994:274) presumably because both are framed symbolic representations.

over, these distinctions are too elastic to have explanatory value since it is circular to attempt to explain global events with reference to an underlying tendency such as post-Fordist consumption patterns, which themselves require explanation, but which are used to exemplify the general trend. This point will be developed with reference to the relationship between communism and (post)-modernity in Chapter 3, but post-modernism does not look like a promising account.

SYSTEM DIFFERENTIATION

Modern cosmology, according to many accounts, began with the Copernican Revolution that removed the Earth from the centre of the universe and understood the cosmos as a complex system of forces. In a similar way, modern social theory began to understand the position of people within the social universe only once the human subject had been de-centred. Stuart Hall (1993:285ff.) identifies 'five great advances' in social theory that contributed to de-centring the subject, namely:

- Marx's claim, that people make history but not in circumstances of their choosing, de-centred human agency and undermined the idea of actor-creators of history;
- Freud and psychoanalysis de-centred our understanding of the self, through the concept of over-determination, whereby psychical phenomena are the result of contradictory processes of repression, displacement and conversion;
- Saussure's linguistics de-centred the author by arguing that language precedes the speaker, who speaks through a system of meanings embedded in linguistic codes;
- Foucault de-centred power and knowledge into the discursive practices of collective modern institutions of workhouses, barracks, prisons, schools, asylums, etc.;
- Feminism de-centres the state and public sphere, by opening up the family, sexuality, housework, the domestic division of labour and so on, to political contestation.[6]

6 Hall does not claim that each of these theories are universally accepted, only that they have each contributed to erosion of the unified concept of the subject.

A major contribution he does not list is systems theory, although this, too, has had an important impact on our understanding of the social universe. The observation that industrial societies exhibit complex and highly differentiated divisions of labour has prompted sociological theorists (from classical political economy, through Durkheim and Parsons to current systems theory) to view social change in terms of adaptation to increasingly complex tasks and environments. Talcott Parsons (1970) argued that social systems exhibit a strain towards consistency (codification and generalization) in which a shared cultural value system restores equilibrium and safeguards continuity. Structural changes follow an evolutionary pattern of increasing complexity and adaptive capacity which permits the inclusion of new units and values according to four functional problems that arise in all social situations. The internal differentiation of any social system involves the sequence: adaptation (mobilizing technical means and resources), goal attainment (setting priorities), integration (achieving co-operation and a sense of solidarity among actors) and latency (tension management and cultural transmission). The Adaptation–Goal Attainment–Integration–Latency (AGIL) schema will be reproduced in each subsystem, and social adaptation is dependent on maintaining boundaries across which exchanges can occur. A very schematic diagram of the social system is provided in Figure 2.1, where various exchanges are illustrated. It might be noted that the economy (adaptation) is dependent upon legal regulation and government intervention from the polity (goal attainment) and this in turn provides administrative co-ordination to the societal community (integration) in return for legitimacy. The fiduciary system (latency) includes households which supply labour, consumption and socialization, but also generates trust in the system, which involves the conditional suspension of continuous calculation. The latter is, as Mayhew (1984) says, fragile but crucial to the accomplishment of social life, as will be seen later in Soviet societies, where levels of generalized trust were very low.

These are, as Niklas Luhmann (1982:55) says, bold and risky assumptions on which to support a whole theory, and much in Parsons's work is dubious and otiose (Morse 1961). Even so, it will be argued in Chapter 5 that this framework might contribute to

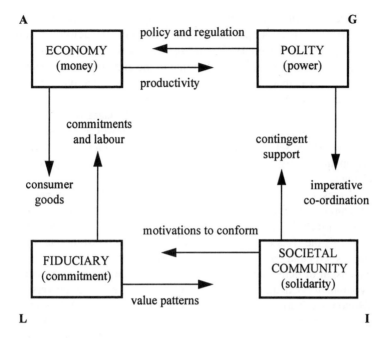

Figure 2.1 Parsons's AGIL schema

conceptualizing social integration and crisis management. Further, it is well known that classical functionalist accounts such as Parsons's had inadequate understanding of conflict (e.g. Alexander 1978; Colomy 1990) and tended to assume that social differentiation and universalistic values arose as a result of automatic social evolution rather than through the gradual hard-fought-for extension of rights and entitlements. Rueschemeyer (1986:171ff.) argues that power is the motive force forming the functional integration of the division of labour and that we should always ask, *for whom* is it efficient, productive and adaptive? The most powerful interests are likely to determine which criteria of 'efficiency' will be selected from among different possible forms of the division of labour. If so, then social evolution represents successive stages in the institutionalization of forms of domination, and although some arrangements might be more efficient and universalistic than others, one cannot explain social change simply with reference to progressive adaptation. Practices that survive in organizations are not necessarily the most 'efficient' ones, but reflect first, a particular configuration of power relations (DiMaggio and Powell 1983), and second, those (such as symbols or articles of faith) that become important to the organization's identity. It is often noted that once these are inscribed into underlying rules of conduct they are likely to be resistant to change (e.g. Zeleny 1985), a phenomenon that is frequently regarded by advocates of change as a cultural lag hindering progressive adaptation. However, we will see in relation to precisely this kind of analysis of post-communism that such arguments involve hegemonic battles for control of the process of change.

However, the notion of exchanges between subsystems need not presuppose social harmony, nor does Parsons's idea of value generalization preclude social struggles. On the contrary, differentiation increases the risks of conflict and also extends the institutional means for its articulation. This can be illustrated with reference to the expansion of democratic rights and social justice, which is part of the evolutionary expansion of values of achievement and universalism (Holton and Turner 1986) which Habermas (1989:374ff.) describes as the 'unfulfilled potential of modernity'. For example, the emerging democratic institutions of early modernity inhabited a male bourgeois public sphere that excluded women and the working class, while the division between workplace and home, central to the concept of a public sphere, presupposed a gendered division of labour between the male realms of economy, politics and the professions versus the female realm of domesticity (Pateman 1988). The exclusion of women was integral to the entitlement of men to democratic participation (Yuval-Davis 1991:63). None the less, the framework of universalistic ethics through which modern societies attempted to legitimate themselves permitted the formation of a discourse of rights and the organization of emancipatory social movements, evidenced in democratic reform movements such as the Chartists, trade union and workers' political parties (Thompson 1991) and feminist movements (Landes 1988:13; Watson 1993). The democratic revolutions bequeathed to women a model for the struggle for rights, a fissure in the construction of the feminine subject (Laclau and Mouffe 1985:117 and 154) through which universalistic values could be extended.

It can be argued, then, that modernity involves expanding opportunities for collective action, indeed social movement activity might be central to the constitution of modern societies (Sztompka 1993:279). At the same time, though, increasing social complexity imposes constraints on action. This is so first because action takes place within networks of unintended and unpredictable consequences; second because co-ordinating disparate and functionally specific actions depend upon markets and bureaucratic organizations, both of which limit the scope of the public sphere (Habermas 1989). On the one hand, then, modernity expands capacities for action within fluid social structures, a view encouraged by the ethic of individualism and achievement in contemporary societies; on the other hand, markets and organizational structures constrain human freedom within rule-bound systems. Thus the duality of action and system has become one of the central problems of sociological theory, that is, how to reconcile the idea of social life as an active accomplishment of purposive, knowledgeable actors *vis-à-vis* the constraints imposed by social structures (Giddens 1979:128ff.).

In modern societies the scope for action expands reflexively with the capacity for knowledge-based intervention in natural and social environments while increasing complexity requires action-systems that detract from the sovereignty of the individual. Giddens (1979) suggests that all social interaction involves the communication of meaning, the exercise of power and the evaluation of conduct. Each mode of interaction deploys a latent structure, respectively, signification, domination and legitimation, through three corresponding forms of knowledge and capabilities. These 'modalities' are, for each case, interpretative schemes, facility (access to resources) and norms, which are properties of communities rather than actors. Action is thus the product of 'structuration', a duality of structure and agency since each are co-present in any interaction. Moreover, structures are both constraining and enabling, a bit like the rules of a game. Rules are constitutive, allowing players to interact, and constraining, defining which moves are legitimate and which are not. While one might accept this, it is questionable whether the actor/structure problem has been solved or simply represented in a different way. The question remains as to whether there is a systematic patterning across the three modes of interaction such that actors' capacities in relation to one mode structure their relations within the others. Further, by focusing on the capacities of the actor, Giddens's concept of structuration ends up collapsing structure (which only exists in so far as it is instantiated) into agency.

Social differentiation theories approach this problem in different ways. Alexander (1990), for example, links increased individual autonomy to the emergence of multi-dimensional social orders, which views complex societies as composed of intersecting and decentred subsystems, each with specific rules and criteria of relevance. Thus actors enter into increasingly voluntary or at any rate horizontal and functionally interdependent relations with one another, by contrast to earlier more hierarchical social forms. Luhmann's solution, though, is bolder: to replace the actor–system dichotomy altogether with one between action and time. Organizational subsystems are self-regulating, autopoietic (homeostatic) and recursive, referring only to their own system elements through which inputs from the environment are processed.[7] In particular, while action occurs within a social present, systems create temporal complexity, giving time to organize a multitude of relational patterns. These 'boundary times' between systems and their environments are essential to the management of complexity (Luhmann 1982:149). In the economy, for example, time boundaries facilitate the possibility of deferring decisions about satisfaction of needs, while providing guarantees that they will be satisfied in time thus acquired. It then becomes possible to believe in a contingent future and conceive of the present as the moment when decisions are made about the future (Luhmann 1992:36). If temporal boundaries disintegrate, with a collapse in the value of a currency, for example, the present moment becomes crucial, since money cannot then store value for use in the future. This leads to the de-differentiation of other social relations, such as a return to barter and dependence on face-to-face encounters, such as occurred in Soviet societies during the fall of communism.

Systems thus limit potentially unlimited communications from their environments through the formation of boundaries such as rules of membership, formal procedures for decision-making and a functionally

---

7 A system as a network of communications (rather than, as for Parsons, shared values) that are ordered so as to remain constant in spite of their dependence upon a more or less inconsiderate and troublesome environment. Systems stabilize by reducing complexity by selecting and channelling impulses from their environment (Luhmann 1982:32).

differentiated internal division of labour.[8] For Luhmann (1982: 230) this is the outcome of three sequential stages of social organization: (i) segmented (patriarchal or kinship) societies, which are then encompassed within (ii) stratified systems, where inequalities of wealth and power appear following the accidental formation of inequality in segmented communities. Hierarchical inequalities perform the dual function of facilitating communication among stratum members, while closing or restricting the communication chances of non-members. However, stratified societies are inflexible and inhibit the formation of (iii) functionally specific differentiated and impersonal roles that are features of modern societies (1982:75). In the third stage, communications are linked to specific entrance and exit rules, such as submission to authority in return for wages, and compared with stratified societies, social relations are more co-operative, formally egalitarian and facilitate multi-directional communication. Rather than exhibit a Weberian command–action structure, modern organizations stress horizontal but functionally specific integration (such as inter-team work) and initiative for contacts flows from subordinates to superiors as well as through commands (Luhmann 1982:32).[9] Stratification and kinship continue to exist subsumed within modern functionally differentiated societies, but with a more open structure and circumscribed functions than previously.

In functionally differentiated societies, exchanges between subsystems occur through steering media, which reduce complexity by developing highly abstract codes through which the system distinguishes itself from its environment (Luhmann 1992:78). In the economy, money acts as a symbolic token, a medium of exchange that can be passed around, thus bracketing time–space by 'coupling insubstan-

---

8 By environment, Luhmann means a multitude of actual and possible events and circumstances (1982:xxvi), made up of other systems, interdependence, temporal relations, the degree of predictability or frequency of surprise. Environments have no clearly defined boundaries but only horizons that imply further possibilities while making it meaningless or inconvenient to pursue them indefinitely. The minimal form of environmental differentiation is the distinction between members and non-members or those who make decisions and those who receive them.

9 Luhmann's analysis resonates with the claim that rigid hierarchies are being replaced by 'adhocracies', flexible systems of management based on informality, decentralization and trust (Mintzberg 1989; Zuboff 1988:401–2). As a depiction of capitalist societies these claims could be accepted only with considerable qualifications, and represent an ideal (if not idealized) type.

tiality and deferral, presence and absence' (Giddens 1990).[10] Money is the paradigm case since (as Marx claimed) capitalism differs from all hitherto existing societies in that here value circulates in money form, which becomes generalized by commodifying social relations that had previously been mediated by reciprocity, obligation, patronage and indenture. The generalization of money facilitated a new measure of equivalence between objects, value, time and   labour, while the commodification of labour meant that the expropriation of a surplus from the production process took on the invisible form value. That is, abstract media of communication are loosened from particular cultural moorings and projected into a global dimension, creating possibilities for highly complex impersonal communications.

Parsons (1970) argued that power has a parallel function in the polity to that of money in the economy, since it is a circulating medium that enables the performance of obligations by those in power.[11] Parsons was referring only to legitimate authority where the mandate of those in authority is dependent on trust.[12] Luhmann, for whom communication is more important for social integration than legitimacy and values (1982:70), emphasizes how, as codes, money and power increase communication possibilities by reducing complexity. In the case of power, political codes are repertoires that schema tize and simplify political discourse (such as progressive or conservative, government or opposition, state or society, public or private interests) and short-circuiting debate by compacting otherwise complex nuances into easily recognizable oppositions.

10 Giddens (1990:23) claims that although the approaches of Parsons and Luhmann have some affinities with his, he does not accept the main framework of their analyses, or the notion of power as a medium of communication. For the purposes of this discussion, though, these differences are not crucial, since they each address the problem of how complex social orders simplify transactions. In many ways, Giddens is less radical than Luhmann in recasting the action/system problem.

11 Later, Parsons (1970) proposed four media: money (in the economic system) power (in the political system), influence (social integration) and value commitment (pattern maintenance) and then added intelligence, performance capacity, affect and interpretation. These developments are not dealt with here since, as Habermas (1989:257) argues, the principles became increasingly unclear, imprecise and merely metaphorical.

12 Giddens's point that power is often based on deception rather than trust (1979:314) missed the point that, as observers, we might regard someone's trust in the authorities as misplaced, but it is trust none the less.

There are some advantages to viewing money and power as steering media as Giddens (1979:338) acknowledges. For one thing it modifies the zero-sum concept of power, in which any class or group has only as much power as another does not have (Poulantzas 1968:151), a view common among élite theories. Rather than regarding power as a possession, the object of contestation, it can be viewed as fluid and (like money) subject to expansion and deflation depending on the extent of trust in the government. Moreover, rather than locate power solely in the state, this implies a more textured and capillary conception of power as dispersed through the social fabric, consequent on the erosion of sovereignty. Sovereign power, initially personalized through the institution of kingship and later made anonymous through a bureaucratic state apparatus, admitted little systemic differentiation and was highly dependent on political–legal regulation, obligations and patronage. Dispersed power, on the other hand, presupposes a multiplicity of authorities and permits higher levels of system differentiation, since steering consequently occurs through media of power, money, collegiality, consent and trust. Thus the transition from sovereign to dispersed power involves a limitation of the remit of the state in favour of self-steering subsystems, which is the ostensible objective of post-communist societies.[13]

A further advantage of viewing money and power as steering media is that it offers insight into the conversion of diffuse dangers into calculable risks, and the transfer of risk between political and economic systems. Social differentiation enables subsystems to maintain sufficient internal complexity to respond to problems generated in their environments (Luhmann 1982:230). For example, the economy has more internal complexity (division of labour, separation between work and household, networks of distribution etc.) than politics, so it has greater opportunity to store and transfer reduced complexity. Consequently, with the evolution of modern societies, the economic system has taken over many risks from politics, since conversion of risks into monetary terms enables them to be digitalized and depoliticized (Luhmann 1992:184). Again, expert cultures have absorbed

13 The notion of dispersed power is similar to Foucault's idea of textured power, which circulates, is never localized here or there, but fractured into multiple sites of surveillance, such as hospitals, schools, prisons and institutional records. But Foucault does not distinguish legitimate from carceral power, with the result that his concept cannot distinguish between coercion and consent.

risks, since their high internal complexity creates capacities for sustaining alternatives, the possibility of variety, dissent and regulated conflict. The use of boundary times to respond to environmental pressures accords systems time to insert their own ways of processing information to respond to outside impulses and select courses of action (Luhmann 1982:145).

With the development of welfare states and interventionist government economic policies, though, the political system reabsorbed risk from the economy, since markets required administration and organization. Although the capitalist economy has greater complexity and flexibility than the political system, it also has greater capacity for disturbing other subsystems and making demands on their performance through cyclical crises (Jessop 1990:334). Further, since the market is not the most efficient provider of welfare goods, such as health, education and infrastructural investment, the political system takes on tasks such as insuring employees against unemployment, protecting firms against bankruptcy, guided investment (for example in depressed regions) as well as general fiscal and economic policy (Luhmann 1982:213). This exchange presupposes a stable boundary between the political and economic systems, rather than a merging of politics and economy which, although aimed at avoiding problems of the blind evolution of self-governing systems, tends to engender further risks, of inflexibility, inefficiency and external costs (Jessop 1990:334).

A systems approach, then, views social differentiation in terms of:

- autopoietic self-closing systems that reduce complexity and risk;
- functional differentiation through AGIL;
- the dominant role of the economy as the main means of co-ordination embedded in cultural values of universalism and achievement;
- stratification based on achievement rather than ascription;
- impersonal complex networks of social interaction steered by symbolic exchanges such as money and power.

Let us now examine some of the problems with this approach.

SYSTEM AND LIFEWORLD

Modern social systems involve complex internal differentiation which facilitates simplification of otherwise unmanageably complex exchanges through symbolic tokens, such as money. However, two points should be noted. First, the upshot of this line of analysis is that increasing differentiation and complexity would render an attempt to rule from a single undifferentiated centre uniting political, economic and cultural controls increasingly difficult (Arato 1991:19; Luhmann 1982:239). Contrary to Weber's expectation that organizations will tend towards optimal centralization and hierarchy, it seems that these are limited by potential overload from the environment in response to which organizations decentralize in order to select and process information. However, while it would be difficult to dispute this general observation, it tells us little about social actors, the capacity of the system to delay crisis tendencies, or whether and how newly differentiated spheres exert an influence on events. Second, systems theory is flat (Zolo 1990–91) in the sense that its model of functional integration does not account for the ways in which structural relations like gender, ethnicity, class (and the relations between them) are encoded and reproduced in impersonal exchanges. As Giddens comments (1979:341) power may be a medium but it is always exercised over someone, it is hierarchical and, to some degree therefore, *is* zero-sum. Luhmann acknowledges that the economic subsystem has primacy but attributes this solely to its capacity for absorbing complexity. But the economy constitutes structural relations of production and distributing resources, and whether or not the resultant inequalities are functional for selecting communications (as Luhmann suggests) they are hardly likely to be conflict-free. Systems theory, especially Luhmann's version, stresses communication rather than value consensus and has no way of accounting for either conflict or integration other than with reference to homeostatic communications. Thus the use of systems concepts needs to be balanced by reference to socio-cultural practices which regulate the ability of systemic media to co-ordinate impersonal action. Let us look at each of these issues.

System formation is actually an uncertain process that demands a high degree of tolerance for indeterminacy especially where traditional instruments of power become marginalized and destabilized. To respond flexibly to environmental change, alternatives need to be built into the system to generate future options. However, since in such a system complexity itself (rather than shared values) has to become a stabilizing factor (Luhmann 1982:161) there is a high risk of regression to earlier forms. The emergence of open systems depends upon interim solutions remaining sufficiently stable to perform the transition – an example might be the nation-state which institutionalized impersonal governance in place of personalized rulership, representing an increase in the political system's ability to process complexity. Such transitions face high risks from the external environment, while cultural attachment to the structures evolved during the *ancien régime* might provide the basis for populist post-crisis settlements that do not greatly diversify organizational systems but none the less release considerable energy (Rueschemeyer 1986:151). This would be the case where revolutionary mass mobilization achieves extensive economic and social transformation without permitting the formation of self-steering decentralized systems.

On closer inspection, then, it seems that social differentiation itself cannot be in the driving seat of social change because it is dependent on other variables, such as the outcome of political struggles or the compatibility between the potential change and existing cultural values. Increases in complexity are followed *either* by altered power relations, pluralization and internal differentiation, *or* by the political system blocking social development and relying on traditional identities such as ethnicity, personalized networks such as clientelism, and autocracy. The latter might occur because of entrenched self-interest among political élites, but more generally because of the limited options for development given in the environment. This suggests that a systems-theory approach will remain of limited value unless the mutual interdependence of systems of power and money with other institutional orders of society is acknowledged.

Habermas describes the latter as the lifeworld,[14] the analysis of

---

14 The concept of the lifeworld, initially derived from phenomenology, is used here in the Habermasian sense of a pre-given basis of experience and medium of social learning. Language and culture embody a stock of knowledge – the stored interpretative work of preceding generations – that renders every new situation familiar, in that understanding takes place against the background of culturally ingrained pre-understandings. This 'pre-reflective background consensus' can become an object of reflection only piecemeal, because we cannot suspend judgement on everything at once (Habermas, 1984:123).

which has been central to Habermas's critique of Luhmann. For Habermas, Luhmann's theory of social differentiation is inadequate, notwithstanding the latter's intellectual debt to the latter on several issues.[15] Habermas concedes that it is possible to analyse societies as self-regulating and self-contained systems: indeed, he regards analysis of the entry of system–environment boundaries into society as the main strand of social theory, from Marx via Spencer and Durkheim to Simmel, Weber and Lukács (Habermas 1991:256). However, an extensive body of sociology, linking, for example, Marx, Durkheim, Weber, Parsons and Polanyi, has argued that even highly abstract and goal-specific exchanges (like markets) are culturally embedded in supportive but constraining social, organizational, institutional and normative frameworks (Jessop 1992). This process, which Weber described as 'societalization' (*Vergesellschaftung*), involves the constant formation and dissolution of social relationships in ways that presuppose conflict as well as co-operation between those involved (Torfing 1991:44).

Confidence, for example, is central to economic life and the boundaries between the economy and other domains are dependent upon the institutionalization of rules, for example against bribery, and separating business from private property, work from family or friendship from business. With the expansion of exchange and credit, new regulatory structures emerged that re-coupled the market to the lifeworld through laws of property and contract (Habermas 1989:261). The development of capitalism entailed an institutional structure of trade associations, information exchanges and networks of non-market contacts. These were limited by the needs of firms to retain competitive advantage, but the expansion of capitalism was accompanied by a process of institutionalization. Members of society, as Durkheim (1984:173) argued, are linked by ties that extend beyond the very brief moment when the act of exchange is accomplished. Thus contracts require large amounts of trust and cultural embeddedness to produce stable patterns of action extending beyond immediate

15 Habermas initiated a joint seminar with Luhmann in Frankfurt in the late 1960s. The publication arising from this dispute, *Theorie der Gesellachaft oder Sozialtechnologie: Was leistet die Systemforschung?* (1971) (Theory of Society or Social Technology: What Does Systems Research Accomplish?) sold over 35,000 copies. The details of the dispute are beyond the scope of this chapter, but further summaries are provided in McCarthy (1978:222–32) and Holub (1991:106–32).

co-presence through space and time (Clegg 1975; Fox 1974). Moreover, corporate trust itself is dependent on institutional guarantees and regulation, is accorded conditionally and is subject to experience.

Complex societies, then, co-ordinate impersonal and disparate exchanges via symbolic tokens, which are effective only if culturally embedded. Thus these systems of exchange are dependent on public confidence and legitimating norms which are not themselves tokens, but are claims to validity, which can be subject to reasoned scrutiny. What is the implication of this? It has been noted that the emergence of modernity involved a changed relationship between the self and authority, and released the argumentative capacity of language – what Habermas (1991:244) calls the 'potential voice of reason which is implicit in everyday communicative practice'. This is implicit in the capacity to give 'yes' or 'no' responses to statements claiming empirical or moral authority. Furthermore (as Durkheim also argued), a condition of participating effectively in modern societies is that members acknowledge that others do not necessarily share their specific beliefs or values. Public interactions thus presuppose a cognitive process in which one acquires the ability to de-centre (Piaget 1965) the original pivotal place which the self occupied in the social world. Post-traditional norms are open to agreement or disagreement; they can be subjected to debate in which actors are expected to provide good reasons for moral injunctions.[16] This is a learning process, an achievement that is matched by progress towards moral autonomy where norms lose their apparently natural validity and require justification in terms of reasoned argument and actors increasingly owe their mutual understandings to their own interpretations (Gouldner 1976:57). In capitalist democracies these learning capacities are increasingly institutionalized in civil law, liberal democracy and

---

16 This rather complex argument, drawing upon Chomsky and Searle's speech–act theory is often misunderstood. Barker (1990:90), for example, suggests that Habermas would be right only if all people thought like philosophers, a view echoed by Piccone (1989) who regards the theory of communication as mystificatory, restricting political participation to intellectuals capable of domination-free discussion. Again, it is claimed that Habermas glosses over structural processes (Benhabib 1981) and wrongly privileges discourse over material bases of social integration that are formed through dependence and violence which later become institutionalized into normatively binding rules (Dux 1991). Critique and defence of Habermas's theory of communicative action are also discussed, for example, in Brand (1990); Honneth and Joas (eds) (1991); Outhwaite (1994); Ray (1993); Thompson and Held (eds) (1982).

citizenship rights, even if these are continually subject to renegotiation.

However, as Weber noted, there is a continual tension between the democratic institutions of the public sphere and the tendency for consent to be circumvented by markets and organizations. Further, it is frequently argued that attempts to impose these institutional systems in cultural contexts where they are regarded as alien to established patterns of cultural reproduction will result in pathological adaptations (Bryant and Mokrzycki (eds), 1994). Habermas (1989:267) argues that areas of life that primarily fulfil functions of cultural reproduction, social integration and socialization, or mutual understanding, cannot be replaced by steering media because these activities cannot be 'bought' and 'collected' like labour and taxes. If systems of power and money forcibly circumvent linguistic and normative structures, that is 'colonize the lifeworld', pathologies, such as loss of meaning, confusion of orientations and collective identities, anomie and withdrawal of motivation will result.

Two problems with this argument should be noted, though. First, it is difficult to justify regarding some areas of social life as normative *a priori*, and others as more appropriately governed by money or power. Second, talk of pathologies is reminiscent of anomie theory which exaggerated the extent to which social action is ever removed from normative constraint, since where people act together at all they do so within social networks. One can avoid the first problem, perhaps, by focusing on the degree to which market forces or bureaucratic power are empirically embedded in cultural practices. This remains agnostic on the *a priori* question but retains the theoretical link between systemic co-ordination and cultural embeddedness. The second problem can be addressed partly with reference to studies of the nineteenth-century process of industrialization which suggest (e.g. Polanyi 1944; Thompson 1991) that the imposition of culturally alien forms of steering generate resistance in the form of social movements defending endangered ways of life, notably the labour movement. But even if social dislocation does stimulate collective action, it is not obvious how we might analytically distinguish 'pathological' from 'normal' responses.

However, I will argue in relation to Soviet socialism that the way in which the system responds to social movements and more covert forms of resistance will strongly influence the resultant configuration.

Where resistance is neither accommodated nor entirely suppressed, a situation results that Alexander (1984) calls a 'columnized society' divided into parallel columns of antagonistic politico-cultural groups. I will argue that in a columnized society the competing spheres of action, official and latent, tend to be symbiotic and latent systems of action increasingly take over the tasks of regulating the official society, with consequences for subsequent developments.

POWER AND LEGITIMATION

The increased capacities for public criticism and debate which complement the decline of pre-modern society render the problem of legitimacy central to the integration of contemporary social orders in both industrial and post-industrial societies. Since the question of legitimation will be important to the subsequent discussion it would be useful to signal some central issues now. It has been noted that as the economy develops dysfunctional effects, risks can be off-loaded on to the political system. However, Luhmann's view that power operates as a steering medium in the same way as money needs to be modified for the following reasons. First, power cannot be manipulated to the same extent as money; it cannot be stored or 'banked'. Second, power has no sign system of equivalents like prices and even if political codes have the effect of short-circuiting debate, they are not abstracted from linguistic interaction in the same way as prices. Third, therefore, power cannot circulate in an unrestricted manner and tends to get bound up symbolically with the person or the context of powerful. Fourth, the exercise of power depends upon what Clegg (1989) calls episodic agency, the ability to control and mobilize organizational resource flows, which in turn presupposes that compliance has already been secured. Fifth, the financing of money (credit) heightens the internal complexity of the economic system, but as power becomes reflexive it creates increasing opportunities for argument and opposition, that is, a process of *de*-differentiation. Finally, the public–legal organization of offices requires legitimation which is more demanding on normative structures than is money. Organizational behaviour is embedded in cultural practices that presuppose reciprocity, trust and informal relations, which Okun (1981) described as the 'invisible handshake', as opposed to the 'invisible hand' of the market and the 'visible hand' of bureaucracy.

These points can be illustrated with reference to Luhmann's account of sanctions that stabilize power. These, he suggests, are physical force, withdrawal of co-operation, loss of membership of organizations, discrediting individuals, breakdowns of technically functional systems and an overload of complexity and uncertainty (1982:151). However, these do not operate in equivalent fashion, since the first four result directly from decisions to deploy sanctions and are variable (they may or may not be enforced); the last two are consequences that follow necessarily from a course of action. Whether or not variable sanctions are enforced might depend on a range of factors such as the legitimacy of the political system, the degree of polarization of the conflict, and the efficiency of enforcers.

What, then, is legitimacy and among whom need it be based to be effective – the whole population, a majority, the administrative staff or certain strata? A classical answer to these questions was provided by Weber, who claimed that every system attempts to establish and to cultivate the belief in its legitimacy, but its form differs according to the types of obedience and legitimacy claimed, the kind of administrative staff developed to guarantee it, and the mode of exercising authority (Weber 1978 I:213). These differences were expressed in Weber's typology of traditional, charismatic and formal legitimacy. Traditional refers to the sanction of immemorial traditions and belief in the legitimacy of those exercising authority under them (e.g. monarchy); charismatic to the belief in the exceptional sanctity, heroism and exemplary character of an individual person (e.g. typically in a theocracy); rational–legal to the belief in legality of enacted rules and the right of those elevated to authority to enact them (e.g. democratic republics). Further, Weber indicated a fourth type, substantive rationality, or the provisioning of given groups with goods under a criterion of ultimate values such as social justice.

However, these types are not really symmetrical since they each presuppose very different forms of social organization. Traditional legitimacy refers to types of beliefs that can be deployed in order to ground legitimacy (such as the Chinese Emperors' Mandate from Heaven) rather than to the qualities of particular individuals holding office. The charismatic type refers to beliefs about the qualities of the leader, although charismatic leaders will often draw upon traditional imagery (such as a prophetic tradition) and Weber also talks about the charisma of office – thus the Pope's spiritual authority derives from his office rather than his person. Formal–rational legitimation refers less to substantive beliefs than to consensus about bureaucratic and democratic procedures. It is worth noting that the fourth category of substantive rationality (which Weber says is 'full of ambiguities') refers both to values and resource allocation but results in a kind of instrumental exchange between rulers and ruled. Given groups are provided with goods under a criterion of social justice, a system also known as 'social eudaemonic' or performance legitimation (Holmes 1993:11). Weber associated this form with 'social dictatorships', such as revolutionary states that distribute welfare in order to secure the loyalty of cadres, a notion that in relation to Soviet societies has been described as covert legitimation (Rigby and Fehér 1982).

David Beetham argues that Weber's schema was conceptual rather than causal, and that he was not able to give a clear account of the structural interrelationships between economy, social structure and government (Beetham 1992:256). Moreover, he criticizes Weber's analysis of legitimacy because in his view it refers primarily to belief or the capacity to generate belief (Beetham 1992:9). In its most extreme form, he says, this understanding would interpret the collapse of state socialism as deficiency of public relations rather than anything wrong with the system of rule. Whether Beetham's interpretation of Weber is fair or not (it might not be) his analysis is interesting in that it offers an approach (in a way not unlike Luhmann) in which performance rather than belief is central. He proposes to deal with legitimacy as a set of multidimensional continua, rules which are jus- tified with reference not to beliefs but to publicly demonstrated consent of subordinates. The latter refers to a subjectively binding force (for whatever motive, love of the leaders or self-interest) which is a public ceremonial declamatory support aimed at third parties who have not taken part (Beetham 1992:18). In similar vein, Žižek (1989:32) argues that cynical distance is compatible with involvement in everyday organizational practices, since people 'know very well how things really are but still they are doing it as if they did not know'. May Day rallies in Red Square and rituals such as elections without a choice of candidates were examples of public displays of unanimity (*edinodushie*) that did not require sincere belief.

It is still unclear, though, how wide the social base of support for such regimes has to be in order for them to be 'legitimate', or conversely how widespread the lack of support to constitute a legitimation crisis. Fehér et al. (1984:138) argue that the Soviet system was 'legitimate' in that its orders were accepted as binding by those who had to enforce them, and there was no compelling vision of an alternative political order to challenge the status quo. However, Holmes (1993) disagrees, arguing that most regimes increasingly addressed the problem of mass popularity, particularly in the 1970s and 1980s. Further, one should not forget the legitimating effects for privileged strata of radical destabilization and even mass terror, where this leads to rapid social mobility, as was the case with the Soviet cultural revolution in 1930s (Fitzpatrick 1979a). This is discussed further in Chapter 4.

Legitimacy, then, is crucial to the ability of the polity to become embedded in the institutional orders of the lifeworld. But how do political systems lose legitimacy? Habermas (1976) gave considerable currency to the notion of a legitimation crisis, of which the collapse of communism might provide an example. Habermas's concept was developed largely (though not entirely) with a view to Western European experience of the post-war corporatist state, so this may not transfer well to the Soviet system. Habermas's theory of legitimation crisis is grounded on a re-modelling of Parsons's AGIL schema via the concepts of system and lifeworld (see Figure 2.2) and the idea of exchanges between three systems, the economy, the administrative state and the socio-cultural system. This is a model with four dimensions: system (divided into economy and polity) and lifeworld (generating legitimation, trust and motivation). Structural contradictions, such as the tendency of the rate of profit to fall, cannot be offset indefinitely but reappear in modified forms as state administration intervenes in the market and takes over functions it previously performed. Here legitimacy was not based primarily on belief so much as on a class compromise that facilitated the redistributive allocation of welfare in exchange for mass loyalty. The principal crisis logic arose because the state was the object of competition between private and public interests in that it both created conditions for capital accumulation and represented public interests via the parliamentary process. By intervening in the market the state is

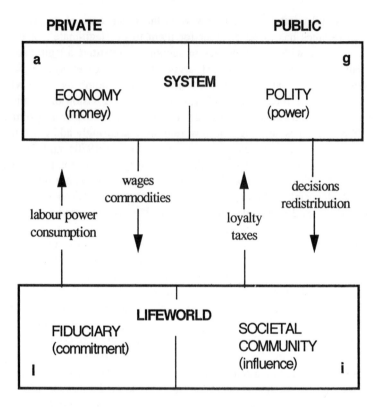

Figure 2.2 Habermas's reinterpretation of Parsons's AGIL

subject to further popular demands for intervention, while having absorbed cyclical crisis tendencies from the economy it is open to administrative overload. Together these tend to produce a fiscal crisis (O'Connor 1973; Habermas 1976) where the welfare state proves to be unsustainable. However, it seemed in the 1970s that to return to market steering and erode the welfare state would disrupt the inter-system exchanges and risk legitimation crisis. Moreover, motivations for compliance might be eroded once the process became visible and the mode of procurement had been seen through (Habermas 1976:70; Pakulski 1986). Western societies may be experiencing the con-sequences of this process, as the Keynesian welfare state is replaced by neoliberal economic policies and a workfare state (Jessop 1992). This is complemented by the erosion, in some cases collapse, of support for European social democratic parties, leaving a political vacuum which populist, regionalist and neofascist groups are attempting to fill.

These problems in advanced capitalism suggest, as Claus Offe (1976) argues, that increasing differentiation does not generate harmony, but rather creates conflicting functions and criteria of relevance within each subsystem, and overall disorganization. Moreover, there is an absence of harmony because each level of social organization is infused with power and hence with conflicts over the appropriation of resources, services and obligations. These power relations are manifest in cleavages of ownership and control (class), sectional interests within organizations, gender divisions and ethnicity. They are mediated and to some extent regulated by the norms, values and institutional practices (that is, by socio-cultural legitimation) but are likely to break out at any time, especially as the overall coherence of the system is placed under strain.

If one turns to Soviet societies it has to be noted that Habermas, like Parsons, presupposed an abstract citizen who was the focus of exchanges between the public and private spheres and who notionally at least consented to a particular form of rule. In Soviet systems the presence of neither could be assumed, which means that discussion of legitimacy will need to examine strategies for generating compliance, and the conditions in which these were more or less successful. Habermas regarded state socialist societies as a variant form of modernity – as 'post-capitalist class societies' – and hence presumably subject to the same crisis tendencies as later capitalism (Habermas 1976:15). Aspects of this thesis might be applicable to Soviet systems, and erosion of the revenue base is certainly present in post-socialism (Campbell 1992), although the Habermasian formulation presupposes that the three subsystems are relatively autonomous, which they were not in Soviet societies. The absence of clear differentiation between economy and polity in socialism would suggest that a different model of integration and crisis is required. It will be argued that rationality crises arose as a result of contradictions in the investment cycle, planning irrationalities and exposure to complex environmental risks, but these could be offset partly by latent differentiation through the second economy. Rationality crises may have been necessary, but certainly not sufficient, conditions for the full-blown legitimation crises of 1989–90. Further, one should bear in mind that these were dynamic systems in which there were, in most cases, successive attempts to disengage economic and political processes which had complex and contradictory effects on social integration. We need to ask under what conditions were motivational outputs forthcoming from the socio-cultural sphere, what choices did households have in provision of inputs into the political system, and how were they structured? This in turn suggests that the problem of legitimacy should be placed within a more systemic context of exchanges between the institutional orders of the lifeworld, and a model to this effect is developed in Chapter 5.

3. State Socialism and Modernity

This chapter discusses some key theoretical approaches to state socialist systems. Chapter 2 argued that regulatory systems embedded in social processes and values were capable of flexible adaptation that avoided over-complexity and unmanageable social conflicts. It further developed a model of modernity as a system of anonymous social interactions regulated primarily through the media of money and power. This is not to say, however, that there is a single organizational form appropriate to modern societies, or that Western capitalist societies should be regarded as the prototype to which others should aspire. Indeed, abstract sociological models might be insufficiently sensitive to differences between empirical social organizations. It was seen how Luhmann argues that in functionally differentiated societies stratification is no longer the primary pattern of differentiation and gives way to an open class structure. He further claims that 'capitalist' and 'socialist' countries do not differ in this respect but only in the extent to which bureaucratic organizations are involved in the reproduction of stratification (1982:244). A not dissimilar view is found in Habermas (1984:282) though his subsequent analysis is more detailed. However, it is far from clear that Soviet and capitalist systems *were* divergent aspects of a process common to complex societies, or whether different trajectories arose out of specific cultural, historical and global configurations.

This chapter re-examines the issue of routes to modernity and industrial society from a variety of perspectives. First, it considers whether one can regard state socialism as a fulfilment of Enlightenment modernity. Second, it critically examines the concept of totalitarianism, both in its original form in the 1950s and 1960s (Arendt; Friedrich and Brzezinski) and more recent variants developed by East European scholars. Third, convergence theorists (e.g. Tinbergen 1959; Kerr et al. 1960; Galbraith, 1972) predicted an evolutionary tendency towards bi-polar convergence between welfare capitalism and state soxialism. Although this approach has been regarded as rather passé over the past two decades or so, it might be argued that 1989–91 was the prelude to a new convergence of post-socialism and capitalism. A number of writers dismiss this point of view a little too hastily and with minimal discussion (e.g. Bryant and Mokrzycki (eds) 1994:2; Offe 1991). The notion of convergence might indeed be inappropriate to understand the post-communist transformation. However, many writers suggest that state socialism was not viable because command economies are inherently incapable of co-ordinating complex social orders. This surely implies that modern societies are constrained by a range of possible, or at least viable, forms of organization, to which they will tend to converge. I will argue here, and in subsequent chapters, that the most significant feature of modern social systems is a reflexive openness to learning which is in turn dependent upon the stabilization of initially fragile complex and highly differentiated systems. Indeed, in a more recent essay, Kerr (1983) develops a 'multidimensional multiway' hypothesis, which suggests that different societies have relatively open developmental trajectories, even if social systems do face constraints that are inscribed in the nature of industrial development itself. However, convergence theories tended to stress the technical as opposed to the social division of labour, and it will be argued that Soviet systems were distinct social formations governed by a logic of development that arose from an ensemble of technical, social and political relations.

SOCIALISM, MODERNITY AND AMBIVALENCE

Many commentators have seen in the Soviet Union a reaffirmation, for better or worse, of Enlightenment values once boldly proclaimed but subsequently eroded. For 'fellow travellers', the Soviet Union represented a return to an eighteenth-century Enlightenment vision of a rational, educated and scientific society based on the maximization of resources and the steady improvement of human nature as visualized by objective brains (Caute 1988:264). During the 1930s and 1940s in particular, Soviet communism was viewed by foreign admirers as a new civilization (e.g. Webb and Webb 1936) in which the Party exercised its will by persuasion (which was what the Enlightenment tradition was all about); ultimate authority rested with the Central Committee but everything was decided by groups and committees. Such enthusiasm was enduringly captured by Lincoln Stephans's comment, on returning from the Soviet Union, 'I have been over into the future and it works' (Caute 1988:26).[1]

Paradoxically, this claim is still accepted, in an inverted way, by those who regard communism as the epitome of modernity, albeit in its most nightmarish form, for whom its collapse portends a crisis of modernity *per se*. Bauman depicts modernity in Promethean terms which are contrasted with the fluid, differentiated and aestheticized cultural forms of post-modernity. Modernity, he says, 'was a long march to the prison. It never arrived there (though in some places, like Stalin's Russia, Hitler's Germany or Mao's China, it came quite close) albeit not for the lack of trying' (1992:xvii). Giddens (1990: 139) similarly describes modernity as a runaway juggernaut of enormous power which threatens to rush out of our control, crushing those who resist it. Again, Marshall Berman (1985) interpreted Goethe's *Faust* as an allegory of modernity's destructiveness, reflected in Stalinist projects such as the White Sea Canal.[2] According to this view, Marxism–Leninism was the archetypal grand narrative of domination (Lyotard 1990) and communism was modernity in its most determined mood and most decisive posture (Bauman 1992: 166).

It is true that this view has a good sociological pedigree. It was the kind of vision evinced in Weber's warnings about increasing bureaucratization and the steel-hard cage (*stahlhartes Gehaeuse*) of rationality. Of course, Weber's model of bureaucratic organization is open to various interpretations (Clegg 1989 and 1994; Chalcraft 1994; DiMaggio and Powell 1983; Ray and Reed (eds) 1994) but a central theme is that 'bureaucratization offers above all the optimum possibility for carrying through the principles of specializing administrative functions according to purely objective considerations' (Weber 1978: 215). In so far as bureaucratic procedures epitomize the modern, its

1 Examples of the Soviet modernist vision are Leonard Sabsovich's anti-urbanist architecture, which envisaged agro-urban settlements powered by a nationwide hydroelectric grid, or Okhitovich's linear socialist cities, which provided the basis for Magnitogorsk. However, by the end of 1930 the utopian architectural schools were being condemned as 'opportunists' and 'leftist phrasemongers' (Starr 1978).

2 Built between 1931 and 1933 largely by zeks, slave labour from the Gulag, the White Sea–Baltic Canal was grandiose and useless, and by 1966 had almost ceased to be used (Hosking 1992:198).

appearance is marked by the decline of what Simmel (1990:457) called the old social obligations, which promotes an atomization of society and the colourlessness of modern life, a cool reserve and anonymous objectivity. Further, for both Weber and Simmel, socialism embodied the complete calculability of life and would therefore represent the logical conclusion of modernity rather than its negation – the dictatorship, as Weber put it of the public official, not the proletariat.[3] Thus,

[s]tate bureaucracy would rule alone if private capitalism were eliminated. The private and public bureaucracies, which now work next to, and potentially against, each other and hence check one another to a degree, would be merged into a single hierarchy. This would be similar to the situation in ancient Egypt, but it would occur in a much more rational – and hence unbreakable – form. (Weber 1978, II:1402)

Schumpeter (1976:386) expected that socialism would succeed capitalism, albeit as a less innovative and more bureaucratic order. Modern organizations, then, were tending towards an optimal type where means (formal procedure, calculability and efficiency) became ends, while substantive values (such as justice, heroism, salvation and self-sacrifice) became matters of personal conviction. One interpretation of this was that rational organizations, as means, were indifferent to the ends to which they were put, which equally could be making money or genocide. For Adorno and Horkheimer (1973:6) bureaucratic, scientific and technical reason (*Verstand*) was a harbinger of totalitarian domination.

According to this conception, Promethean modernity is associated with gigantism, Fordist mass production and consumption; an extensive, corporatist and rationalized state; a secular (and often etatist) ideology; cultural homogeneity governed by the ethos of technology and the culture industry.[4] Moreover, it is claimed that modernity

---

3 Weber did, however, distinguish between two types of planned economy (Planwirtschaft) – complete socialization, where the economy is administered purely as a budgetary unit, and partial socialization of branches of production with the retention of capital accounting. These he said are technically examples of quite different types (1978 I:111). He also noted that the further bureaucratization implied by socialism might not prove possible (1978 I:225).

4 This broad conception of modernization as etatism, rationalization and secularization has been influential among Third World, as well as Soviet, 'modernizing élites'.. Examples include Kemalism in Turkey, Pahlavi Shah's Resurgence Party in Iran and Nasser's Egypt.

involves the development of increasingly subtle systems of control and their incursion into everyday life, particularly through institutions and social technologies, such as Foucault's (1979) carceral or Panoptic society. The less coercive, visible and imposing power becomes through the centralization and mobilization of administrative control, the more pervasive, internalized and 'normal' it appears (Burrell 1988).

However, the nightmare vision of disciplinary power and administrative control built into the fabric of everyday life is based on an over-deterministic view of socio-technical change. Not only is the implementation of these systems more haphazard, partial and fragmented than Bauman and others suggest, but the systems are also blunted by the countervailing power which those subject to them are able to develop (Reed 1991). Further, Talcott Parsons has argued that Weber's formulation of rationalization is not adequate for explaining capitalist economic activity since non-instrumental values have been re-institutionalized as a constraint on the market, especially those for professional services or with a high knowledge content, which, though universalistic and functionally specific in orientation, are subject to the *Gesellschaftlich* rules of professional ethics (Parsons, 1970).[5] Weber's 'rationally controlled action' (*Gesellschaftshandlen*) was only one among several types of purposive and value-rational actions, and modern societies exhibit high structural differentiation of spheres of action which forces actors to choose among pattern variables.[6]

Moreover, the institutionalization of markets, bureaucratic organizations, rationalized work practices and the like did not occur in an unproblematic evolutionary way, but have been subject to resistance, in service of which traditionalistic solidarity has frequently been deployed in innovative ways (Eldridge 1994; Thompson 1991). In the process, the Romantic critique of modernity, a frame of meaning that negates technological and instrumental values in the name of lost

5 Martin Albrow (1994) develops the more general claim that apparently impersonal and goal-rational organizations are actually highly charged with emotion.

6 In every situation actors choose between five polar orientations: collectivity–individualism; affectivity–value neutrality; particularism–universalism; ascribed status–performances (what people achieve rather than what they are); diffuseness–specificity. The first three couplets are stances towards the self while the last two are towards object relations. For Parsons they must be resolved in one way or the other – one cannot have both at the same time.

authenticity, became part of the repertoire of modern worldviews.[7]
That the dislocation of pre-industrial forms of life was the price paid
for enhanced freedom and control over the natural world is deeply
ingrained in modernity's self-understanding. Thus as well as rationalized spheres, the socio-cultural system of modern societies contains
counter-cultures which can be drawn upon by social movements
seeking a return to pre-modernity. Examples include craft communi-
tarianism, which aspires to unravel the web of a highly differentiated
division of labour (Smith and Thompson 1992); or deep ecology
movements, which insist on the need to establish meaningful relations
between the human world and the world as a global context
(Blumenberg 1985; Luke 1988).

If this is so, then how should we evaluate the different claims concerning modernity and Soviet systems? It is worth noting the congruence between Romanticism and the ideal of revolutionary heroism
(Löwy 1979). On one hand, the revolutionary tradition from 1789
through 1848 to 1917 has been associated with the birth of modernity
and a decisive break with feudal bonds (e.g. Habermas 1990; Touraine
1990). Yet, on the other hand, modernity is associated with Weber's
notions of disenchantment, rationalization, organizational impersonality and formal legality. From the standpoint of the latter, the claim
that Soviet systems were 'modern' would be hard to defend. In terms
of a sober 'Weberian' vision of modernity, the charismatic ideal of
selfless revolutionary heroism, of shock workers and Stakhanovites,
what Jowitt (1983) calls the amalgam of bureaucratic discipline and
charismatic correctness would appear to have more in common with
the *pre*modern cult of warriors upholding 'honour' as prime virtue
than the modern ethos of disenchanted scepticism.[8] Janos (1991) argues
that the Soviet Union was a garrison state ruled by a political class
whose self-justification derived from the external orientation of a
militaristic ideology which in turn justified a barracks economy and

---

7 For example, Marx (1973:162) saw 'the bourgeois viewpoint' as caught in an
   antithesis between itself and Romanticism, the longing for the 'original richness' of
   pre-modern forms of life. Similarly, Ferenc Fehér (1986) argues that Romantic anti-
   modernism and the idea of 'authentic man' rescued from industrialization are
   fundamentally modern constructs.

8 Indeed, Weber's fragmentary analysis of communism suggested that it was a pre-
   capitalist ethos based on the comradeship of rebellious soldiers, the utopian
   mentality of intellectuals and the revolutionary aspirations of the peasantry (Turner
   1994).

society. Again, Fehér et al. (1984:210) argue that, 'the ethics of Bol-shevism are in themselves a manifestation of ... the de-enlightenment process. Loyalty and obedience to the sovereign as supreme values belong to a world prior to enlightenment'. These would include the ethic of vigilance (*bditelnost*), military preparation (*voennaya pod-gotovka*) and struggle (*borba*), which successive mobilization campaigns during the 1920s and 1930s attempted to inculcate (Slepyan 1993).

Modernization is actually, as Weber and Simmel were well aware, an ambiguous process in which actual outcomes, such as the institu-tionalization of particular organizational forms, represent only one of a number of possible constellations (Wellmer 1983). It is better under-stood, as Arnason (1991 and 1993) puts it as a field of tensions, a highly contested terrain subject to competing claims for its appropria-tion, which cannot easily be subsumed within a unified theory.[9] Arnason claims that within the civilizational paradigm of modernity, alternative forms and 'counter-paradigms' appear via the selective appropriation and reactivation of traditions within a modernizing vision. Russia's peripheral position in Europe, combined with its internal 'Asiatic' influences, Arnason claims, fashioned an alternative modernizing paradigm that both challenged Western modernity and offered a proto-type that claimed to prefigure its future (1993:22ff.). The continuity of Russian traditionalism within Soviet Marxism was ensured partly through the incorporation of the élitist–populist revolu-tionary tradition of Chernyshevsky and Tkachev within Leninism (Arnason 1993:64–8), and the absorption of the Tsarist bureaucracy into the Soviet apparatus after 1917 (Fainsod 1963:250).

Thus Arnason's notion of a counter-paradigm of modernity avoids the simplistic subsumption of the Soviet experience within the frame-work of Western modernity. However, it does imply that there is a core model of modernity to which other societies either approximate or eventually fail. Moreover, the notion of Asiatic backwardness is problematic for reasons that will become apparent. Jowitt (1978:34),

---

9 Lash (1988) identifies two phases of modernity – 'early' and 'late' – the former characterized by foundationalist and absolute beliefs (such as the Reformation, or revolutionary heroism); the latter by organizationally complex, value-relative and pluralistic systems. This does not help much, because the late period seems to overlap with what is also called post-modernity and anyway these two phases should not be conflated (as in Bauman and Lyotard).

on the other hand, argues that the novelty of Leninism was its fusion of charismatic authority with organizational impersonality in which the Party rather than particular individuals was invested with heroic authority. The vanguard ethic places the Party as the sole legitimate source of political initiative and proletarian correctness, above the constraints of legality, a principle established by the Bolsheviks in the 1918 coup which ended the Constituent Assembly, an act justified in the name of higher charismatic authority, of revolutionary will over historical conditions.

STALINISM AND 'TOTALITARIANISM'

The idea that totalitarianism and modernity are inherently, as opposed to contingently connected has been influential (e.g. Giddens 1990:172). In Friedrich and Brzezinski's (1964) classical account, totalitarianism involved:

1. an official ideology covering all vital aspects of existence focused on a perfect final state of mankind;
2. a hierarchically organized single mass party led typically by the dictator and intertwined with the government bureaucracy, consisting of a relatively small percentage of the population who are unquestioningly dedicated to the ideology;
3. terrorist police control, directed not only at 'enemies' of the regime but against arbitrarily selected classes of the population;
4. near-complete monopoly of all means of effective mass communications (press, radio, cinema);
5. near-complete monopoly of all means of effective armed combat;
6. central control and direction of the economy.

This list is not necessarily exhaustive, and other traits might be added, such as economic autarky, closed frontiers, or an obsession with borders (Waller 1992). The technological aspect of totalitarianism is particularly striking in the secret police terror, technically enhanced possibilities of supervision and control of movement. Likewise the centrally   directed   economy   presupposes   the   reporting, cataloguing and calculating devices provided by modern technology. In short, Friedrich and Brzezinski argue, four of the six traits are technologically conditioned, which reflects a trend in modern civilization towards greater organizational size, such that totalitarian societies appear to be 'merely exaggerations, but none the less logical exaggerations, of the technical state of modern society' (1964:11–12). Weber's iron cage lurks in the background.

The atomization of society, as both a precondition for and consequence of totalitarianism, is a theme in Hannah Arendt (1967), who argues that support for totalitarian parties arises from 'mass society', where large numbers of people are not integrated into intermediate social groupings, such as social classes or community organizations. Loss of integration among non-élites allows the rise of new élites bent on total mobilization, while loss of ties with community creates an atomized society that is readily mobilized, creating conditions for the dictatorship of demagogues. Echoing Adorno and Horkheimer, Arendt suggests that 'the subterranean stream of Western history has finally come to the surface' – a claim echoed more recently by Václav Havel, for whom totalitarian society is the distorted mirror of the whole of modern civilization (Havel 1988).[10]

For Horváth and Szakolczai (1992) totalitarianism, unlike later concepts, was cognizant of the centrality of the party apparatus in social organization. Arendt regarded totalitarian organizations as representing a new type, divided into a Front Organization of members and sympathizers on one hand and élite cadres to whom access is tightly regulated on the other. Real power, though, rested with secret police who aimed at transforming human nature, a point reiterated by Friedrich and Brzezinski, for whom the totalitarian movement seeks to extend this power into every nook and cranny of society, geared to a futuristic orientation, grandiose schemes of social reconstruction which are the basis for the extension of totalitarian power to all segments of

10 This reflects the influence of Heideggerianism in Czech philosophy. Patocka wrote of the triumph of impersonal rationality as the individual is both the victim and the instrument of the system. Havel, like Belohradsky, warned of something 'far more serious' in this form of rule: 'the inevitable consequences of rationalism' of the break with Naturwelt, of an immediate pre-rational empathy with nature. In Havel (1988) this connection was explicit. He wrote of his childhood 'intuition' that the smoking factory chimney was a violation of nature, representative of a breach in the natural order of things.

society (1964:131–2). There is no legality in this system because it is dependent on arbitrary lawlessness, while the population is mobilized against imagined enemies in a perpetual state of crisis, such as the fear of capitalist encirclement, 'counter-revolutionary plots' such as the Donbass mine and Shakhty trials (1930), the trial of Mensheviks (1931), and waves of purges throughout the 1930s. Real mass terror, moreover, begins *after* political resistance is liquidated, when it takes genocidal proportions – millions in concentration camps and forced labour as well as rapid élite circulation. Of 139 members of the Soviet Central Committee elected at the XVII Congress (1934), 110 had been arrested by the XVIII (1939), and of 1,966 delegates to the former 1,108 were arrested and only 59 took their places at the latter. That whole populations or groups (e.g. Estonians, Jews, doctors, engineers, kulaks) can be deported, subject to famine, forced labour or mass execution, indicates the prerogative sovereign power of the state over society (Arato 1982; Fraenkel 1941).

However, a range of objections have been levelled at the totalitarianism concept (Solomon (ed.) 1983). Analytically the concept is tautologous to the extent that it is derived from the regimes (Nazi Germany, Stalinism) to which it is retrospectively 'applied'. However, its adequacy even as description of Soviet society under Stalin has been questioned, especially by the so-called Revisionist school,[11] who have argued that Stalinism was not visionary or utopian but in many respects conservative; that the regime had less control than is often claimed, since its strategy was improvised, reacting to the unintended consequences of policies; that the strata to which Stalin appealed for support were active in pursuing the purges. Thus the initiative to an extent came from below; the terror had grass-roots support and this should cause us to revise the traditional view of society as an object of totalitarian terror. Let us briefly elaborate each of these.

Stalinism was not visionary or utopian but was actually the conservative Thermidor reaction that many Bolsheviks had feared since 1917 (Daniels 1993:102–5). The First Five Year Plan (1928–32) is often cited to highlight features of totalitarianism, especially all-embracing controls to effect an ideological reconstruction of society. Yet totali-

11 Includes Sheila Fitzpatrick, Arch Getty, Rittersporn and Thurston, and draws exten-
    sively on data from the Smolensk archives at Harvard. 'Members' of the school are
    not of one mind. Getty (1985), for instance, took issue with Fitzpatrick's collective
    social mobility thesis while she has disputed aspects of his account of the Purges.

tarian theory cannot explain why the Cultural Revolution (1928–30) was abandoned after Stalin's 'dizziness with success' speech (March 1930) when former advocates of radical change were condemned as Trotskyites, wreckers, opportunists and so on. This Great Retreat was driven by unanticipated responses to the chaos of the Five Year Plan and the discovery that militants such as the Komsomols were often disrespectful of the new communist power (Hough 1978:251). Subsequently, many young advocates of the cultural revolution were purged in 1937–8 along with the old revolutionaries (Fitzpatrick 1978). Further, despite the terror, an actual differentiation occurred between law and society, public and private, Party and state, which was signalled by the abandonment of Pashukanis's concept of the post-legal order. His arrest and disappearance in 1937 marked the consolidation of the legal system and the defeat of utopian expectations of a withering away of the state.[12] Even the revolutionary politicization of society is premised on a strategically narrow use of political decision-making power in which the complexity of the political system is less than that of society. Accounts of Soviet systems in terms of 'state vs society' and 'atomization' are therefore likely to prove simplistic and we need to examine their dynamics as (partially) differentiated systems.

The concept of totalitarianism as utopian reconstruction further ignores the extent of re-traditionalization that took place under Stalin after 1931. Along with the conformist ethos of the new social stratum of party officials, family life was extolled, divorce made more difficult, abortion prohibited in 1944, and homosexuality criminalized. Indeed, Filtzer (1992b:177) comments that it would have been difficult to build up the nuclear family as an authoritarian structure if women had been freed from domestic burdens. Stalinism required a re-traditionalization of culture and the subordination of women in the workplace and at home.

A further illustration of this cultural re-traditionalization is found in the way history teaching returned to 'important events, personages

12 A leading figure in the Revoliutsiya prava group, Pashukanis argued that law was the juridical expression of commodity exchange and that as this is superseded by planning, law and the state would wither away. In the early 1930s, Pashukanis was influential in promoting simplification of the criminal code, the establishment of comrades' courts and the expansion of psychiatry into the criminal system. However, the 1936 Constitution differentiated punitive criminal law from civil law, and protected personal property (Sharlet 1978).

and dates': Ivan the Terrible and Peter the Great were once again national heroes (Hosking 1992:215–16) and Stalin's mythical simple-minded account of Russian history (the *Short Course*) became a canonical text.[13] Rather than promote a utopian, modernist recon-struction of society, Stalinist culture was conservative, a development which Vera Dunham (1976) suggests reflected the victory of the young, careerist, status conscious petty-bourgeois (*meshchanstvo*) over the revolutionary intelligentsia. This new class surrounded itself with chintz curtains and polka-dotted tea cups, thick pile carpets red-plush hangings and monumental architecture.

Moreover, even under Stalin the regime had less control than is often claimed, and its strategy was often improvised, reacting to the unintended consequences of policies over which complex struggles were taking place. Between 1933 and 1936 there were three attempts to exercise central control through Central Control Commission (TsKK) – the purges (1933–35), verification of documents (1935), and exchange of Party cards (1936). Party records between 1933 and 1934 (when membership fell by 33 per cent) show a chaotic situation, rather than calculated bureaucratic operation (Lewin 1978). The second verification in 1935, however, was 'less arbitrary than one might have thought' and the majority of offences were non-ideological, usually corruption and infraction of rules (Getty 1985:85). Further, Thurston (1986) suggests that these campaigns had public support, and argues (again from the Smolensk archive) that following Kirov's assassination (1934), which signalled the opening of the purges, popular feeling was against enemies rather than the state. Some radi-cals attempted to realize the 1936 Constitution and use it against the bureaucracy, and in 1937 at Magnitogorsk, workers turned the purges against managers. Thurston found little proof that everyone was affected by an atmosphere of totalitarian terror, in which 'anyone could be next'.

Indeed, for Getty (1985:112) the NKVD[14] Chairman, Nikolai Yezhov, was 'a radical anti-bureaucrat who mistrusted economic managers, searched for class enemies, a puritanical and vigilant

13 The Short Course was to be an object of private contemplation, not to be read in groups since this might engender discussion (Kharkhordin 1993).
14 Narodny Kommissariat Vnutrennikh Del (People's Commissariat for Internal Affairs), later of course the Komitet Gosudarstvennoy Bezopasnosti (Committee for State Security).

investigator'. There was, he suggests, a Trotskyist network in the leadership of 1936 (1985:122) and their purge culminated in the Novosibirsk trial in November 1936 of former Trotskyists accused of sabotage.[15] At the February 1937 Plenum of the Central Committee, Stalin attacked patronage, and local cliques in the apparat called on the masses to 'verify' leaders. *Pravda* denounced party fiefs, called for rank-and-file criticism regardless of person and allowed dissatisfactions at local level to be voiced, to the extent that the NKVD tried to defend some accused leaders (Rittersporn 1979). The centre wanted to use mass resentment to force compliance by officials and in the 1937 Party elections over half (30,000) of the local and regional lower-level Party leadership was ousted. This was followed by an atmosphere of crisis and the arrest of Marshal Tukhachevsky and leading Red Army Generals on charges of espionage.[16] The crisis presented a potential challenge to the state, and the trials of Bukharin, Rykov, Yagoda and Rakovsky shifted blame for the disorganization on to the former opposition.

Stalin appealed to distinct strata for support, and the Great Purges actively involved significant groups of the population (Hosking 1992:206). These included a core of new technical graduates (*vydvizhentsy*) who were subsequently dependent on the regime's patronage. Sheila Fitzpatrick (1979b) insists on the need to differentiate 'society' to make visible the inter- and intra-class/stratum including those within the bureaucracy. Further, there were hierarchies among workers, divided into unskilled 'new workers' (from villages) and 'old' (from cities) and convict, semi-free and bureaucratically created strata. Totalitarian theory does not examine the ruling stratum and the way in which purges resulted in the formation of a new privileged caste (Hosking 1992:206). The core of the upwardly mobile group were the new technical graduates who took the place of 'bourgeois specialists' and Red Directors'.[17] Indeed, for Fitzpatrick,

15 Most accounts, however, suggest that there was no Trotskyist organization by the early 1930s. For example, Andrew and Gordievesky claim, 'The real reason why Trotskyists had disappeared from view within the Soviet Union was simply that ... they had in fact disappeared': the Trotskyite–Zinovyevite Terrorist Centre was a fantasy (1991:148–9).

16 Like Deutscher (1990), Getty thinks 'maybe there was a plot' among army officers, although most sources conclude that there was not.

17 The Red Directors, appointed after 1917 on the basis of political and organizational reliability but with limited technical education, were removed wholesale from key

who echoes Mannheim's concept of a political generation, social mobility was the key to purges, since the leadership appealed to the young, talented and ambitious, upwardly mobile, who were recruited into the managerial strata.[18] The trial of Pyatakov (Deputy Commissar of Heavy Industry) was a signal for the mass demotions and arrests of the old managerial–technical élite, while others enjoyed rapid promotion. In the period 1928–32, 152,000 leading cadres were graduates; during 1933–37 there were 266,000, and by 1941 89 per cent of cadres were graduates, the majority of whom survived the purges (Getty 1985:112). Industrialization further created an expansion in posts – between 1928 and 1932 the number of engineers rose from 18,000 to 74,000 and professionals in administration from 63,000 to 119,000. The majority of these posts were filled by former workers, who accounted for half the directors of industrial enterprises by 1933. By 1952 36 per cent of the Central Committee came from the *vydvizhentsy* (Fitzpatrick 1979b). Purges opened doors to dizzy opportunities (Hosking 1992:196) and simple denunciation (*donos*) was often sufficient to have a competitor removed, since the NKVD had to fulfil targets.[19] That the leadership acted with the collusion of a significant section of the population, which became a loyal cadre stratum, challenges the view of 'society' as the passive object of 'totalitarianism'.

So extensive was grass-root support for the terror that Getty (1985) and Fitzpatrick (1979b) describe it as a 'revolution from below'. Rittersporn (1979) argues that the struggles of 1936–38 were unleashed by popular discontent with the arbitrariness, corruption and inefficiency of the ruling stratum, a claim supported by the Smolensk archives, which have five dossiers filled with complaints from that city's regions in 1936. Jerry Hough (1978:246) argues that Arendt's

administrative posts in the Great Purges. There is not space here to detail the shifting balance between expertise and political criteria in appointment to the Soviet bureaucracy, but this is discussed by Hough (1969) and Fitzpatrick (1979a and b).

18 Most of the Brezhnev generation came from this cohort, which made up 50 per cent of Ministers and Deputy Ministers (57 of 115) by 1952. By 1980 half of the Politburo were from the generation which had experienced rapid social mobility. Kosygin, for example, graduated in 1935 from Leningrad Textile Institute and by 1937 was director of a textile factory and by 1939 Commissar for the Textile Industry.

19 In its omniscience the NKVD did not require its intended victims to have committed specific 'counter-revolutionary' acts. Those about to finish terms in camps could be re-sentenced since the NKVD 'knew' beforehand that they would again violate Article 58 on counter-revolutionary crimes (Gelb 1993).

image of a terrorized and atomized society bears 'no relationship to the reality of the time' since the mobilization programme was an attempt to integrate not to atomize inexperienced workers and peasants. None the less, one effect of the purges, combined with the Five Year Plans, was to create high levels of social disorganization, and Filtzer (1992b:236) argues that Stalinism did not lead to a totalitarian society but one almost totally unorganizable and dysfunctional.

However, these claims have been controversial and subject to a number of objections. First, the moral objection that the Revisionists tend to minimize the terror by emphasizing other developments. Millions, and not merely members of the élite, were affected; hundreds of thousands were involved in administering the terror (Cohen 1986). Second, social mobility was two-way and few cities grew as large as the Gulag capitals – as millions moved upward, millions moved downward into a Gulag hell (Ginzburg 1981). To write of the 1930s while ignoring the *zeks* is like writing a history of the ante-bellum South without mentioning slavery (Cohen 1986). Third, claims that the Party was weak are challenged, since millions were murdered despite 'weak' Party machinery. The presence of factional struggles demolishes the monolithic façade but does not explain the bloodshed nor how terror entered the pores of everyday life (Kenez 1986). For some, totalitarianism did capture definite aspects of the experience of Stalinism (Horváth and Szakolczai 1992), such as the total claim of the regime on its population, and the process of plebiscitary mobilization. Even if the revisionists are correct to identify the complexity of Soviet life, they blunt the political cutting edge of social history (Eley 1986). Conquest (1990) argues that the capriciousness of the terror gave it great effect, and that arrests 'eased off' to one million a year by 1939 because it had achieved its purpose, although Thurston (1986) questions the evidence for this figure.

However, totalitarianism could not account for the decline of terror. Friedrich and Brzezinski suggest rather weakly that terror 'can decrease as a new generation rises' (1964:301) and a managerial class might be bound by the constraints of industrial society rather than ideology. Daniels (1993), for whom totalitarianism was the outcome of revolutionary processes of *longue durée*, argues that the demise of these systems is attributable to a kind of routinization and that they will eventually 'lose their thrall', a position which requires a more elaborate sociological theory than he offers. The concept came to be regarded as somewhat passé following the détente of the 1960s, and the de-Stalinization of the Soviet Union under Khrushchev. The XX Congress (1956) was followed by gradual legalization, such as the 1958 new criminal code which removed offences such as 'enemy of the people', 'counter-revolutionary activity' or doing something 'analogous' to a crime. Debate continued as to the permanence of this relaxation but the Soviet Union under Khrushchev was widely regarded as 'no longer totalitarian'.

None the less, a central aspect of the concept lived on in the notion of the progressive destruction of civil society and the absorption of all forms of social life by the state. Civil society literature is premised on what Arato (1982), following Offe and earlier work by Fraenkel (1941), calls the 'domination of the prerogative state over society'. Moreover, the concept has regained considerable currency among East European scholars in the 1980s. Friedrich and Brzezinski (1964: 137) had suggested that, once the system became stable, totalitarian terror came into its own and embraced the whole society, so that many felt hunted even though the secret police did not touch them. This is echoed in Lovas and Anderson's (1982) concept of 'friendly repression' and other recent accounts of the concept. Before the 1989–90 uprisings, Havel and Rupnik stressed the continuity of domination between Stalinist and post-Stalinist forms of rule, arguing that the system's dominance had become more effective since the demise of Stalinism. Rupnik (1988) argued that although the rule of the Party is never total and, as totalitarianism dispensed with terror, the system paradoxically became more 'truly totalitarian'. For Rupnik this 'post-totalitarianism' phase displayed several features. Party officials were secure from terror; there was an appearance of legality; Marxist–Leninist ideology was disorganized and everyday life was depoliticized; this was accompanied by the survival of totalitarianism control within the Party.

This form of rule was allegedly more successful than earlier totalitarianism because it adopted the mantle of rationality and legality.[20] Similarly, Elemer Hankiss argued that by the 1960s the paralysis of Hungarian society under totalitarian rule had reached its limits, to be

20 Fehér (1986) cites the use of mental hospitals to detain dissidents under Khrushchev and Brezhnev as indications that some re-enlightenment had taken place since repression had to appear in the guise of science.

followed by liberalization, which was a more sophisticated policy of domination (Hankiss, 1990:49). However, this argument was seriously flawed since legality opened up the possibility of a private sphere free from state intervention and therefore of independent activity. Indeed, the history of the Communist Parties of Eastern Europe is one in which major social conflicts have arisen in part from divisions within the ruling élite (Kecskemeti 1969). The initial transition from Stalinist terror to a more open regime in Hungary and Poland during 1953–55 was not an automatic process, but was rather the result of the mobilization of intellectuals, journalists, members of the Politburo and, increasingly, workers and students, who were able to make advances against the Stalinist faction within the élite. It is true that in Hungary this ended in the catastrophe of 1956, and that in Poland the initial hopes invested in Gomulka and decentralized self-management were to be disappointed (Ascherson 1988). Yet the history of Soviet societies over the past four decades is one marked by struggles, sometimes covert, sometimes open, which took place both within and outside the Party–State. Thus the claims of the 'post-totalitarian' theorists had little prima facie plausibility prior to 1989 and now have none at all (Arato 1991). The trends they identified were actually systemic management strategies, which (unwittingly) prepared for the dissolution of the system. Like the post-Weberian control models noted above, these arguments over-totalize the capacity of the system to exert effective domination. Theorists of totalitarian mass movements explain the genesis but not the trajectory of the movements once in power and the theory exaggerated the élite–mass dichotomy.

Rather than evidence of excessive power, the terror was the consequence of a deficit of power in the system, evidenced, for example, in mobilization campaigns that were often ineffective, frustrated by apathy and competing organizational goals between party officials and mass organizations (Slepyan 1993). If a system lacks adequate internal means to regulate the variation of its contributions, its political élite is likely to 'blame' forces in the environment for organizational failures. The result is a simple image of the environment and categorical moralizing form of processing experience such as conspiracy theories (Luhmann 1982:149). The preoccupation with spies, wreckers, foreign encirclement, counter-revolutionaries, and so on, which created the conditions for mass terror, was the result of the political system's incapacity to respond flexibly to its environment, as well as an over-burdening of feasible objectives. In the post-Stalinist period, depoliticization was a means by which the state was differentiated from institutional orders of society without calling the leading role of the Party publicly into question (Staniszkis 1992). This represented an expansion of power in the political system through a technocratic rather than a politicized ethos. By the 1960s, local Party organs had acquired considerable latitude to deal with local officials, enterprise managers and government departments, and were not tightly locked into a command–action hierarchy (Hough 1969). It was at this point that the possibilities of a convergence between the two systems became apparent.

TECHNOLOGICS AND CONVERGENCE

The theory of functional differentiation implies that there is an optimal organizational form at which industrial societies process complexity most efficiently. This raises the question of whether there is a core model of modernity from which one deviates at one's peril, or whether, on the contrary, there are multiple forms of modernity that will vary with particular local configurations of social organization. Further, while it is reasonably clear that routes from pre-modern to modern society have been varied (Moore 1969) there may nevertheless be a tendency towards cultural, organizational and economic homogeneity once an industrial system is in place (Almond 1987). This view suggests a social logic inscribed into technical forms of organization. The emergence of welfare capitalism and post-Stalinist communism in the 1950s, along with détente in the 1960s, encouraged the belief that the two systems were indeed converging (Tinbergen 1959; Kerr et al. 1960; Kerr 1983). This thesis is not particularly new. Saint-Simon envisaged industrial society as an organic system governed by an educated élite who would formulate a public policy of 'Christian Industrialism', combining economic efficiency with distributive justice. For Marx, the more advanced society showed, to the industrially less advanced, an image of its own future. The influence of Weber's view (1978 II:1402) that 'the future belongs to bureaucratization' has already been noted. Schumpeter (1976:129) similarly argued that mankind was not free to choose since 'things economic and social move by their own momentum and the ensuing situations compel individuals and groups to behave in certain ways whatever they may wish to do'.

Was state socialism, then, a divergent path to modernity, in which the necessary functions were performed by substitute agents, or a fundamentally different logic of development? Under the influence of managerial revolution theorists (e.g. Burnham 1964), Soviet-type systems were viewed as variants of the phenomenon of industrial society which, after 1917, bifurcated into capitalist and non-capitalist forms still unified by an underlying logic. Classical convergence theories identified a range of logical possibilities, shown in Figure 3.1, especially row 2a. First, mono-polar convergence on communism, in which the capitalist world conforms with Marxist expectations, is the Soviet counter-paradigm of modernity that was echoed by fellow travellers such as the Webbs and Steffans. Second, varieties of bi-polar convergence, as East and West both balance state ownership, a private sector, a decentralized and differentiated economy, and worker participation in management. These contain various options, such as Tinbergen's (1959) strong convergence thesis that envisaged that both systems would develop optimum forms of welfare and the market, state intervention and private ownership, egalitarian income distribution and so on; Kerr et al.'s weaker claim (1960) that industrial societies would tend towards various combinations of plan, market, managerialism and corporatism; and 'hybrid' systems interposed between East and West resulting from reform communism and consisting of quasi-pluralism, administrative market and second economy (Hankiss 1990). According to Kerr (1983:18), the basic structure alleged to give rise to this logic consists of:

- skilled and productive industrial workers who are mobile, educated and rule-following;
- large enterprises, cities and state intervention capable of generating consensus;
- a managerial–professional occupational hierarchy;
- acceptance by workers of the economic structure based on their sharing the gains of industrialism, and growing security and influence over the workplace.

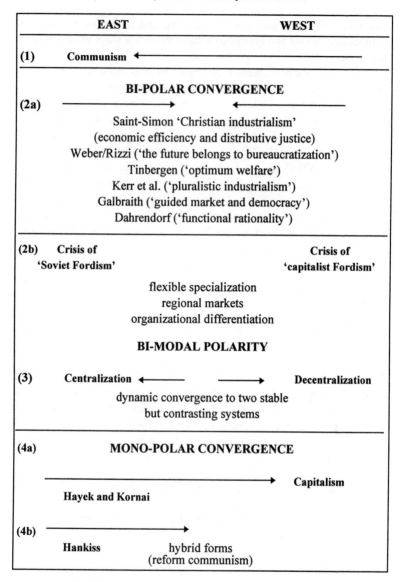

Figure 3.1 Models of convergence

Third, bi-modal polarity in which each system stabilized and co-existed around divergent organizational forms (Pryor 1973). Fourth, there is the opposite form of mono-polar convergence, the Hayekian dream of capitalism worldwide, a view encouraged now by the collapse of communism (Fukuyama 1992; Kornai 1990a).

Kerr (1983) re-assessed earlier versions of his thesis in the light of concerns about the future of growth, leadership changes in the USSR and the renewed Cold War, the cultural contradictions of capitalism between egalitarianism, meritocracy, individualism, and the exhaustion of the welfare state in both East and West. He develops a differential model of three levels of potential convergence and continuing diversity (in the early 1980s) between capitalist and state socialist systems. Level 1, which displayed most convergence, was that of science, technology, productive resources and organization, and patterns of work and daily life. Level 2 consisted of opposing imprints arising from divergent élite patterns (the bourgeoisie in capitalism; revolutionary intelligentsia in state socialism) and created bi-polar diversity in political systems. Level 3, culture including gender attitudes, religion, nationalism and ethnicity, is subject to the most varied imprints of pre-industrial beliefs and behavioural patterns. This revised model to some extent answers Archer's (1990) criticism that Kerr did not address the cultural dimension of development, although his conception of levels is still rather crude and does not elaborate the various mediations between them.[21]

Further, this modified convergence thesis has a rather dated conception of industrialism which seems to identify closely with Fordist production regimes and regulatory systems. Looked at through the post-Fordist literature, a different pattern of convergence might be proposed, since the type of organizations once believed to be most effective (the monocratic, command–action hierarchies which the Soviet systems in some ways exemplified), face increasing pressures towards diversification as the environments with which they deal

---

21 Alexander (1995) argues that later modernization theory reconceptualized convergence to allow for parallel but independent pathways to the modern, but by then it was too late. Critical sociology had begun to narrate the social in a new way, in terms of the polarity between capitalism and socialism instead of between tradition and modernity, and the modern came to be viewed through negative categories of exploitation and bureaucratization. Perhaps so, but there were still problems with the revised theory, as there are with Alexander's partial rehabilitation of convergence, which is discussed in Chapter 7.

increase in complexity (Weick 1979). Literature on the crisis of Fordism suggests that in advanced capitalist countries the logic of centralized control is giving way to an 'organizational smorgasbord' on which 'organization becomes the art of deconstructing organizations that can re-organize themselves' (Stark 1992b:57). This argument revolves around four structural developments: the unpredictable and uncontrollable disruptions to standardized methods of organizational management caused by more sophisticated information technologies (Castells 1989; Scarborough and Corbett 1992); the centrality of expert knowledge and power within the much more decentralized and dispersed corporate forms emerging in the 'information mode of development' (Castells 1989); the extreme economic fragmentation and segmentation which these socio-technical changes generate (Piore and Sabel 1984); and the 'hyper-differentiating' cultures which are both cause and consequence of these transformations in the material base of advanced capitalist economies (Crook et al. 1992). According to David Harvey (1994: 185–6), a new regime of 'flexible accumulation' will entail a mix of highly efficient Fordist production regimes in some sectors and regions combined with flexible technologies and organizational forms that provide the socio-technical, economic and administrative capacities demanded by globalized capitalist competition, particularly in the finance, service, high-tech and knowledge-intensive sectors.

Robin Murray (1992) suggests that 'Soviet Fordism' was an application (and exaggeration) of the organizational forms of capitalist Fordism, such as the synchronization of production flows, gigantic scale and product standardization.[22] Examples of this model might be the Chelyabinsk tractor factory built by Ford in the 1930s, which had a higher caterpillar output than the USA (Murray 1992), or the East German *Kombinate* in the 1960s (Voskamp and Wittke 1991). From this point of view, the crisis of communism could be understood in terms of a global crisis of the Fordist regime of accumulation (see row 2b in Figure 3.1). These changes indicate that post-socialist societies

---

22 The Bolsheviks' well-known admiration for Taylorism resulted in an attempt to apply principles formulated for the enterprise to the whole society. Murray does point out that, unlike the capitalist version, Soviet Fordism lacked the 'pull' of monetary demand and the 'push' of the threat of unemployment. Further, for capitalist enterprises, anticipated profit stimulates rationalized work organization, whereas Soviet enterprises were geared to the fulfilment of physical planning targets, with results described in Chapter 4.

encounter a world of diverse organizational forms where the complexity and volatility of socio-technical and political-cultural developments outrun the control systems made available by rational bureaucracy. A possible future for post-socialism that has shown some potential in Hungary (Neumann 1992) is the evolution of flexible decentralization, self-management, the growth of regional and local markets, horizontal integration and the expansion of civil society, that is, sophisticated and open structures for managing complexity and impersonality. Even so, the evolution of these kinds of structures might be fettered by inertia, problems of integration in the global economy, the historical pattern of capital investment, problems of identifying and sustaining national competitive advantage, shortage of appropriate skills, or lack of foreign investment (these are discussed in Chapters 7 and 8).

Kerr (1983:81) acknowledges that a single optimal economic system is a day-dream and, like Kornai (1980), proposes a model of choice among 'package deals'.[23] But if this is the case the question remains as to the range of variation circumscribed by the organizational structure of each system and at what point the existing package becomes unworkable. Which options are viable within the constraints of the existing system and which would require a fundamental reconstruction? These issues featured prominently in debates about reform communism in the 1980s (e.g. Arato 1982; Fehér et al. 1984). In order to develop this we need to theorize social evolution on different dimensions of language, culture and communication, through dimensions of production, where nature is appropriated for human needs; socialization, where inner nature (or personality) is adapted to society through communicative action; and system maintenance through steering capacity, which increases with successful adaptations to environmental disturbances. Successful adaptations are those which are consistent with the continued identity or goal state of the system and protect its core social relations. Learning capacities are not one-dimensional and open up different kinds of potentials along the dimensions of production, socialization and systemic regulation (Habermas 1979:120). This is not envisaged as an autonomous process,

---

23 These (ideologically rather loaded) choices are between economic efficiency and income inequality; individualism and full employment; dispersion or concentration of power, reflecting Kornai's neoliberalism.

but rather, as Rueschemeyer (1986:171) stressed, one driven by the outcomes of power struggles which select from among different forms of social differentiation.

The following is a schematic approximation of the principle of organization in the two systems (see Figure 3.2) which will be elaborated in this study.[24] The range of variation in capitalist societies is determined by the principle of profitability which operates in both *laissez-faire* and the Keynesian Welfare State (KWS) versions. In the former, conditions of profitability are given by the national and overseas markets, in response to which investment and profit fluctuates with high risk of social dislocation since welfare is discretionary. In the latter, enterprises mould environments and the state budget acts as a 'shock absorber' through the KWS. Despite state regulation, though, enterprises remain self-financing, capital is alienable and remains independent of the state.

However, the range of variation in socialist societies was determined by the integrated administrative hierarchy where capital merged with the state and investment decisions were not governed by profitability. In the Stalinist growth model, production was determined by volume in the central plan and since enterprises were not self-funding they were not constrained by resources or overheads. The limits of growth were thus the de facto macroeconomic ratios of the budget, and plan fulfilment rather than resource management was the central objective. On the other hand, reform communism introduced decentralized enterprise budgets with elements of self-financing (but still subsidized) marginal private property (e.g. allotments) with a state distribution system, and production measured in value. However, money still did not become the socially generalized form of value, nor does differentiation between polity and economy proceed to the point where the latter is absorbing complexity and risk from the former. Convergence theses exaggerated the range of internal variation each system could permit without threatening its core structure of accumulation. Rakovski (Kis)[25] (1978) argues that in statist systems the range

---

24 Some of these oppositions are matters of degree but the model emphasizes aspects where change would presuppose an alteration in the balance of power and level of system differentiation.
25 'Rakovski' was a pseudonym for Janos Kis, one of the leaders of the Hungarian Democratic Opposition, which was one of the first opposition groups to emerge

CAPITALISM	STATE SOCIALISM
Class-based system of allocation	Status-based system of allocation
Means of production owned privately (with extensive state investment)	Absence of large-scale private production (with exceptions, e.g. Polish agriculture)
Investment decisions led and limited by anticipated profit	Dissolution of boundaries between state and economy
Social development and state intervention follows logic of capital accumulation	Profit subordinated to state policy and availability of resources
Insolvency results in bankruptcy	Soft budget constraint
Crises of over-production	Shortage economy – crises of investment exceeding available resources
Money as the social form of value	Money was not the real medium of exchange. Capital goods circulated through inter-departmental requisition
Wages cover necessary subsistence costs	Consumption goods (housing, domestic fuel, transport, food) subsidized
Capitalist proprietor commands labour through the wage contract and legal framework	No wage contract. Apparatus that controlled means of production also controlled labour
Trade union collective bargaining (giving way to plant negotiations)	Trade unions little independence. But informal enterprise-based agreements gave labour some control over labour process
Taxation system presupposes juridical citizen and contract with the state	Redistributive economy presupposed subject of sovereign state
Formal–legal legitimacy	Substantive legitimacy
Political pluralism and public sphere constrained by commercial and technocratic systems	Political monism but increasing pluralism in post-Stalinism

Figure 3.2 Capitalism and state socialism

during the 1980s. Kis was a youthful revisionist of the Budapest School, but later evolved into an advocate of Western capitalism and describes himself as a 'socio-liberal'. Between 1988 and 1992 he chaired the Free Democratic Alliance, later the Alliance of Free Democrats.

of variation, for example the extent to which they can move towards market systems, was limited by the exigencies of the central planning bureaucracy that cannot hand over steering to the market without abdicating. Likewise, Bahro (1977:222) claims that even when reforms were at their height,[26] the system did not go so far as to establish the autonomy of industrial enterprises or even let them pay an obligatory calculable tax. Thus the notion of an evolutionary bi-polar convergence driven by a logic of industrial society is implausible when set against the particular form of systemic regulation in Soviet states. The latter were neither a distorted reflection of ugly tendencies within Western modernity (as some versions of totalitarian theory suggest) nor were they a divergent route to the common goal, an industrial society. On the contrary, it will be argued, Soviet systems represented a specific socio-economic form of peripheral modernization.

None the less convergence theories perhaps deserve reconsideration in view of dominant interpretations of the collapse of communism. Many accounts assume that the eventual collapse of communism represented a version of mono-polar convergence (row 4 in Figure 3.1) resulting from the disintegration of the Soviet system. One explanation of Soviet economic stagnation in the 1970s and 1980s highlights the incompatibility between the form of social organization (the plan, state monopoly, bureaucracy) and the technical requirements of the division of labour (Gomulka 1986; Winiecki 1986a and b). Gomulka argued that the system had achieved success in expanding the rate of capital accumulation, mobilizing labour participation, and R & D investment. However, the system of centrally-directed extensive growth had reached an international growth equilibrium and in the absence of efficiency-enhancing institutional changes – substantial exposure to market competition and financial imperatives – the economy would stagnate further (1986:57). This again suggests that there is a technical logic to the division of labour in industrial societies with which certain social forms are incompatible (which may be true) *and* that this necessarily creates mounting political pressure within the system to change, which is a more doubtful proposition. Rather, the socio-cultural system cannot be considered independently from the

26 The pre-1980s reforms, such as the Liberman Reforms in the Soviet Union (1967–68); the Hungarian New Economic Mechanism (1968) or the DDR's New Economic System (1963–67).

economic–technical division of labour, and might actually facilitate change which preserves the core identity of the system. There is no single organizational form appropriate to modern societies, and the experience of state socialism combined with its mode of integration into the global economy might generate a developmental trajectory divergent from that of Western Europe.

4. Mode of Domination and Legitimacy

This chapter develops the concluding remarks in Chapter 3 into a model of the mode of domination in Soviet societies. There is fairly wide agreement that their organizing structure was exhibited in the system of nomenklatura appointments, the origins of which lay in the aftermath of the Russian revolution. I argue that unlike capitalism, where a surplus is appropriated in the form of value, the nomenklatura appropriated a surplus product which was divided between accumulation and differentially allocated consumption. This generated new forms of horizontal and vertical stratification and social tensions that required co-ordination, since coercion was insufficient to guarantee the reproduction of the mode of domination. Following the discussion in Chapter 2, it is appropriate to ask what was the Soviet principle of organization or its defining structure, and what constituted change within, as opposed to change of, the system?

On these questions, though, there is little agreement. Controversy surrounded the issue of whether the nomenklatura constituted a social class, or if it did, what type of class it was. As a distinct privileged stratum within a bureaucratic hierarchy, the nomenklatura defined collective interests and entered into structurally antagonistic relations with direct producers (Nove 1975). Some have suggested that the nomenklatura performed functions of capital and were therefore a state bureaucratic bourgeoisie; others, such as Djilas (1957), Rakovski/Kis (1978), or Konrad and Szelenyi (1979), wrote of a New Class of technocrat-managers, and Fehér et al. (1984) of a more loosely-defined 'corporate ruling group'. On the other hand Staniszkis (1992) proposes a systemic approach that avoids attributing agency to a particular stratum – a view that will be considered at the end of this chapter. I will argue that reproduction of nomenklatura privileges was embedded in the redistributive economy, which was a complex system of allocation steered by power, which constituted stratified consumption cleavages and minimal social integration.

MODE OF DOMINATION

It is fairly clear that placing Soviet systems into the analytical frameworks of Western social theory has proved problematic (Staniszkis 1992:3). Indeed, the discussion of convergence theories indicated that there has been dispute over the degree of systemic difference between state socialism and capitalism, in response to which two analytical strategies have been either to suggest that the Soviet systems were really variants of something else, such as (state) capitalism or Asiatic despotism, or to regard them as a new social formation *sui generis*. To some extent these debates were more matters of rhetoric than of substance, especially when argued from doctrinaire standpoints. Even so, they are still relevant to the problem of locating the systemic dynamics and tensions of Soviet societies and pose questions about new structural antagonisms and contradictions taking shape in postcommunism.

State Capitalism

Those who claim that the Soviet systems were 'state capitalist' argue that because the state bureaucracy performed the functions of capital, the system itself is capitalist. Frederick Pollock (1978) developed the theory of state capitalism, initially in relation to the Third Reich, which was subsequently extended to Soviet societies.[1] State capitalism was seen as a post-market society where, freed from private capital and the constraints of a bourgeois constitution, the state increases production in economically retarded territories at a rate only seen in the early stage of capitalism (Horkheimer 1940/1973). However, more recent accounts entail a kind of convergence thesis which claims that monopolization and state regulation in capitalist economies finds a parallel in Soviet systems, where the bureaucracy performs

[1] Lenin referred to Soviet Russia as 'state capitalist' but specifically in relation to the New Economic Policy (NEP).

the role of the collective capitalist, or the 'personification of capital' (Cliff 1968:117; Callinicos 1991:39).

Bureaucratic state capitalism, it is argued, fulfils the historical mission that Marxism attributes to the bourgeoisie, to increase in the productive forces of social labour and the socialization of labour.[2] More specifically, Cliff argues that the law of value[3] did not operate directly in the Soviet Union which was the 'negation of capitalism on the basis of capitalism itself' (1968:110). Prices lost their regulatory function and the whole economy was organized like a single enterprise (1968:150). It was none the less integrated into the world economy, principally through military competition, which absorbed a high percentage of surplus product and intensified the rate of exploitation. Thus the absence of extensive markets or private productive property does not preclude the description of Soviet systems as capitalist, or 'militarized state capitalism' (Callinicos 1991:19). Subordination to global capitalism required the Soviet Union to maximize the productivity of labour to extract the maximum surplus from direct producers, even though labour was not commodified. The ratio between surplus value and wages (s/v) was determined by the mode of integration of the Soviet Union into the world economy, especially through military competition with the West which necessitated the subordination of consumer goods to high rates of capital investment and armaments production. Indeed, the militarized police state in which trade unions and other forms of independent workers' political representation were repressed permitted more draconian labour discipline and hence a

2 Critics of this thesis such as Mandel often make the point that none of its advocates can say exactly when capitalism was restored in Soviet Russia. However Cliff is fairly explicit that it was during the First Five Year Plan that the state began primitive accumulation.

3 The law of value claims that under capitalism the commodity form expresses a social relation between producers whose labour is also turned into a commodity. However, the extraction of value from the productive process gives rise to a crisis tendency, expressed in the formula $s/c+v=p$, where the ratio of surplus value (s) to the cost of production is equal to the rate of profit (p). As the organic composition of capital rises, that is, as the fixed costs of raw materials and machinery (c) rise relative to variable costs (v) the denominator ($c+v$) must rise relative to the numerator (s) and the rate of profit must fall in the long run. This remains the logical tendency of capitalism, even if it is 'offset' in the short term by factors such as colonialism, state intervention or international trade. The hypothesis is difficult to test, given the complexity of global capital and the variation of necessary labour time and rates of exploitation in different parts of the system.

higher rate of exploitation of the Soviet proletariat than in Western capitalist democracies (Cliff 1968:159).

Further, Wildt (1979) argues that capitalism was not defined by the commodification of labour but rather by capital accumulation through exploitation of labour power. In these terms the Soviet bureaucracy was a ruling class in the Marxist sense, that is, an aggregate group defined by a common relationship to labour and the instruments of production. Again, for Castoriadis (1978/9) a new social group can create and impose relations of production corresponding to its domination, which facilitate its social reproduction through new forms of power, as occurred in slave societies and the contemporary bureaucratic regimes in Russia, China and Eastern Europe. In the latter, he argues, the state is dominated by the Party which unifies the dominant group. It is still part of the socio-historical universe of capitalism, however, because its goal is the rational mastery of nature through unlimited expansion of productive forces, an obsessive preoccupation with economic development, rationalization and control of all activities, and an increasingly elaborate division of labour and planning.

However, the concept of state capitalism operates with a vague notion of 'capitalism' which is dissolved into formulations like 'production for production's sake' or the accumulation of a surplus – descriptions that conceal more than they reveal about Soviet systems. It was suggested in Chapter 3 that capitalism refers to a system where, despite state regulation, substantial means of production are privately owned; investment decisions are led by anticipated profit; economic rationality steers social development, including the pattern of state intervention. Money is the social form of value, which begets more value within a division of labour where the capitalist proprietor has command over labour, although this is circumscribed by the conditions of the wage contract within a legal framework.

Further, the capitalist state is differentiated from economic reproduction along several dimensions which permit complex exchanges between power and money. Parsons and Smelser (1966:83) point out that the primary source of capital is the polity via the creation of credit, government protection of industry, subsidies and direct control of enterprises. This exchange is premised upon the differentiation of economy (the adaptive subsystem), the polity (goal attainment) and the household (latent pattern maintenance). Thus the state is excluded from the production process, and economic policy (goal attainment) responds to outputs from the economy, rather than becoming involved with the details of capital accumulation. The use of law and money as steering media is constrained by the constitutional tax-state since both mechanisms work at a distance from real economic agents. State intervention is motivated largely by the potential for market failure, but this withdraws money from the immediate circuit of capital, provoking fiscal crisis which in turn prompts the rolling back of the state. The separation between state and economy creates scope for conflicts of interest and priorities so government policies do not necessarily reflect needs of capital (Jessop 1990:356). Thus it is possible to have a Labour or Social Democratic government while capital remains dominant in the economy (Poulantzas 1968:130–41).

However, none of these conditions obtained to any significant degree in Soviet systems. On the contrary, in state socialism the dissolution of boundaries between state and economy resulted in profit being subordinated to the vicissitudes of state allocation and the appropriation of use-values. Money was not the medium of exchange, since the majority of capital goods circulated through interdepartmental requisition (Mandel 1977:567), and consumption goods (especially housing, domestic fuel, transport and food) were heavily subsidized. This in turn resulted in production that could not satisfy solvent demand, thus instead of periodic crises of over-production, Soviet systems were subject to permanent crises of under-production (Voslensky 1984:142). There was no wage contract between employers and employees, since the apparatus that controlled the means of production (such as Gosplan in the USSR) also commanded labour, set rates of pay and consumption subsidies. It is true that an unconsumed surplus product was accumulated by a bureaucratic élite, and that wage labour was general throughout the system, but neither of these in themselves render Soviet systems 'capitalist,' since both can be found in complex pre-capitalist societies. Similarly, Soviet systems could not be described as 'capitalist' simply by virtue of their linkage and subordination to the global economy, any more than could, say, the Ottoman Empire in the nineteenth century. This subordination might in the long term erode state accumulation and it will be argued in Chapter 6 that the opening of some centrally-planned economies (especially Hungary and Poland) to foreign debt and imported technology in the 1970s and 1980s left them vulnerable to inflation and other external constraints (Andreff 1992). However, that gradual integration into the global economy eroded the integration of these systems, indicates their incompatibility with global capitalism, rather than being a sub-species of it. The main purpose of the designation 'state capitalism' is rhetorical, I suspect, to keep intact a unilinear conception of history in which the only post-capitalist society will be a genuinely socialist one, rather than acknowledge that there are diverse paths to and from modernity.

Asiatic Despotism

A different and influential thesis is that Russian post-revolutionary modernization took place in conditions of socio-economic under-development (which is indisputable) in the course of which Russian cultural specificity reasserted itself. Mihály Vajda (1988) argues that only in European history, following the Carolinian Empire, is a stable separation between state and civil society institutionalized, giving birth to the self-positing individual and swift disintegration of tra-ditions. Not unlike Wittfogel (1959), this suggests that Russian devel-opment followed an 'Asiatic' rather than 'European' trajectory. Wittfogel argued that Stalinism was the contemporary manifestation of an age-old Asiatic power system, a claim that is repeated in Arnason (1993), Deutscher (1990) and Szamuely (1988). Deutscher argues that through Stalinism, 'defeated Tsarist Russia was imposing her own standards upon victorious Bolshevism' (1990:357). Again, Pellicani (1989) argues that the Bolshevik Revolution was an Asiatic reaction against the West, and Vajda (1988) like Arnason (1993) regards Bolshevism as a hybrid of Western industrialism (electri-fication plus soviets) and Asiatic statism.

Bahro (1977) claims that Soviet systems represented a non-capitalist route to modernity where, in the absence of feudalism, state societies rather than capitalism developed. Here the Asiatic mode of production is the connecting link between the patriarchal phase of primitive society and class societies of Asia, where priests, temple cities and the division of labour between administrative and religious functions, circumscribed class societies without private productive property based on tribute, which supported a strong centralized state.[4]

---

4 The central features of Marx's concept of Oriental Despotism were: communal

The peculiarity of Russia compared with Western capitalism lay in features such as service land holding (*pomestie*), state peasants, tribute, the bureaucratic pyramid, and towns that were administrative and garrison stations without burghers. By the early twentieth century, Russia combined Asiatic elements (a multinational state and tradition of autocracy from Baty Khan to the Tsars); a psychology of primary patriarchy; semi-feudalism that had not been fully liquidated; and a fragmented industrial base with a modern proletariat. The Bolsheviks replaced Tsarist bureaucracy with a Soviet one, which achieved more labour discipline and intensified exploitation than was previously possible. Stalin's colonization of Siberia, for example, would have been impossible without slave labour in the camps (Bahro 1977: 128ff.). However, this system could not enforce the same intensity and productivity of labour as capitalism since it was based on simple reproduction, not qualitative development.

Bahro is right to suggest that a modernizing state can deploy only the cultural and material resources that are inherited from an *ancien régime*, and that these are likely to impose their character on to new social forms. As Korosić (1988) argues, Soviet bureaucracies could accomplish only primitive accumulation based on labour mobilization, and were unable to develop functionally integrated economies of scale, as a result of which bureaucratic co-ordination was overloaded. Indeed, the state has a leading role in early modernization which requires taking resources and people out of agriculture, to permit primitive accumulation, increase productivity and reduce the necessary costs of labour, by providing cheap food, for example. According to Barrington Moore, the taming of the agrarian sector has been a decisive feature of the whole historical process of modernization (Moore 1969:429) which has involved restructuring agrarian social relations either through violent elimination of the traditional landed classes (as in Russia)[5] or co-opting and subduing them (as in Britain). In the

labour in villages; agro-hydraulic irrigation which required public works (e.g. aqueducts), in turn requiring a centralized state funded by tribute; cities were undeveloped garrison towns; absence of classes and struggle, creating static and stagnant societies without history, since the unchanging social infrastructure opposed human intervention of the environment by labour (Shanin 1983).

5 This is not to say that it was accomplished effectively even on its own terms. Citing evidence that the Soviet state actually subsidized agriculture during the 1930s, Seldon (1983) argues that 'the case ... that imposed collectivization is an indispensable measure for rapid industrialization can no longer withstand scrutiny'.

contemporary world, developing states approach this problem in a variety of ways, but whether small-holder production is maintained with more squeezed out of it, or whether servile labour is aggregated on large units (as with collectivization), the extraction of agricultural surplus requires strong political controls (Ray 1993: 88–9).

However, this does not mean that all developing states are 'Asiatic' or reducible to pre-capitalist conditions, a claim that would anyway be quite inapplicable to Central and Eastern Europe. This approach possibly expressed the frustration, felt by East European dissidents, with the immobility and deeply conservative nature of these societies (Fehér et al. 1984:38) but the analysis did not approach Soviet societies as integral systems. The notion that they were 'Asiatic' was at best a weak analogy, since in Marx's Asian mode of production the state received tribute from economic units independent of its own activity, rather than in the Soviet case from directly owning and managing them. Indeed, collectivization destroyed what was left of one of the important 'Asiatic' institutions of pre-revolutionary Russia, the *obshchina* (village community). This is not to deny, though, that certain aspects of Russian state culture were recomposed into the new system, such as the Table of Ranks (see below).

The New Class

The Soviet system was a social formation *sui generis*, not a subspecies of capitalism nor an 'Asiatic' vestige. This point of view is echoed by a number of theorists who argue that the bureaucratic élite constituted a 'New Class', a term popularized by Djilas (1957:44), the core of which lay in its exclusive right to distribute national income, set wages, direct economic development and dispose of nationalized assets. Rakovski (1978:15) argued that Soviet-type societies were neither socialist nor capitalist, nor a mixture of the two systems, but a class system *sui generis* existing alongside capitalism. It has been seen how the core of Stalinist society was created in the Great Purge of 1937–38 which removed almost the entire top stratum of industrial managers and party and government personnel. The *vydvizhentsy*, typically in their thirties, were communists with working-class background or experience of productive work, newly graduated from engineering school, working as plant engineers, and often simultaneously completing diploma work on dissertations, who frequently stepped or stumbled into their places (Fitzpatrick 1979a:242).

It is still not entirely clear, though, to what extent this created a dichotomous social structure such as that suggested by Konrad and Szelenyi (1979). They claim that Soviet systems were dominated by the New Class of the intelligentsia in uneasy alliance with the bureaucracy. Planners and intellectuals were two class factions, defined by their possession of technical expertise and bureaucratic power rather than private property, who disposed of a social surplus over which the direct producers had no control. Each maximized resources that as planners they could dispose of directly, and as intellectuals, indirectly (Szelenyi 1979). According to this view, the power of the bureaucracy was central in Soviet development until it was challenged by democratization and economic reform movements in the 1970s. This 'quasi-opposition' from within the Party empowered intellectuals to make redistributive decisions and began their road to class power (Konrad and Szelenyi 1979:201).[6]

Voslensky (1984) and Zemtsov (1976 and 1985) share with these writers an (albeit looser) notion of the New Class, pointing to the ability of the bureaucratic élite to consolidate its position via the intergenerational transmission of cultural capital. This took place through access to élite schools and universities, foreign travel, dachas and privileged occupations, as well as the opportunity to amass private fortunes through influence and connections (*blat*) (Zemtsov 1976:23). Fehér et al. (1984) argue that the term 'class' might not be appropriate to describe this élite which was defined neither by property nor by market relations, and prefer to speak of a corporate ruling group.[7] However, they posit the 'corporate ruling group' as the

---

6 Szelenyi (1988) substantially revised his view to the effect that 'The bureaucracy proved to be more stubborn than we anticipated'. However, if it 'was less inclined to make concessions in its dealings with the intelligentsia than we anticipated, it proved to be more flexible toward private business particularly the petty-bourgeoisie'. He insists, though, that 'the core of our book on the intellectuals was quite correct' in identifying the 'real social trends in the Soviet Union and Eastern Europe' (Szelenyi 1988:216–17).

7 So-called on the grounds that it is broader than the bureaucratic élite yet lacks the dichotomous relations defining classes. The corporate ruling group includes administrators, technical experts, cultural élites, and members of the apparat.

structural core of Soviet systems which is if anything a more ambiguous notion than the 'New Class'.

Central to this view of the Soviet system is the Party list, the nomenklatura, which controlled appointments to all significant positions, and this mechanism of élite recruitment created a clientelistic mode of domination and social regulation specific to state socialist societies. This was a bureaucratic system of control established in the 1920s by the Orgburo which (ratified by the Central Committee) controlled appointments to all significant positions, including nominally 'elective' ones (Hough 1969:153; Rigby 1988). Its chief instrument was Orgraspred (Organization and Assignment Department) which in the late 1940s split into Departments of the Party, Trade Unions and Komsomol. The nomenklatura was a list both of posts and of suitable personnel, which was updated by the NKVD/KGB and Cadres Department. At Central Committee level the nomenklatura included all-Union commissars (ministers), Republic Prime Ministers, diplomatic officials, senior members of the judicial system and bureaucracy, armed forces and NKVD officers, newspaper editors, leading members of trade unions, creative unions and mass organizations, and enterprise directors. At Republic, oblast (region) and raion (district) level similar posts were filled from a local list (Hosking 1992:210). In Hungary, by 1949 over 90 per cent of newly appointed high-level bureaucrats were from the Party list (Hankiss 1990:45).[8]

The Soviet nomenklatura consisted of about 700 in 1918, 100,000 by the 1930s and 250,000 by the 1980s (about 0.1 per cent of the population) according to Voslensky (1984:95). Mandel (1992:83) puts the figure at 300,000–400,000 that is, about 0.2 per cent of the population. Matthews (1978) provides a breakdown for the later 1970s which amounts to 271,000 (about 0.2 per cent of the workforce), comprising;

- party bureaucracy: 200,000;
- industrial managers: 5,000;
- intelligentsia: 10,000;
- doctors: 7,000;

8 A similar pattern developed in other communist regimes. In Poland by 1953 only 2.2 per cent of managerial positions were filled by non-members of the Party, compared with 17 per cent in 1949 (Majkowski 1985:100).

- legal officials: 2,000;
- editors and senior journalists: 17,000;
- military, police, and KGB officers: 30,000.[9]

The system displayed what Foucault (1979) described as the art of rank, where every position was classified according to a complex system of categories,[10] and its exceptional comprehensiveness converted its occupants into a distinct social category defined by common behavioural, attitudinal and organizational characters (Hill 1988). As with any stratification system, though, there is the problem of defining clear boundaries, which might render the term nomenklatura as vague as 'partocracy' or 'bureaucracy' (Rigby 1990a:6). However, the upper echelons of the nomenklatura were strategic élites who shared access to economic and cultural resources, earning at least 4,000 roubles per month when the average in the USSR was 240 (Matthews 1978:30). They were further marked out by spatial segregation in the cities, where accommodation was often differentiated among creative, scholarly and technical-managerial roles. Thus exclusive nomenklatura districts appeared, such as Kotelnicheskaya naberezhnaya (Moscow, Lenin Hills); Buda Hills (Budapest); or Rezidentsiya Boyana (Sofia).

The nomenklatura consumed part of the surplus product but largely through non-monetary privileges. According to Zaslavsky (1982) Soviet money income differentials of 1:20 or 1:30 were transformed into a ratio of about 1:100 when non-monetary advantages were included. Privileged consumption rights included additional payments such as: the so-called 'thirteenth month'; the Kremlin ration, allowances of medicines, meals and normally unavailable luxuries for the Central Committee; chauffeured transport; exclusive medical services; foreign travel; rest homes and dachas. The nomenklatura had privileged housing allocation, where the average space was six square

---

9 Horváth and Szakolczai (1992:223) emphasize, however, that the nomenklatura should not be confused with the apparatus of full-time party workers, since these constituted mutually exclusive categories (even if there was some circulation of individuals between the two) between decision-makers (nomenklatura) and functionaries with an organizational power base.

10 For example the head of an *obkom* was a 'category III group 26 official'. Several people have noted the similarity between this system and the Petrine 'Table of Ranks' (e.g. Fehér et al. 1984:34).

metres per head (nine for intellectuals) but the nomenklatura were entitled to 74 sq.m. Finally, education, such as access to a higher educational establishment (Vysshee Uchebnoe Zavedenie, or VUZ) was an important means of intergenerational accumulation and transfer of cultural capital.[11]

At the centre of the system is the nomenklatura, or New Class, which is organized, ideologically integrated and internally differentiated and which exercises power through the Party–state organs. The surplus is produced by arbitrarily setting the price for labour such that low value is placed on producers and very high value on the nomenklatura (Timofeev 1985). Further, when fewer goods are available than could actually be bought, real wages are low and the rate of exploitation is high. Effective wages are reflected in the amount of actual goods and services that can be purchased, and the difference between money wage and its purchasing power (the reverse of capitalism) is a form of coerced saving (Voslensky 1984:162). In this model the intelligentsia (as will be seen shortly) are in the ambiguous position of sharing in the surplus product, but facing this same discrepancy between wages and purchasing power, since they did not have access to the consumption outlets of the nomenklatura proper.

However, this is not to say that even the rule of the nomenklatura was secure or complete. Ticktin (1976) argues that the nomenklatura's control over the surplus was only partial, for four reasons. First, because value did not circulate in monetary form, nomenklatura privileges were highly visible unless clouded in elaborate secrecy; second, the inefficiency of the economy restricted possible consumption; third, (after Stalin) managers exercised weak control over labour and their orders were often countermanded by the workers; fourth, productive property was not disposable. Hence the life-style of nomenklatura of lower rank than Party élite, was probably less privileged than their comparators in capitalist societies. Szelenyi comments that

---

11 The result was a complex and cross-cutting system of stratification. In Bulgaria, for example, there were five grades of hotels on the Black Sea coast for different levels of Party employees. The highest grade was for employees of the Central Committee, and the right to holiday there extended to poorly paid low status employees (author's observation).

[i]t is extremely difficult to compare the general level of social inequalities between different socio-economic formations ... [However] a department head in the Central Committee or Central Planning Office – a major power figure in the redistributive power hierarchy – who makes daily decisions affecting hundreds of millions of Forints, Zlotys or Leva will be satisfied with a two-bedroomed flat of $55m^2$ on a crowded and ugly new housing development. ... I am inclined to believe that even if we can speak about a new ruling class in East European state socialism then it is the most miserable privileged class in the history of mankind. (Szelenyi 1979)

Further, the nomenklatura were subject to high levels of personal, and to an extent, collective insecurity. Again, the absence of money as an impersonal media of communication meant that the nomenklatura were directly dependent on personal connections. According to Voslensky, recruitment to the élite was particularistic and clientelistic, operating through 'recommendation' of individuals from higher to lower committees, although in the 1960s Hough detected evidence of appointment according to merit, which suggests more impersonal criteria (1969:175). Even so, the extensive latitude they enjoyed in dealing with local officials, enterprise managers and government departments created considerable scope for discretion and a degree of flexibility. This further created the opportunity for the consolidation of sectional interests, complex intersections of vertical and horizontal differentiation which were mediated by a clientelistic reward system (Majkowski 1985; Rigby 1990b:69).

Class Power or Sovereign Power?

These considerations have led a number of writers to question whether it is appropriate to regard the nomenklatura as a class at all. Mandel (1992), following Trotsky, speaks of a bureaucratic caste, and Jowitt (1983) and Staniszkis (1992) of a neo-patrimonial estate. Mandel (1992:6) disputes the notion of the bureaucracy as a New Class on the grounds that the bureaucracy was a social layer that did not have the cohesion to act as a social force (1992:175) reflecting as it did an unstable equilibrium of class forces and hybrid of allocative and commodity-producing economies. The bureaucracy was parasitic and, unlike a real ruling class, was unable to base its material privileges on the coherent functioning of the economic system. Privileges and guaranteed consumption provided no motivation for increased productivity but led rather to stagnation, waste and decline (Mandel 1977 and 1992; cf. Ticktin 1987; Gomulka 1986:42–61).

This seriously questions the extent to which the bureaucracy or New Class was the subject or architect of the system. After all, the NKVD itself was subject to purges, coinciding, for example, with the execution of three of its Chairmen, Yagoda (1936), Yezhov (1938) and Beria (1953). Despite the slogan '*kadry reshayut vsë!*' (cadres decide everything!) hundreds of thousands were sent to their deaths during the purges (Rigby 1990b:6), which suggests that sovereignty emanated from elsewhere in the social system. Not only this, but Staniszkis (1992) argues that the system embodied political power without substance, and relations of production without economic subjects. Fehér et al. (1984), too, come some way towards this, suggesting that the productive principle of modernity became detached from the constraints of civil society and converted into pure domination. The core of this formation is not described in terms of a class or even a mode of accumulation, but of a goal-function, *Zweck der Produktion*, production for its own sake.[12] This was inherently irrational since without free social articulation of needs there can be no consistent social rationality. Where the only restraints on production are those set by the extent and technical composition of resources, rather than by demand, needs are channelled into pre-figured forms in a system that is brutally enforced, producing both excess and scarcity to an unparalleled extent (Fehér et al. 1984:236).

Here power resided with the sovereign Party, not the bureaucracy. Indeed, the Soviet sovereign has never been the bureaucracy although the leaders are selected from its ranks; the bureaucratic mode of the execution of power is a consequence of the system of domination and not identical with it, even less its cause (Fehér et al. 1984:175). Hence, rules could be invalidated by a phone call or so formulated that their application could not be rational. This is true, too, of the nti-corruption campaigns, which for Holmes (1993:274) are evidence

12 The key characteristics of *Zwecke der Produktion* were the abolition of the market which blocks the road to the future since it leaves open no mechanism for contingencies; dictatorship and de-enlightenment; no objective basis of calculation and especially no calculation of human price; and a 'guaranteed society' which is the opposite of the welfare state, since it requires the atomization of the individual (Fehér et al. 1984:244–7).

of leadership drives for popular rational–legal legitimacy. All Soviet leaders, beginning with Lenin, regularly blamed the inefficiency of the system on the bureaucracy; they launched campaigns against it, and its lack of initiative and narrow-mindedness. Thus the bureaucracy only had what Fehér et al. (1984:175) call 'emanated-executive power' from the corporate ruling group. When Andropov and later Gorbachev attacked bureaucratic inefficiency, they were not really breaking new ground but conforming to this tradition of periodic anti-corruption campaigns that did not restore discipline, but re-set limits of personal appropriation and *blat* (Timofeev 1985). Andropov's campaign against corruption, like Aliev's in Azerbaijan (1969) or Shevardnadze's in Georgia (1973), was a campaign of mass mobilization which demonstrated the vulnerability of individuals and their dependence on patronage of superiors (Voslensky 1984).

However, despite these insights, the designation 'dictatorship over needs' is open to serious objections. Like totalitarian theory, it oversimplifies Soviet societies into élite–mass or state–society. At a conceptual level Fehér et al. do not clearly differentiate *Zwecke der Produktion* from Weber's *Wertrationalität* of which it seems to be a special case, their claims to the contrary notwithstanding (1984:138). At an explanatory level, the whole framework of dictatorship over needs is geared towards presenting the system as an immobile dead end (1984:243). Thus they are unable to account for change of the system (e.g. the appearance of glasnost) except as ruses of the ruling group (e.g. Fehér and Arato (eds) 1989) and cannot identify any dynamic that might account for subsequent events.

Despite their de-centred conception of sovereign power, Fehér et al. still credit the ruling group with excessive ability to realize the hegemonic project of domination as an end in itself. Yet the power of the nomenklatura was highly diffuse, and emanated from the systemic organization, since an individual's privileges were dependent upon his or her position in the hierarchy. In this context the main defence the nomenklatura could provide were groupings of mutual support and client networks, such as Khrushchev's buddies from the Ukraine; Brezhnev's mafia of Dnepropetrovsk; or Gorbachev's friends from Stavropol. Being embedded in clientelistic structures meant that the intergenerational transmission of cultural and material capital was uncertain, since membership was dependent upon the continued approval of superiors and local party organs, rather than an independent base. During the Stalin period, officials were denied personal a ssets and their dependence on Stalin's personal patronage was reinforced in various ways.[13] After Stalin, the nomenklatura consolidated into cadre-patrons, or what Jowitt (1983) calls 'political principals', overseeing a system founded upon an administrative hierarchy within a fiscal corporation.

The nomenklatura system was a formidable machinery of patronage extending to every professional or political function in the country. However, Party officials were not yet a social class with means of perpetuating their power and privilege through property or the control of expert knowledge. In many ways the history of Soviet Russia might be regarded as the history of their efforts to extend this power and privilege into a permanent secure and accepted acquisition (Hosking 1992:84–5). Voslensky (1984:240) noted that by the 1980s the New Class was coming to feel anxious that its rule was terminable without notice since it lacked an independent base of ownership in civil society. Members did not own the source of their benefits but enjoyed the privilege of benefices,[14] even if there was a tendency for these to become fiefdoms, attached to a person rather than the office. To understand the dynamic of system we need to understand the ways in which nomenklatura privileges were embedded in complex exchanges of power and patronage.

MODES OF SOCIETALIZATION

Thus far it has been argued that the Soviet systems were hierarchical-bureaucratic societies in which the nomenklatura system was the dominant mechanism of stratification. However, it was argued in Chapter 2 that for a structure of domination in a social system to be reproduced it must be embedded within institutional orders of the lifeworld. One of the central problems encountered by Soviet systems was their weak mode of societalization (Jessop et al. 1993) arising

13 Such as the packets of money, often of insubstantial amounts, which were delivered from Stalin to high-ranking officials (Voslensky 1984:214).
14 These are a form of patrimonial subordination, a lifelong not hereditary remuneration for its holder in exchange for his or her real or presumed services, the remuneration is an attribute of the office not the incumbent.

from the fusion of the economic and political mechanisms, the excessive demands on the planning process posed by a complex economy,
and the difficulties of generating legitimacy and mass compliance
with decisions from the political system. These limited the self-
regulating capacities of the system, creating weak institutional
adjustment, a limited range of development strategies, and forms of
crisis management that undermined economic viability (Kaminski
1991:11). More will be said on this in Chapter 5, but for the moment
I propose to examine the extent to which the domination of the
nomenklatura was embedded in the institutional orders of society.
This will be done first by examining the problem of legitimation, and
then the redistributive economy which institutionalized the power of
the nomenklatura.

Legitimation

It was seen in Chapter 2 that there is disagreement over the nature and
importance of legitimacy, particularly over the significance of beliefs,
as opposed to public ceremonials or instrumental bases of acquiescence. I will argue that while instrumental accounts explain periods of
integration in Soviet societies, in order to understand the underlying
dynamic of these systems, legitimacy needs to be situated within a
context of rationalization and learning. The importance of a sense of
dynamic process here is apparent if we consider whether the domination of the nomenklatura was legitimate at all. The answer will differ
considerably depending upon the period in question – whether one is
talking about Lenin's dispersal of the Constituent Assembly in 1918;
Stalin's cultural revolution; the Great Patriotic War; the August 1991
attempted coup, and so on. One's answer will vary, too, in response to
the question, legitimacy for whom? Both these questions require us to
address the dynamics of integration and crisis in Soviet systems.

Fehér et al. offer what I have elsewhere called a minimal concept
of legitimation (Ray 1993:90ff.) which suggests that the Soviet Union
at best enjoyed negative legitimacy. That is, it was legitimate only to
the extent that while at least one part of the population, perhaps only
the Party, acknowledged it as exemplary and binding, the other part did
not confront it with an image of an alternative order equally as
exemplary (Fehér et al. 1984:138). Moreover, this minimal legitimacy

applied only to the Soviet Union since the rest of Eastern Europe experienced a protracted legitimation crisis (1984:138). One reason for this was that State Socialism in Russia (and Yugoslavia) was indigenous, while in Central Europe it was imposed by foreign occupation, and was always regarded as such by the majority of the population.[15] Eastern Europe could persist in continuous legitimation crisis without collapse so long as members of the Party retain their belief in the exemplary character of the order and continue to find it binding, although they add that such survival is unlikely (1984:138).

Pakulski (1986) argues that the concept of legitimacy is not appropriate to Soviet systems, where it is better to speak of conditional tolerance. Legitimacy involves the belief in the legality of rules, voluntary consent and procedural rationality (bureaucracy and rational–legal principles). By comparison the Soviet systems were not rational–legal since formal regulations played a minor role compared with informal and arbitrary activities; depersonalization was weak and clientelism and informal arrangements were strong; there was a blurred division between official and private spheres with prerogatives of office extended to family and friends; meritocratic criteria in recruitment and promotion were weak and, in the case of nomenklatura appointments, highly secret.

In the light of subsequent events, and the collapse of self-confidence among communist élites in 1989–91, combined with their inability to call upon Soviet support, these accounts initially appear plausible. Ziółkowski claims, for example, that but for the intervention of the Red Army (or its threat) communism would have fallen long before, in the 1950s, which appears to confirm the idea of a permanent legitimation crisis (Ziółkowski 1990:51).

However, Fehér et al.'s diagnosis was vague and did not offer any explicit analysis of the dynamic forces at work, beyond suggesting that there was a crisis waiting to happen. Holmes (1993:18-22), too, objects to their analysis of legitimation on four grounds. First, the vision of alternative order (e.g. Western social democracy) might be less important than the availability of its means of attainment. Second, Fehér et al. could not predict the circumstances of the crisis that

---

15 On this basis, we should probably also distinguish between the legitimacy of the Russian Federation, until recently, as opposed to that of the other Soviet republics, especially the Baltic states.

actually occurred in the same way across Eastern Europe and the Soviet Union, which weakens the view that there were fundamental differences between them. Third, their understanding of legitimacy is not subtle enough to account for differences of pacification among different regimes, such as Kádárism in Hungary after 1956 as opposed to normalization in Czechoslovakia after 1968. Fourth, they do not distinguish legitimacy deficit (the chronic condition) from legitimacy crisis (which is acute), nor the legitimacy of the regime from that of the system. Problems with the former have less immediately threatening implications for social integration than do problems with the latter.

There are problems, too, with David Beetham's claims that rules are justified with reference not to beliefs, but to the publicly demonstrated consent of subordinates. The latter have subjectively binding force irrespective of motive, whether love of the leaders or self-interest, in the form of a public ceremonial for the benefit of observers (1992:18). Why people turn out for work on a Saturday without pay, for example – whether it is because the local mayor is a relative, or because they will move up the queue for a new apartment, or because they are committed communists – is irrelevant to the importance that these rituals have as public displays of support for the regime. However, this account offers an insubstantial basis for long-term social integration, since there is evidence that forcing people to make public commitment to things they do not believe generates cynicism and pathologies, such as alcoholism, apathy and interpersonal violence (Hankiss 1990; Slepyan 1993; Timofeev 1985). Since these in turn erode motivations to work and publicly affirm the regime, by encouraging withdrawal and apathy, they are actually dysfunctional from the point of view of legitimation. Beetham depicts a situation in which considerable routinization of 'loyalty' has already taken place and become blasé.

Fehér et al. discern three phases in the development of Soviet legitimacy. During the first, the Leninist–Jacobin phase, the Party was content to justify itself with reference to the exigencies of international revolution, and did not seek legitimacy.[16] In the second, the Stalinist phase, the goal of socialism in one country required that the

16 They do not deal extensively with the NEP which, if not about legitimacy, none the less recognized limitations to prerogative power.

state secure authority for mass mobilization, which took the form of totalitarian charisma – the total subordination of civil society to the state. Post-Stalinism, the third phase, has reinforced habitual traditionalism, patriotism, rule by a gerontocracy (Brezhnev's generation), claims to the historic right of the Party to rule, and general depoliticization of society.[17] It is in the latter phase that public display of support becomes routinized.

It is worth noting in passing that even with Stalinism there was an interplay of traditionalist and revolutionary strands of legitimation (Deutscher 1990:515). Stalinist traditionalism included Slavophilism, rehabilitation of the Orthodox Church and patriotism, family values and anti-Semitism (e.g. Wistrich 1992:177ff.) which harked back to Tsarist ideologies. Further, it was seen in Chapter 3 that what Fehér et al. describe as totalitarian charisma – the cult of Stalinism, ethic of self-sacrifice, mass mobilization – actually had an ambiguous relationship with modernity and they were themselves in many ways traditionalist, invoking as they did a quasi-religious confessional personality and a warrior ethos of the revolutionary hero.

However, this caveat does not detract from the point that there *was* a gradual routinization and instrumentalization of legitimacy claims with the emergence of post-Stalinism. David Lane (1979) argues that to compensate for a lack of formal procedures for generating consensus, the Soviet state closely linked social integration to the system of resource allocation. Maria Márkus (1982) suggested that covert legitimation rendered people dependent on, and acquiescent to state agencies for their material well-being. Márkus argues that the official ideology, or overt legitimation, is verbal ritual, whereas covert legitimation takes the form of redistributive policies, full employment, widened access to education, income maintenance, housing subsidies, health and welfare, social mobility and social security. This notion of functional legitimacy (Staniszkis 1992:101–2) is similar to Weber's substantive rationality which he associated particularly with post-revolutionary regimes that create loyal cadre strata,[18] and appears

17 This is a rather loose usage of the Weberian concept of traditionalism, which described societies with a simple division of labour where 'fear of magical evils reinforces the general psychological inhibitions against any sort of change in customary modes of action' (Weber 1978 I:36). Gerontocracy is found with primary patriarchalism, and in both cases 'there is a complete absence of personal staff' (Weber 1987 I:231)!

18 This is often misunderstood. Barker (1990:49–50), for example, assumes that it

again in the idea of a corporatist social contract between rulers and ruled or Pakulski's conditional tolerance (1986:35).

After Stalin the system began a transition of *longue durée* from a plebiscitary dictatorship to a more formalized bureaucracy, in a way consistent with Weber's expectation that 'the more bureaucratization advances and the more substantial the interests in benefices and other opportunities become, the more surely does the party organization fall into the hands of experts. ... As a rule the party organization easily succeeds in this castration of charisma' (1978 II:1131–2). Indeed, after the end of Stalin's purges, when tenure became secure, nomenklatura office holders formed a self-perpetuating bureaucratic élite usually appointed for life, and enmeshed within a complex system of patronage.

Taken together these various approaches create multidimensional ways of understanding possible bases for legitimacy claims in Soviet systems. Legitimacy might pertain to beliefs about the social order, which might have traditional, charismatic or formal–rational bases. Or it might take the form of an instrumental exchange between rulers and ruled, such as that often associated with Kádárism in Hungary. Again, legitimacy claims might appeal to an élite cadre stratum or attempt to win the loyalty or participation of wider groups in the population. Legitimacy claims might, in short, be instrumental, normative or procedural, and might appeal to élites or masses. See Figure 4.1 for examples of each of these combinations, which will be referred to again.

The particular character of legitimacy claims will be structured by interactions between the mode of domination and the institutional orders of society. Thus when we speak of legitimacy we look at an ensemble of social relations and embedding of steering media in social institutions. As charismatic-substantive claims become routinized there is a tendency to rely more on instrumental and depoliticized modes of legitimacy. However, instrumental expediency is a less secure basis for embedding the social system than either charisma or formal procedures for negotiation and adaptation. The way is open for a situation where eudaemonic legitimacy first erodes

refers to belief in the absolute validity of an order as an expression of ultimate values. However, redistributive justice, in the form of rewards for the loyal cadre stratum, suggests a more instrumental exchange.

	Elite Cadre	Mass Loyalty
Instrumental	Social mobility (*vydvizhentsy*)	Redistributive economy (Kádárism)
Normative	Vanguard ethos (Leninism)	Mobilization for communism/motherland (Great Patriotic War)
Procedural	Technocracy (Andropov)	Pluralism/Reform Communism (Glasnost)

Figure 4.1 Modes of legitimacy

charismatic heroism, replacing absolutist claims with tacit understandings between rulers and ruled, but this itself runs into trouble as the state faces resource problems such as fiscal crisis and international debt.

Redistributive Economies

It has been noted that the nomenklatura were defined by consumption privileges rather than by ownership of the means of production. This idea is elaborated further in what Szelenyi, Hegedüs, Tosics and others have called the 'redistributive economy'. Following Polanyi's distinction between transactive (market) and dispositive economic relationships,[19] this refers to a system of state-regulated collective consumption, where the state redistributes a surplus which was not accumulated in personal incomes but which was directly centralized in the state budget and reallocated according to centrally defined goals and values (Szelenyi 1979). The principle of resource allocation in redistributive systems is administrative power, even if goods and services are commodities, since prices are determined by decisions of

19 Both types of society can have trade and money, but in the dispositive type prices are not regulated by the market, but fixed by a sovereign authority. In the transactive type traders exchange goods at market prices (Polanyi 1944).

the authorities (Konrad and Szelenyi 1979:51). Thus the pattern of resource allocation is likely to coincide with the dominant lines of political power (including influence, special connections, reciprocal networks and so on) rather than market position. Szelenyi (1979) claims that the redistributive economy created new inequalities as a result of the existing distribution of power in the system, although this thesis is questioned by other writers.

The housing debate provided an example. In the housing sector the state was owner of extensive housing stock, and rents were not linked to property values but were kept low and administratively allocated. However, the 1950s goal of completely nationalized housing was not realized anywhere and a private sector of inherited, private rented and self-built dwellings existed alongside the redistributive sector. The state remained dominant in housing construction (building for both rent and sale) and tightly regulated the private sector, thus Soviet housing systems were mixed economies.[20] This created options of both exit from one sector into the other, and voice in the form of applications which might invoke influence and patronage (Hegedüs and Tosics 1990).

In the Bulgarian[21] state socialist system, the market was greatly restricted, although it did not eliminate private ownership and to some extent it was promoted (World Bank 1990). By the 1980s, some 70 per cent of new construction was offered for sale, although the procedures for purchasing or renting dwellings involved bureaucratic allocation. Whether for sale or rental, the principal means of allocation was that of municipally constructed apartments, where a norm of 90 sq. m. per family operated. The purchase of apartments was financed through loans from the State Bank, at about 33 per cent total interest on the amount borrowed and the usual mortgage repayment period was 25 years. In order to buy, a deposit of 30 per cent of the apartment price was required. There was no automatic right to buy, and

20 Hegedüs (1987) says that the ratio of state:private housing in Hungary varied between 30:70 and 75:25, depending on the method of calculation. What is crucial is the definition of state finance, and whether National Savings Bank money, housing associations and   public co-operatives belong to the state or to the marketized sectors.

21 These observations are based on interviews in Sofia in 1990, and I am indebted to Professor Stoyan Kambourov and the late Lyuben Nikolov for their assistance with this.

families could wait years for their application to purchase to be processed.

Data now available suggest that the upper nomenklatura had access to apartments larger than the norm (up to 500 sq. m.) and 90 per cent loans from the State Bank. Further, networks of influence and negotiation seemed to work on at least three levels. First, new apartments were allocated directly by the municipality to people on the waiting list, where points would be awarded based on factors such as existing housing facilities, family size, length of time on the waiting list, level of consumption (a family owning a car would have fewer points) or amount of money saved towards the deposit. Alongside such formal–rational criteria, there was a substantive–rational distribution mechanism, according to which prioritized categories, such as ethnic minorities (especially Roma), those with special occupational needs, leaders of 'mass organizations' or 'active fighters against Fascism' had priority.

Second, housing would be allocated en bloc to employers and enterprises, such as the university, large industrial plants, or government departments. The size of this allocation was a matter for negotiation between these interests and the municipal housing authorities, and the outcome was dependent on the balance of power in these committees. For enterprises, their ability to offer their employees housing was important to corporate planning (whether they could increase their labour-force for example) and to labour relations within the organization. Having been granted blocks of housing, there was then a third level of allocation within the enterprise, which was structured according to a mixture of formal–rational and informal criteria.

During the 1970s and 1980s, there was a debate centred upon the effects of state redistributive policies. Szelenyi concluded that state redistributive economies had regressive effects and perpetuated consumer inequalities,[22] since higher status groups, the better qualified with higher than average income, were heavily over-represented in the redistributive sector of the urban housing system and correspondingly a negative correlation was found between income and home ownership.

---

22 Similarly Krejci (1976) argued that, while in terms of power and control the 'most relevant dividing line within contemporary Czech society ... [was] ... the functional division between managers and producers', in terms of the distribution of consumption resources, the most marked division was in the quality of housing.

The working class, especially the semi-skilled workers, had to build their own homes because they did not have access to the redistributive sector. White-collar workers received 50 per cent more subsidy than blue collars who in turn received more than agricultural workers. Consequently the state allocates the surplus in favour of higher income groups by forcing those with less income to pay the total cost of their housing from wages or salaries which did not allow for housing costs. Despite the original goal of solving the housing shortage, in Hungary in the 1960s investment in the state sector was not forthcoming because of a lack of lobbying within the planning process (Hegedüs and Tosics 1990) and the system remained producer-dominated (Pickvance 1988; Hegedüs and Tosics 1990; Tosics 1988).[23]

In the Soviet Union rents rose three times between 1928 and 1961, but in 1961 rent ceased to be a fiscal levy and became symbolic and nominal, creating the illusion of free accommodation. However, Soviet sociologists have documented the existence of extreme inequalities in the distribution of housing between social groups, in that access to housing was determined by social status and 'subjective factors', that is corruption and patronage. Bessonova (1988) argued that control over accommodation constituted a crucial component in an employers' reward system (the most prestigious aspect of their office was to distribute flats from their own departmental housing stock) and concludes that it was the administrative system itself which made housing the lever for enserfing (*zakreposhchenie*) the worker. With over 40 per cent of state housing owned and allocated by employers, considerable variations in living standards could result from clientelistic networks through which a large group of people received housing without joining the waiting list as perks of their position. This seems to bear out Horváth and Szakolczai's observation that the real strength of the Party resided not in institutions or structures, but in keeping individuals in a state of personal dependence (1992:141–2).

---

23 This principle was replicated in other spheres, too, since higher income groups made more use of medical services (and access to better facilities) and stayed longer in education (and attended more specialist schools) than lower income groups (Szelenyi 1979).

However, the relationship between social class differentiation and housing allocation was complex. In relation to Hungary, Pickvance (1988) makes similar claims to Bessonova, as does Ciechocinska (1987) for Poland. Hegedüs, however, claimed that in Hungary inequalities of access declined after 1971, suggesting that state allocation was not inherently inegalitarian. On the basis of a study of Prague, Musil (1987) argued that socialist cities showed an increase in heterogeneity of macrostructure (i.e. social mixing) but homogeneity of microstructure (i.e. segregation in inner-city and older regions).[24] In two Hungarian cities, Szelenyi (1983) found that

> traditional vertical inequality was ...accompanied by specific horizontal inequalities. Among people within similar social categories there were the elderly who had homes, and the young who did not have them yet; there were the original urban residents with homes and the newer immigrants [to the city] without them; ...Among people of the same income, working together in the same workshop or office, there would commonly be tenants, sub-tenants, bed-tenants and boarders in workers' hostels – and the lucky tenants of whole houses or apartments were privileged like princes. (Szelenyi 1983:34)

None the less, Szelenyi argued that, among those in urban centres with secure tenure, the pattern was for higher bureaucrats, intellectuals and technicians to live in larger accommodation, while clerical workers, service workers, skilled, semi-skilled and unskilled workers lived in smaller accommodation (1983:67).

THE SOVIET SOCIAL SYSTEM

It is often suggested that, in contrast to capitalist democracies, state socialist systems were fused hierarchical societies where the 'Party–state' constituted the peak of an organizational hierarchy to which

---

24 Musil argued that overall social ecology (in Prague), that is, the macrostructure, became more heterogeneous (e.g. variance in social ecology was explained by social class to only 17 per cent in 1970, compared with 35 per cent in 1930). But within the microstructure, homogeneity was increasing. This was so both at the good quality housing end of the spectrum, where higher bureaucrats and those of financial means were concentrated, and at the lower end, where there was a concentration of the elderly, less well qualified, and marginal ethnic groups, such as gypsies.

other institutional orders were subordinate, and in which they were treated as equivalent (e.g. Jessop et al. 1993:6; Kaminski 1991:8). However, there are some problems with this view that arise from the degree of separation that inevitably evolved between economic and political subsystems. This can be illustrated in several ways. First, officials, especially in enterprises, were not effectively controlled by a unified Party–state. On the contrary, the Party was often unsure of the political reliability of cadres, hence the periodic attempts to 'verify leaders'. Second, Stalinist purges aimed at bringing the apparat under the control of the Central Control Commission (TsKK) actually submerged the country into crisis, and during the 1960s (especially after the removal of Khrushchev) the apparat won security of tenure, from which it follows that there was an institutionalized (albeit weak) division of powers among the security apparat, the Central Committee, enterprise managers and the Party apparat. Third, planning quotas were experienced by enterprises as outputs from an administrative subsubsystem within the polity that required a response which in turn required time boundaries and internally closed communications. Fourth, the recalcitrance of the economy confronted by planning decisions – resistance by enterprises and workers led to a decline in charismatic mobilization and an increase in incentives to plan fulfilment – indicates that for the polity, too, the economy represented an external environment. A rudimentary closure of subsystems *vis-à-vis* environments was thus occurring, especially by the late 1950s.

Soviet systems were complex bureaucratic structures with dual systems of authority running from the Central Committee through the Party apparatus, shadowing the administrative hierarchy of planning boards and ministries, down to single enterprises or villages (Lovenduski and Woodall 1987:93). I have argued elsewhere (Ray 1994) that this was not a formal–rational type of bureaucracy, but an estate or patrimonial system in which there was an unclear division between the office-holder and private appropriation. The transition from Stalinism to post-Stalinist societies, which occurred once the accumulation potential of terroristic–heroic mobilization reached its limits, involved a gradual depoliticization and routinization of social life. This routinized apoliticism, however, prevented the institutionalization of political pluralism (Staniszkis 1992; Jessop et al. 1993) and the post-Stalinist state was left with a problem it never solved, of attempting to sustain monocratic political control in an increasingly differentiated society. Thus the state remained central to the distribution process via the redistributive economy which was a means of establishing functional legitimation among significant groups in the population, while securing the loyalty of the nomenklatura and the bulk of the intelligentsia. Social stratification in Soviet societies remained bureaucratically constituted and more akin to the kind of stand structures (*ständische Herrschaft*) described by Weber (e.g. 1978 I:232–3), where administrative staff appropriated particular powers and corresponding economic assets, than to social class relations in a system of property and contract. The redistributive economy was a system of bureaucratic resource allocation that generated structures of privilege which constituted the nomenklatura as a privileged location. The 'rule' of the nomenklatura was embedded in complex systems of patronage and the influence exerted in the redistributive economy governed by the media of power rather than money.

In this sense, then, it might be accurate to describe the form of rule as a 'partocracy'. However, a limitation of this view, and one that is shared by the New Class thesis, is its attempt to define the system with reference to its central *subject* rather than the system of social relations within which particular social locations are embedded (Staniszkis 1992). Socialist societies were highly complex systems of stratum differentiation along lines such as complex administrative hierarchies; Party/non-Party membership which could cut across occupational stratification (Majkowski 1985); socio-spatial differentiation (Szelenyi 1983:34); generational, gender and ethnic stratification (Lovenduski and Woodall 1987); not to mention the new patterns of cleavage resulting from the economic liberalization (Szelenyi 1988). Yet Fehér et al., Arato, and Konrad and Szelenyi attempted to encapsulate Soviet systems in terms of dichotomous models such as *Zweck der Produktion* vs need articulation, or the planner–redistributor vs the producer. The problem with these dichotomies was that they attempted to operate simultaneously on system-analytical and subject-analytical levels. Thus, with Fehér et al., dictatorship over needs was enforced by the corporate ruling group (a sociological category) which it is assumed will succeed systematically in achieving its goals, and ensuring that reforms are self-limiting. This conceptual tendency is even more marked in Konrad and Szelenyi (1979) whose notion of the class power of the intelligentsia is open to the further objection that it cannot identify any defining characteristic for a stratum which is itself highly differentiated internally, yet manages to organize its collective interests systematically. Arato ambiguously argues that the process of depoliticization (liberalization) is a regulative process, aimed at protecting the central principle of organization, although 'it is not consciously directed by a social agency, whether the latter be a "class", an "order" or even the party élite itself' (Arato 1982).

Even so, Arato usefully shifts the terrain of theorization towards systemic regulation, which might provide a framework for understanding the subsequent crisis. The over-extension of the state imposed huge regulatory demands as the nomenklatura imposed its goals throughout the apparatus (Boella 1979). The state combined functions of employment, welfare and socio-cultural reproduction, which gave rise to the continual threat of administrative crises. This had implications for the legitimacy of the system because it made relative advantage visible and prevented the economic system (money) absorbing risk from the political system that would have made the position of the nomenklatura more secure. The deep insecurity of the nomenklatura was linked to the overburdening of the redistributive system with allocation, legitimacy and reproducing nomenklatura privileges.

Figure 4.2 outlines a preliminary model of inter-system exchanges in Soviet-type systems, based on Habermas's model of system and lifeworld, introduced in Chapter 2. At the level of the system, the economy (adaptation) and the Party–state bureaucracy (goal-attainment) exchange non-consumed surplus (the basis of nomenklatura privileges) against political management of the economy and clientelism. Organizational behaviour is thus embedded in cultural practices that presuppose reciprocal trust and informal relations, which Okun (1981) described as the 'invisible handshake', as opposed to the 'invisible hand' of the market and the 'visible hand' of bureaucracy. From the socio-cultural subsystem (the lifeworld) the community (integration) is as Habermas (1982:283) argues, a largely fictional creation of mass organizations and sham public life, which none the less provides the Party with displays of conformity and 'loyalty'. Households (integration) exchange labour power and consumption

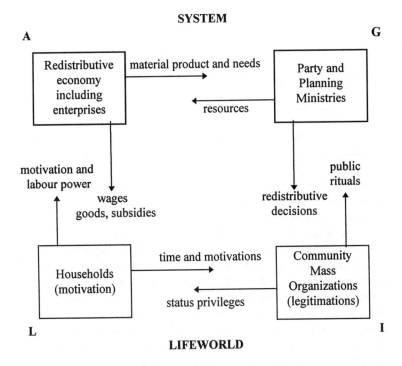

Figure 4.2 Preliminary model of the Soviet social system

against wages, commodities and subsidies from the state economy, which the Party hoped could be traded against socialization and motivation. The latter is an important source of functional or instrumental legitimacy in that the community is dependent on the state to provide income and services such as housing, fuel or public transport. At this stage this model is schematic, but Chapter 5 will examine how the system generated crisis tendencies and could function only through the operation of latent forms of integration in the second society.

5. Systemic Crises in State Socialism

By the late 1980s, the term 'crisis' was appearing with increasing frequency in relation to Soviet systems, especially with the advent of glasnost which allowed steering problems to become more visible.[1] Slightly earlier, Fehér et al. (1984:21–2) had predicted that a new global crisis was again approaching East European societies since 'the very consequences of the working of this system undermine the social basis on which its post-Stalinist stabilization has rested to date'. Moreover, it has been noted already that Fehér et al. regarded Eastern Europe (as distinct from the Soviet Union) as experiencing a protracted legitimation crisis (Heller 1982; Fehér et al. 1984:152).[2] However, writers who predicted imminent crisis tended to regard its presence as endemic and its meaning as self-evident, rather than develop a crisis theory as such. In particular, it is often assumed that economic and administrative steering problems automatically spill over into political and cultural spheres to create a general awareness of crisis among the population. However, this does not necessarily happen, partly because social systems institutionalize strategies of crisis management and partly because latent forms of integration arise, with the effect of compensating for crisis tendencies.

Arnason (1993:27) argues that Soviet regimes were not self-closed systems, did not have a system identity, but on the contrary were always limited, fragile and, in the case of Eastern Europe, superimposed from without.[3] Consequently, he argues that they cannot have experienced a systemic crisis but instead disintegrated under the

---

1 Birman (1988), Connor (1991), Davis and Scase (1985), Comisso (1990), Fehér and Arato (1991), Flaherty (1992), Lemke and Marks (eds) (1992), Ost (1989), Shoup (1989) and Ticktin (1992), to cite just a few.
2 Arnason (1993:27) points out that crises in the Soviet system were often predicted but only in general terms without specifying under what conditions they might arise.
3 Similarly though from a systems–theoretical perspective, Zeleny (1985) argues that while capitalist societies are autopoietic, communism was allopoietic, that is, neither self-closing nor self-maintaining.

combined weight of self-destructive trends, oppositional social movements, the strains imposed by competition with the West, and geopolitical factors such as the inability of the Soviet Union's decomposing economy to withstand its global military commitments (1993:180ff.). I do not dispute the relevance of these forces, as the analysis in this and the following chapter will show, but it is difficult to analyse factors such as 'self-destructive trends' unless one presupposes that Soviet socialism was a system, that is, a pattern or structure of intended and unintended actions and mutual interdependencies that were reproduced through time and space, while maintaining discernible boundaries with multiple environments. This chapter will describe the principle of organization of Soviet systems in order to identify the crisis tendencies that developed along with changing forms of social regulation.

THEORY OF CRISIS

In sociological literature, crisis theory has often addressed capitalist societies and cannot easily be transferred to Soviet systems. Much of this theory has addressed consequences alleged to arise from politicizing and therefore de-differentiating the economic and socio-cultural spheres. Habermas (1976) and Offe (1976), for example, were concerned with whether capitalist states could regulate the economy without politicizing it, or at least retain stable boundaries between the politico-administrative, economic and ideological subsystems. This problem is less relevant to state socialism, where crises worked in the opposite direction. That is, communist states attempted to offset the effects of excessive political regulation through increasing reliance on the monetary exchange which was a process of de-linking to reduce the fusion of political and economic imperatives. To understand this process, we need to examine the specific structures and action systems of Soviet-type societies.

However, despite the centrality of crisis to analysis of the end of communism, the concept is rarely theorized, writers often assuming that its meaning will emerge through diverse illustrations. After considering various approaches, Holmes defines crisis as a critical juncture or watershed, a point at which a system and/or regime is uncertain about its future direction and/or is seriously threatened by external forces or through its own internal contradictions ... or an interaction of these. (1993:35)

The problem with such a loose definition is that it can describe almost any imaginable crisis but hardly offers a differentiated or explanatory model.

This is true, too, of some otherwise highly theoretical accounts such as Arato (1982 and 1991), who offers a theory of the structural contradictions of state socialism but offers no theory of crisis itself. Again, Ticktin (1992) assumes that economic problems combined with structural contradictions will spill over into crises of social integration, that is, legitimacy crises. Writers frequently conflate crises of the regime with those of the system, or at any rate do not clearly distinguish one from the other. Mandel argued that since the Brezhnev era, the Soviet Union had gone through a 'real crisis of the regime' (as opposed to an unreal one?) evidenced by ageing leaders, immobility in the face of political choices, rigidity and ineffectiveness of the dominant ideology, slow economic growth, shortages, stagnant living standards, technological backwardness, social conflicts (1991:32–44) and an 'ideological–moral crisis' in the form of corruption and alcoholism (1991:101). This suggests that crisis can be understood as an accumulation of empirical failures or deficiencies, but Mandel does not offer a theory of crisis dynamics themselves nor the process whereby they are transferred among institutional orders of society. Again, his position is tenable only if one assumes that steering problems necessarily precipitate or at least threaten a breakdown of social order.[4]

Colin Hay (1993) points out that a crisis is a moment of decisive intervention or rupture (from *krísis*) in which the existing order cannot

---

4 A regime has a good chance of withstanding economic failure while it is perceived to offer a plausible mode of crisis intervention, or even failing this to be the best available. Further, the crisis of confidence in a government (as occurred in Poland after 1981) need not involve rejection of substantive cultural values within which a system is embedded. Again in Poland during the 1980s mass support for social justice, workers' control and secure employment was at variance with the shift towards anti-socialist values among both old and new élites – the Polish United Workers' Party (PUWP) Government and Solidarity (Walicki 1991a). This is discussed further in Chapters 6 and 7.

be preserved in its present form but does not necessarily precipitate the collapse of institutional structures, even though it will be perceived to threaten them.[5] Subjective awareness of crisis is crucial to its existence, since to be a moment of decisive intervention, crisis must be perceived as such, and involves constructions, simulations (Hay 1995) and metaphors (Mesjasz 1992) of latent contradictions or failures.

According to this definition, Fehér et al.'s notion of permanent legitimation crisis (which is echoed by Arnason 1993:138) is a contradiction in terms. A perpetual crisis would be one that did not directly threaten the stability of the system, nor result in decisive intervention for its resolution. An unresolved crisis would rapidly degenerate into catastrophe, a disintegration of the system, which would be its resolution. However, even if crises cannot be perpetual, one might none the less speak of a persistent legitimacy deficit, or again, following Hay (who borrows the term from Gramsci), of a catastrophic equilibrium. This is a potentially crisis prone yet relatively static conjuncture where submerged social unrest gives rise to localized resistance but only occasionally to overt national protest (Hay 1994 and 1995). The system is nevertheless seeking a longer-term stability that proves to be elusive.

Three questions are important here. First, how might we distinguish crises of and in a system? Second, how are steering problems articulated into conscious awareness that 'something needs to be done', and among whom does this awareness need to surface? Third, what types of subsequent modes of crisis intervention are likely to be successful or unsuccessful and why? Let us look briefly at each of these.

Crises within a system are not necessarily system-threatening. Regulatory regimes are always penetrated with conflicts of interests, and forms of crisis management are inscribed in the existing pattern of institutional relations. Although temporary institutional solutions cannot indefinitely confine crises, the existence of imbalances does not indicate the impending collapse of the system. On the contrary, crises might occasion an adaptive reshaping of structural relations, as occurred during the post-boom fiscal crisis of the state in the

---

5 Similarly, Holton (1990) points out that the concept is derived from drama or medicine and refers to crossroads, bifurcation points, moments when intensification of process requires some resolution which might be positive (healing) or negative (death).

advanced industrial world during the 1970s, which facilitated the extensive restructuring of the relation between capital, labour and the state that is loosely known as the 'rolling back of the state'. This is actually a misnomer, since during periods of restructuring the role of the state is likely to be more rather than less extensive. However, the result was that capital became more flexible, less heavily taxed or subject to bureaucratic constraints, and labour movements were considerably weaker by the 1990s than they had been in the 1970s. Crises in an accumulation regime then, can facilitate adaptive restructuring, although (to reiterate the point made in Chapter 2) this is not a quasi-natural evolutionary process, but the outcome of power struggles between interests embedded in the accumulation process (Rueschemeyer 1986).

When accumulation problems become unmanageable, however, we can speak of potential crisis of rather than in the accumulation regime (Jessop 1990:309). The question, which is especially relevant to understanding the crisis of communism, is what mechanism translates a crisis *within* to one *of* the system (Hill 1992)? Rationality problems and crisis tendencies can appear at different levels within the system – socio-cultural, economic and political subsystems – and the deeper the crisis, the more likely it is to threaten the identity of the system (Berber 1992). A crisis is likely to become system-threatening when failure on a lower level amplifies the crisis to a higher level, or erodes the performance of systems high in information, such as planning. This process can be displaced through compensating latent mechanisms of integration. It was seen in Chapter 2 that social differentiation facilitates this process of displacement, for example by allowing the transfer of risk from the polity to the economy whereby steering problems in the latter are depoliticized and do not then threaten the identity of the political subsystem.

What is meant by deepening of a crisis? We could consider for the moment the simplified model of socialist systems outlined in Figure 4.2 above, which depicted exchanges between the political and economic subsystems on the one hand, and the socio-cultural sphere on the other. Risks arising from productive activities (economic steering) are reduced by the polity through planning directives and subventions, while the polity siphons off the unconsumed surplus from the productive sector through administered procurement prices and taxes.

However, both the economy and polity are dependent on inputs from the socio-cultural subsystem and for habits of acquiescence to be transmitted through socialization. In the case of the polity, redistributive decisions and organization are dependent on sufficient legitimacy, or at least compliance, for directives of the Party to be binding. In the case of the economic subsystem, production is dependent on motivations and labour from households, in return for personal and collective consumption goods and wages. Dislocations in steering are likely to have amplifying knock-on effects throughout the system. For example, a deficit of consumer goods had de-legitimating effects which some states (e.g. Hungary and Poland during the 1970s) attempted to finance through foreign borrowing. This, however, opened the economy to the effects of cyclical pressures from global financial markets and rising debt repayment ratios, which in turn had de-legitimating effects as state budgets and consequently collective consumption, were reduced.

However, steering crises in socialist systems did not necessarily manifest themselves as legitimation crises because of the existence of institutionalized forms of crisis management. Lehman (1988) warns against a binary opposition of crisis and stability since societies are multi-layered systems in which conflict and consensus coexist and serious steering problems are compatible with continued viability. In Soviet societies there were tendencies towards the diffusion of steering problems as well as their amplification. I will argue that two processes here were crucial to the regulation of state socialism: crisis management and latent forms of integration.

State socialist systems institutionalized adaptive agents of planning who were supposed to perform functions of crisis avoidance. That is, they were to systematically anticipate and analyse deficiencies and limitations of stabilizing activity, a task rather optimistically described by Cornelius Disco as characterizing a 'smart bureaucracy'. This

not only pursues the formalized and rule-bound deployment of centralized authority in the tradition of its Weberian ancestors, but also senses, theoretically comprehends, plans and selectively reconstructs its particular environment. While so doing it pays particular attention to the effects of its own interventions, utilizing each instance as a learning experience in which to sharpen and streamline future policy. (Disco 1987:51)

It has to be said that one hardly recognizes the Soviet bureaucracy here. Even so, crisis management will be a process of trial and error and its content determined by balance of political forces (Jessop 1990:30). Its aim is to avoid spill-over of rationality crises into crises of motivation (identity or values) or of legitimation (public support). Offe (1976) suggests that the success or failure of institutionalized practices of crisis avoidance might depend on the availability of legitimation and ideological resources, the depth of steering problems, and experience of earlier adaptation. Further, the efficacy of responses to crises is likely to depend on structural constraints on goal preferences for crisis intervention (Jessop 1990:9–10). In communist systems, crisis management could not be allowed to undermine the Party's access to disposable resources, or legitimating values such as the myth of the vanguard. The success of crisis management will be further conditioned by the degree of congruence between crisis perception by planners or other relevant state agents in relation to latent rationality problems, along with the unintended consequences of intervention.

However, in statist systems, the boundaries between the polity, economy and socio-cultural systems are weak and potentially prone to a rapid deepening of crises as these spill over from the economy into planning, administrative and socio-cultural spheres.[6] In this context latent mechanisms of integration are crucial. These include covert legitimation (Rigby 1982); covert pluralism (Jessop et al. 1993); symbiosis between official and informal economies and social spheres (Hankiss 1991). Even so, an adaptive 'solution' to systemic crisis at a lower level can still disturb reproduction at a higher level because subsystem outputs become dysfunctional. For example, as we shall see in more detail shortly, the emergence of an informal sector in state socialist systems, which was an adaptive response to systemic failure, resulted in a gradual loss of legitimacy for the political subsystem and motivation crisis in the socio-cultural sphere.

None of this, however, accounts for the appearance of crises themselves. One theme in crisis theory locates the organizational basis for contradiction in the way in which enterprises and the planning

6 It is true, however, that administrative failure is hard to define because it disorganizes social life within a certain threshold of tolerance that is likely to vary in different circumstances and, unlike bankruptcy, for example, offers no unambiguous criteria of failure.

authorities are embroiled in a kind of contradiction between action and system. Marx's theory of the tendency of the rate of profit to fall (TRPF) is a prototype for this idea, since it effectively claims that in the capitalist system what is rational from an individual perspective might be dysfunctional from a system perspective. According to the TRPF individual capital units can only accumulate in such a way as to increase their organic composition, which in the long run reduces the average rate of profitability in the system.[7] In state socialism different kinds of steering problems arose as unintended consequences of institutional arrangements which could not easily be changed, partly because they were rational from the standpoint of the individual actor or enterprise but not from that of the system. For example, it was rational for managers of socialist enterprises to maximize the utility of their resources through ad hoc agreements with the workers to fix production norms, to hoard labour and materials or to underestimate the enterprise's productive capacity in negotiations with planners (Filtzer 1992b). But micro-level strategies created or exacerbated macro-level irrationalities, shortages and imbalances, partly because they entered information flows, which in turn made adaptive practices even more rational for individual enterprises. These conflicting rationalities arose from a set of structural and organizational contradictions that will now be examined.

IDENTITY OF THE SYSTEM

This section identifies the systemic origins of the crisis of Soviet socialism, which first requires a statement of the core elements of the system, distinguishing between the principle of structural domination and the steering subsystems responsible for production decisions, legitimation and motivation. The mode of domination was the rule of the nomenklatura status system based on appropriation through privileges and client networks. However, in order to reproduce itself in a changing environment, the mode of domination will draw upon cognitive and normative learning capacities that take the form of exem-

---

7 See Chapter 4, n.3 (*passim*). I am not concerned here with the question of whether Marx's theory of the TRPF is accurate, but rather with a model of internal contradictions between action orientations and the system.

plary alternatives inscribed into socio-cultural resources. These together constitute the principle of organization which refers to the capacity of society to learn without losing its identity (Habermas 1976:4–8) or, as Arato (1982) puts it, the limits of staying within those limits. In modern social systems the principle of organization is structured around three dimensions – productive forces and exchange (the economy); identity-securing interpretations (norms); institutional steering (the polity). The principle of organization circumscribes the range of possible variation consistent with the continued identity of the system, and co-ordinates two dimensions: capacities for systemic steering and the scope for the deployment of cognitive and moral learning. Further, regulatory strategies protect the identity of the system through co-option, crisis management, or the displacement of conflicts to social locations where they present least threat. Thus, complex social systems tolerate relatively high levels of internal conflict and crisis potential without disintegrating. However, Habermas's concept suggests that attempts to resolve steering problems have crisis effects if the learning capacity of system limits further development of the principle of organization at normative and cognitive levels.

Andrew Arato (1982:203) defines the principle of organization of Soviet systems as an 'industrial redistributive command economy', which dominated the economic and normative–cultural spheres (a somewhat modified version of which is shown in Figure 5.1). The key units in this model are system integration, social integration, and stratification plus latent integration which was not part of Arato's model and will be discussed later. Each of these appears in three sub-systems, adaptive (economic), goal attainment (state), and cultural. The following analysis will examine the increasing tension between the structural core of the state socialist model and its adaptive strategies.

The Stalinist (and to some extent post-Stalinist) growth model was driven by extensive development, where the goal was to increase the absolute surplus product over the proportion consumed (Ticktin 1992:147), which is amenable to central direction and implies relatively low levels of social differentiation. Extensive growth corresponds to the stage of primitive accumulation in the development of capitalism, which in particular involved proletarianization of rural labour and the forcible extraction of absolute surplus value from

	ECONOMY	STATE	CULTURE
System integration	Redistributive command economy	Party–state bureaucracies	Dictatorship over socialization
Social integration (legitimacy)	Welfare Functional dependence	Substantive justice Vanguard party	Social solidarity Collectivist ethics
Stratification	Redistributor/ redistributed Skill and education	Hierarchical politiocratic	Mass organizations Privatized
Latent integration	Second economy informal networks	Symbiosis with informal networks	*Nalevo* and *delat' plan* Culture of illegality

Figure 5.1 Principle of organization in state socialism

agrarian producers (Moore 1966). The goal of Stalinist economic development recapitulated the central dilemma of industrialization, namely to convert peasant labour into an industrial proletariat while increasing food production and preventing traditional rural habits (e.g. fragmented cultivation) from dissipating productive gains. New techniques of specialization and capital investment in agriculture were needed to cover the 'release price' of rural labour. This is the output lost through the departure of labour and the extra productivity of industry needed to equip agriculture with the means of increasing productivity. The release price will tend to fall with the commercialization of agriculture, which offers incentives to productivity through increased rural purchasing power, creates dependence on the industrial sector for machinery, and encourages a shift from subsistence to accumulation (Seton 1961). This does, however, presuppose some transfer of value back from industry to agriculture.

In the Soviet model, collectivization was crucial as a means of effecting both the elimination of smallholders (*kulaks*) and the extraction of value from *kolkozhy* (collective farms) via procurement quotas (Cliff 1968; Ticktin 1992:147). However, this closed off the possibility of either increased commercialization or functional interdependence with industry, opting instead for coercion and famine (for example in the Ukraine in 1932) as a means of reducing the release price of rural labour, which was paid through procurement quotas.[8]

The central features of the Stalinist growth model, then, outlined on the left of Figure 5.2, involved subordination of the economy to the

CORE SOVIET MODEL	MARKET SOCIALISM
Rapid extensive growth	Intensive growth
High centralization	Decentralization
Capital goods priority	Consumer growth
Output measured in volume	Output measured in value
Forced collectivization	Private plots encouraged
Import substitution	Competitive advantage and specialization
State ownership and direction of economy	Core (state) economy and second (private) economy
High per cent of GDP accumulated	Lower accumulation
Soft budget constraints	Shadow calculations to discover market clearing prices
Market as temporary expedient	Guided market – enterprises responsible for debts
	Managerial incentives to profitability
Cycle of investment and shortages	Market-led cycles regulated through indicative planning
Official policy of wage equalization	Wage differentials as incentives

Figure 5.2 The core Soviet model and market socialism

capital goods sector; a high percentage of accumulated GDP; output targets set by volume; forced collectivization as a basis for the extraction of a surplus for industrial and military growth; import substitution and economic autarky; high centralization combined with campaigns of

8 The volume of grain procurements taken by the state from collective farms, for example, rose from 14.7 per cent of total yield in 1928, to 26.4 per cent in 1930, 34 per cent in 1933, and 39.4 per cent in 1935 (Hosking 1992:166; Seton 1961). That is, nearly 40 per cent of the grain harvest was transferred from the countryside to the towns.

mass mobilization. Soft budget constraints (Kornai 1986) meant that the only effective constraints on production were the availability of resources allocated through the plan, since enterprises did not face the possibility of bankruptcy.[9]

This autarkic path of development, which has been described as 'Fordism in one country' (Voskamp and Wittke, 1991) was a kind of parody of Western productivism which fetishized output and techno-logical development while acknowledging no human or ecological costs (Fehér et al. 1984). Soviet modernization was achieved initially through intensification of heavy industrial production and collective consumption, combined with the heroic goal of achieving a higher stage of modernity than that represented by capitalism. Thus, frontier expansion (e.g. into Siberia) could be pursued without intensifying the productivity of labour through the introduction of new technologies.

The Stalinist accumulation strategy, though, ran up against self-limitations, which subsequent Soviet governments attempted to rectify. Terroristic control of labour was eventually limited by an acute labour shortage which actually increased the power of labour in the production process. This was illustrated by high labour turnover, which undermined plans (since these assumed a stable plant workforce) and created poor labour discipline, which was met in turn by repressive labour laws in the 1940s.[10] However, even these had a limited effect, as enterprise managers had to gain the compliance of the workforce, especially in the face of acute shortages of materials and machinery, since maintaining production was dependent on the innovation and co-operation of operatives (Filtzer 1991 and 1992b). The nomenklatura was engaged in a struggle for control of the labour process and securing motivational inputs from the socio-cultural system, which was all the more acute since the cost of eliminating effective political activity was to turn it into general discontentment with the labour process. Worker resistance was manifest in the system's

9 Budget softness refers to the ability of the unit to *co-determine* its own budget by influencing the terms of contract between it and its income source. The greater that ability is, the greater the degree of softness (Gomulka 1986:86). This is then a relation of power to command resources, which is inscribed into the mode of domination.

10 Growth in the informal bargaining power of labour in post-Stalinism in illustrated by the steady rise in average industrial wages from 66.1 roubles per month in 1950, to 88.9 in 1960, to 216.4 in 1986 – an average annual rise between 1960 and 1986 of 2.4 per cent – while incomes of the intelligentsia rose by only 1.76 per cent.

chronic inability to organize inputs, sabotage, slow working and withdrawal of labour into private activities such as cultivating small-
holdings (Manchin 1988; Szelenyi 1988). In addition, there was what
Hankiss describes as 'withdrawal into apathy', disengagement from
public life and 'escape into illness', evidenced by high rates of
alcoholism (Hankiss 1990:45).

Extensive accumulation was dependent on mass mobilization,
draconian labour discipline, and *zek* labour, which was in turn
dependent on the terror to provide an adequate labour supply.
However, this terroristic mode of regulation, combined with the
effects of the war in which 25 million Soviet citizens had been killed,
created a demographic crisis since 10–20 per cent of the adult male
population were in the camps. Stalinism had further encountered
limits of the application of terror, manifest in resistance and uprisings
in the camps (Hosking 1992:328), and a kind of mobilization exhaustion. Mass mobilization was legitimated through the myth of the vanguard ('there are no citadels the Bolsheviks cannot storm') but, as I
argued in Chapter 4, this ethic appealed essentially to the elite cadre
stratum. The failure of many speed-up and mobilization campaigns
(Slepyan 1993) during the 1920s and 1930s indicated that attempts to
instil charismatic enthusiasm in the Soviet population often foun-
dered, and the production process faced a chronic deficiency of motivations (Filtzer 1992b:8). Thus the diminution of terror after 1953
reflected in part the search for a new legitimacy base under Khrushchev, which the XXII Congress (1961) attempted to address through
new growth objectives and economic decentralization, combined with
public condemnation of Stalin (Whetten 1989:35).

The central goal of the Party in the post-Stalin period was to shift
from the exhausted extensive growth model to intensive growth
through increasing labour productivity. This, however, required
extensive changes – the reduction of supply shortages; improvements
in quality of capital and consumer goods; less variability in production;
availability of consumption goods, as a reward for labour. However, I
will argue that these goals were continually frustrated by the learning
capacity of the system – especially since the myth of the vanguard
would have been compromised by increasing diversity and plurality
(Fehér et al. 1984; Staniszkis 1992; Swain 1992). This was not, then,
merely a problem of solving structural economic problems through
technocratic solutions, as many reform communists imagined, but was

rather a problem created by limits inscribed into socio-cultural processes of socialization.

These were problems of institutionalizing sufficient social differentiation to permit mediated information flows and time boundaries for effective decision-making. Lenin proposed to run Soviet Russia as a single organization , 'the whole of which will have become a single office and a single factory, with equality of labour and pay' all under the leadership of the armed workers (Lenin 1969:93). However, as Nove (1991:37) and Sayer (1995) argue this was always unviable because the structure of a single organization cannot be transferred to the social division of labour comprising intersecting subsystems and hundreds of thousands of production and consumption decisions which elude the possibility of central design. A social division of labour entails an unprecedented division of knowledge which stretches beyond the comprehension of any single mind or organization.[11] Planners attempted to replace impersonal, indeterminate decisions with personal will in the forms of quotas and fixed prices. The complexity and unpredictability of demand in industrial societies (Nove 1991; Swain 1992) mean that it is impossible for a central authority to flexibly control millions of prices and production decisions. Attempts to do this result in what Djilas (1957:99) described as anarchy, wastefulness of fantastic proportions with no way of adjusting to world prices, which the illusion of 'planning' conceals.

This is not to say that planning *per se* necessarily generated systemic irrationalities, but rather the particular mode of producer sovereignty which was an expression of the mode of domination.[12] The weakness of cost restraint (soft budgets) meant that the planning cycle was governed by the limits of physical resource constraints (Nove 1991; Kornai 1986 and 1990a; Dallago 1990). Permanent full

11 Sayer (1995) suggests that Hayek's distinction between the economy and a catallexy might be useful here. The economy is used in the restricted sense of clusters of economic activities organized for specific purposes and which have a unitary hierarchy of ends (such as households and firms) while a catallexy is a mass of innumerable economies without specific, common purpose – the product of spontaneous growth rather than design.

12 Neoliberal economists tend to address these inherent planning irrationalities as though a system of regulation could be studied in abstraction from its institutional and regulatory forms. They contrast actual features of an extant system with an ideal-type free market economy (which, as Glasman (1994) suggests, exists only in a computer game) and assume that the failure of the former can be attributed to its distance from the latter.

employment of reserves created a chronic shortage of labour and investment for growth which had a number of self-limiting consequences for the system, reflected in the decline in earlier high rates of growth.[13] The appearance of rationality problems can be illustrated with reference to the following examples.

Hoarding. The redistributive system generated little pressure to be efficient and chronic shortages were created through the hoarding of labour as a flexible factor used to process raw materials in-house (Stark 1992b). Enterprises would understate their productive potential to obtain manageable targets, and over-indent inputs of energy, raw materials and labour (Smith 1993:37). This was a spontaneous process which by the 1960s was converting the earlier core model of the command economy into an economy of barter through interdepartmental co-ordination, an *ekonomika soglasovanii* (Naishul, 1993). Access to funds, then, depended less on financial soundness than on success in bargaining, which in turn favoured the large enterprises (Swain 1992:127). The extent of hoarding by enterprises was reflected in the rising levels of inventories which, between 1956 and 1965, accounted for 33 per cent of industrial assets in Czechoslovakia; 28 per cent in Poland; 33 per cent in Hungary; 20 per cent in the GDR. The long-term deceleration of the economy was marked by increasingly severe investment cycles and dependence on technology imports (Goldmann and Kouba 1969). The uneven pattern of investment further created specific sectoral cycles, such as the excessive upswing in investment in the chemical industry in the Soviet Union during 1958–65 which surpassed the possibilities for training, designing and producing machinery (Gomulka 1986). Thus shortages of materials and lack of maintenance were endemic in the production system and represented 'anticipatory competition' (Filtzer 1992b:134ff.). Hoarding was a kind of the functional equivalent to the profit motive, since it

13 Published GDP growth rates were often inaccurate of course. During the Gorbachev period percentage annual rates for the Soviet Union were published with a retrospective inflation adjustment: 7.2 (1951–60), 4.4 (1961–65), 4.1 (1966–70), 3.2 (1971–75), 1.0 (1976–80) and 0.6 (1981–86). This declining curve is due in part to exhaustion of extensive development, rising energy costs, and poor work motivations in a system where there was little to consume with increased earnings (Walker 1988:53ff.). Even so, during the Eighth and Ninth Five Year Plans (1966–75) steel output rose from 91 to 141 million tons p.a.; coal from 587 to 710 m. tons p.a.; petroleum from 243 to 491 m. tons p.a. See Bratkowski (1993) for a discussion of the use of statistical indicators.

presented the enterprise with a set of unintended systemic constraints that called for a particular pattern of game rational behaviour (Birman 1980 and 1988).

Imbalances. The volume of aggregated output which was used as an indicator of plan fulfilment was divorced from economic reality (Brus 1988; Šik 1976; Nove 1991). Planners knew that enterprises hoarded labour and materials and allowed for this in plan targets. In turn, managers further under-reported inventories in order to anticipate planners' adjustments (Nove 1991:81) which created opacity and indirectness in communications. The planning system encouraged falsification of data (Harrison 1993) which meant that worsening conditions were largely invisible. Inflation, for example, was hidden through the practice of re-describing goods and selling them at higher prices than previously. One consequence of these imbalances was the practice of *storming* which reflected bottlenecks in the production process. In order to meet monthly targets, on which bonuses depended, all hands, workers, clerical and management, would be deployed in production. At a Vilnius television factory, for example, Martin Walker reported that workers never used a screwdriver in the last week, the screws were hammered in, connections slam-soldered and parts cannibalized from other TVs (Walker 1988:42). Storming was, none the less a rational response to the imbalances in the plan and illustrates how micro-level adaptations could be in contradiction with macro-systemic goals.

Departmentalism (vedomstvennost) *and localism* (mestnichestvo). Functionally differentiated and complex systems institutionalize specialization that avoids the need to consider everything in the context of everything else. Soviet systems were highly differentiated bureaucratic orders but each department was supposed to issue decisions while considering the overall context of the central plan. Further, each ministry and department accumulated power and resources often duplicating functions performed elsewhere – such as the twenty-five ministries in Pavlodar oblast each with its own quarry and building factory (Nove 1991:75). This kind of self-supply was related to the formation of sectoral interests, which were dependent upon the patronage and clientelism that redistributive economies sustained, against a background of chronic scarcity (Bunce 1983). While the creation of privileged sectors might have generated loyalty and dependence (and hence contributed to micro-social integration), the coalescing of sectoral interests (heavy industry, the mass public, specialists, or consumer lobbies) created conditions for recurrent fiscal crisis (Campbell 1992).

CYCLICAL CRISES WITHIN STATE SOCIALISM

The planning mechanisms, then, gave rise to systemic contradictions which limited the self-regulating capacities of the system (Kaminski 1991:11; Nove 1991:103) through a series of what Habermas (1989: 384) calls 'self-blocking mechanisms' in which a massive waste of resources was combined with the systematic creation of shortages (Arnason 1993:105). The drive for quantitative growth, regulated through planning targets, created little incentive for enterprise managers to maximize the efficient deployment of resources. Rather, it was in the interests of enterprise managers to maximize accumulation of their plant's resources by underestimating its productive capacity; establish a large wage fund by hoarding labour; anticipate supply shortages (of spare parts, labour and raw materials) by accumulating reserves to be bartered in the future with other enterprises, while subunits within enterprises capitalized on blind spots (Nove 1991:103; Sakwa 1990:268; Stark 1992b). Modernization, such as the introduction of new machinery, was resisted since this would have pushed up the norms for the future or made workers redundant (Filtzer 1992b:25).

The result was a hollowed-out plan in which the control of the centre gave way to cyclical bottlenecks resulting from unbalanced growth (Bauer 1978; Birman 1988). These arose because of a cycle of investment hunger and shortages leading to resistance and informal exchange. The priority given to the capital goods and military sector (Department 1) was a consequence of the political priorities of extensive growth, which was also the rationale for the guiding hand of the vanguard party. The political power of the large state monopolies through ministries and the Central Committee meant that their interests were never neglected in the plan (Gomulka 1986:227–50). This combined with soft budgets and the practice of anticipatory competition to cause high self-consumption of resources in Department 1 where output was limited only by the physical extent of resources, machinery and labour motivation. This in turn limited the supply of machinery and resources for the consumer goods sector (Department 2) in two ways. First, the chronic shortage of consumer goods and housing exacerbated the motivation crisis and worker resistance, which further exacerbated the rationality crisis by slowing down production and under-fulfilling the plan. Second, even if Department 2 were given priority, the shortage of suitable machinery increased the pressure to increase the output of capital goods, which further fuelled the self-consumption of resources in Department 1. Thus the economy was prone to periodic crises of over-investment, and a lag and echo effect of 10–15 years in which competition among enterprises for resources accelerated new waves of investment (Marrese 1981; Goldman and Kouba 1969; Flaherty 1992; Zloch-Christy 1987).

However, despite these systemic irrationalities, this was still a self-regulating and self-maintaining system (Zaslavsky 1985) in which a pattern of crisis and intervention could be identified, as shown in Figure 5.3. The pattern of disjointed growth identified above would continue until it became critical, that is, until it reached the threshold of political tolerance (such as Poland in 1956) at which point, when subjective awareness of crisis dawned among the party hierarchy, the political centre intervened to correct imbalances. The lack of surplus labour, and self consumption by Department 1, created a chronic resource deficit that was filled, if at all, through technology imports which resulted in chronic balance of payments problems, debt and dependence (Bratkowski 1993).

This self-devouring cycle drew capital away from other vital areas, especially the consumer sector, to preserve the accumulation regime. According to Flaherty (1992) these cycles were the result of post-Stalinist corporatism which transformed the plan into a résumé of branch proposals. For Flaherty chronic over-investment in Department 1 was evidenced by the fact that the proportion of GDP allocated to consumption actually fell during the Soviet period and accumulation efficiency fell by 53 per cent between the late 1960s and the 1980s.[14] Thus by the 1980s the Soviet Union had one of the highest

14 According to Flaherty (1992), the percentage of GDP devoted to consumer goods in the USSR was 60 in 1928; 38 in 1940; 31 in 1950; 27 in 1960; 26 in 1970; 26 in 1980; 24 in 1986. However, according to other sources (*SSSR v tsifrakh v 1989g.*) consumption percentages (excluding alcohol) during the 1980s were: 1980: 41.20; 1985: 39.38; 1986: 40.05; 1987: 40.85; 1988: 40.46; 1989: 40.58.

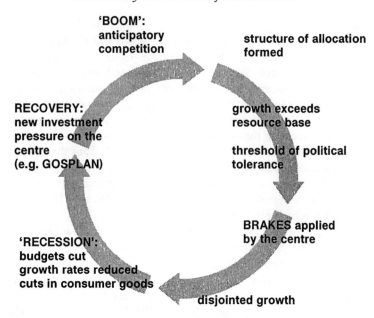

'BOOM':
anticipatory
competition

structure of allocation
formed

RECOVERY:
new investment
pressure on the
centre
(e.g. GOSPLAN)

growth exceeds
resource base

threshold of political
tolerance

BRAKES applied
by the centre

'RECESSION':
budgets cut
growth rates reduced
cuts in consumer goods

disjointed growth

Figure 5.3 Cyclical crises in state socialism

rates of investment in the world but produced virtually zero growth. This cyclical pattern of growth and recession is indicated in Figure 5.4, which shows eleven violent swings of expansion and contraction in five socialist countries during the post-war period. Production rose during the high levels of investment in the early 1950s, and fell thereafter, to rise in the later 1950s with post-Stalinist reinvestment and stabilization; falling again in 1960–63, rising again in the mid-1960s and early 1970s. If these are viewed as a single chart (Figure 5.4) then it is clear that, although the intensity of the swings varies in different countries, and some specific timings vary (e.g. Bulgaria is counter-cyclical in cycle VII but enters recession in VIII) there is an overall similarity, suggesting an underlying pattern common to Soviet societies.

Further, by the 1960s long-range problems in the Soviet economy were apparent. Much national product growth resulted from oil and gas production which involved high capital and investment costs.

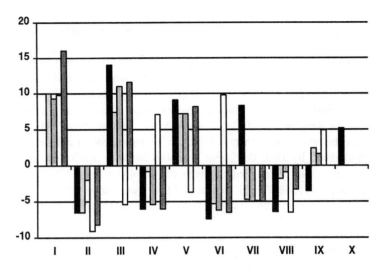

■ Bulgaria □ Czechoslovakia ▤ Hungary □ Poland ▥ USSR

Cycle	I	II	III	IV	V	VI	VII	VIII	IX	X
	1950–52	1953–56	1957–59	1960–63	1964–67	1968–71	1972–75	1976–80	1981–85	1986–88
Bulgaria		−6.50	14.00	−6.00	9.10	−7.40	8.30	−6.40	−3.50	5.20
	1950–52	1953–56	1957–61	1962–65	1966–69	1970–75	1976–78	1979–84	1985–88	
Czecho–Slovakia	10.00	−6.50	7.40	−0.80	7.20	−5.30	−4.70	−1.80	2.40	
	1951–53	1954–56	1957–60	1961–65	1966–69	1970–74	1975–77	1979–85	1986–88	
Hungary	9.30	−2.00	11.00	−5.40	7.20	−6.20	−5.00	−0.90	1.60	
	1950–53	1954–63	1964–68	1969–70	1971–75	1976–78	1979–82	1983–85	1986–88	
Poland	9.80	−9.10	−5.40	7.10	−3.70	9.80	−4.90	−6.50	4.90	3.90
	1950–51	1952–53	1954–56	1957–63	1964–68	1969–73	1974–78	1979–88		
USSR	16.00	−8.20	11.60	−6.00	8.20	−6.50	−5.00	−3.30		

Source: Kolodko (1992:6)

Figure 5.4 Growth cycles in centrally planned economies, 1950–1988

Since 1945 each one per cent increase in growth had required a 1.4 per cent increase in investment and a 1.2 per cent increase in raw materials supply (Guber 1985). Moreover, as the geographical integration of the USSR weakened with population dispersal, so problems associated with the extensive developmental model accumulated. For example, the cost of coal from Siberia doubled with every 1,500 km., hence nuclear reactors were situated in the more populous western USSR (Walker, 1988:70). Between the 1950s and 1980s the annual growth rate fell from 11.4 per cent to 3.6 per cent and although by 1980 the USSR produced twice as much steel as the USA, its output of finished products was smaller (White 1992b:106). Aganbegyan (1988:37–80) commented that 'our country produces four and a half times more tractors than the US in order to produce a smaller quantity of wheat'.

These blockages were exacerbated by closed communication systems within the Party and planning bureaucracy where the absence of public scrutiny and participation facilitated the disregard for resource constraints (Gomulka 1986:227–50).[15] Thus these investment cycles were peculiar to this form of socialism (Gomulka 1986:28) because of the close relationship between the investment cycle and political unrest which affects investment priorities, which in turn reflected the close linkage outlined in Chapter 4 between resource allocation and legitimation.

RANGE OF VARIATION

The Soviet systems none the less demonstrated a capacity to adapt, partly because they contained exemplary models of alternative organizational forms that defined the scope for learning and flexibility. This range of variation is customarily understood as the oscillation between 'plan' and 'market'. However, this was not a late innovation, but was inscribed in the learning capacity of the system from the early years.

---

15 Further, poor feedback resulted in a tendency to assume that any success was the desired result of policy rather than a short-term and unintended consequence, as with the Polish Net Material Product growth during 1970–75, which was the consequence of relaxed import restrictions combined with energy price rises which opened credit lines to Eastern Europe, especially Hungary and Poland (Gomulka 1986; Ray 1993:99).

Since the NEP in the 1920s, increasing the scope for market allocation had been available as a palliative for steering problems with the command economy, even if officially only as a temporary expedient.[16] For example, in order to expand food production during the Great Fatherland War, the *zveno* (link) system enabled families to take over stretches of *kolkhoz* land and sell surplus produce on private markets, but despite the arguments of some economists, the system was not extended after the war.[17] Even so, private plots remained on collective farms and successive attempts to remove them failed.[18] During the 1950s Soviet agricultural policy attempted to solve the problem of rising labour replacement costs through incentives to increase rural productivity. Hence delivery prices rose 200–500 per cent; delivery norms were lowered; arrears were cancelled; equipment was transferred from Machine Tractor Stations to farm management, which were to switch to full cost accounting. In addition, urban female labour was mobilized into industry through increased welfare and child-care facilities (Seton 1961), though at lower wages than male workers, thus reducing industrial reproduction costs (Filtzer 1992b).

As an international order, moreover, Soviet systems contained a considerable range of scope for variation, the clearest examples of which are:

- The NEP and its derivations, such as the *zveno*.
- Bloc countries in which collectivization was not pursued after

16 The key features of the NEP were: a mixed economy in which the commanding heights of the economy (banks and large manufacturing) were under public ownership while smaller enterprises and most agriculture developed privately. Prices fluctuated according to market conditions and wage differentials increased. By 1926 industrial production had risen to its pre-war level but no surplus was produced from agriculture for industrial investment.

17 Collective farms provided equipment, animals and fertilizer for link workers. Voznesensky (Chair of Gosplan) and Andreyev (Politburo member responsible for agriculture) favoured the continuation of the *zveno* after 1945, but in 1946 Stalin ordered that all land farmed under this system be returned to the collective farms (Hosking 1992:288).

18 Private plots were highly productive, partly because they grew high value crops such as onions and grapes rather than rye or wheat (Nove 1991:94). Controversy over the link system revived after an experiment in Krasnodar oblast in which 10 workers increased by three times the yield of a plot normally cultivated by a brigade of 80. Extension of this scheme, however (which was also implemented in Kazakhstan), threatened the organizational base of the rural Party in *kolkhozy* and was not developed (Hosking 1992:288).

1956, notably in Poland where 89 per cent of agriculture remained privately owned and the average holding was five hectares as opposed to 5,000 in Soviet Union.[19] In Hungary collectivization was placed on a voluntary basis in the New Course announced by Prime Minister Imre Nagy in 1953 (Kecskemeti 1969:45–6).

• The Yugoslav model of self-management and state co-ordination with extensive market and competition between worker co-operatives (Horvat 1976). Although this system was not generalized throughout the bloc, workers' councils as democratic regulators in industry (effectively a substitute for political democracy) were periodically debated in other communist states (Federowicz 1994:21).

• The Hungarian New Economic Mechanism (NEM; see below) as an alternative mode of system regulation (Bauer 1978; Swain 1992; Nove 1991).

This range of variation was elaborated into a concept of an alternative system of market socialism by economists such as Oskar Lange and Ota Šik (1976) and Alec Nove (1991), which is summarized on the right of Figure 5.2. Market socialism involved economic decentralization and the measurement of output in value rather than volume; a core state economy distinct from a second, private economy. A 'guided market' would enable enterprises to make investment and production decisions; managers would have incentives to run enterprises at a profit and would be responsible for debts; wage differentials would act as a stimulus to increased productivity. In some models the system of central planning would remain, but with shadow

19 As elsewhere in the socialist bloc, the Polish Government instigated a 'campaign against the *kulaks'* in 1945, confiscating all arable land in excess of 50 hectares, but the majority of land was owned by peasant farmers (with an average holding of 5.4 ha.). In 1956, following massive peasant resistance, collectivization was abandoned, and Gomulka increased credits to private farmers while state land was leased (1 million ha. between 1957 and 1960). By 1988, 82 per cent of capital goods, 66 per cent of consumer and 70 per cent of the tertiary sectors were publicly owned. However, in agriculture, 79 per cent of food production came from private plots. There were 5,107 state farms (average size 1,000 hectares) but 2.6 million private farms of over five hectares and 1.2 million under five hectares (Lovenduski and Woodall 1987:87 and Majkowski 1985).

calculations through which prices would be mathematically calculated in an attempt to discover market-clearing prices.

These ideas were influential in the Hungarian NEM (1968) which involved the following features:

- elimination of compulsory plan instructions;
- abolition of central allocation of materials and products;
- plan fulfilment ceased to be the basic success indicator;
- new indicators included fulfilment of contractual deliveries to the Council for Mutual Economic Assistance (CMEA); growth of labour productivity; consumer goods supply;
- bargaining about plan figures ceased to be the main activity of managers and state;
- the NEM thus removed the main reason to distort information.

In this combination of plan and market, the state retained control of capital goods, distribution, infrastructure and agriculture but a market economy was allowed to grow up alongside. This was increasingly responsible for the distribution of consumption goods and the service sector, while rural small-holdings and co-operatives were formed to make dual use of state property. Personal incomes from the private sector were allowed to grow, along with a decentralized banking system through which, from the late 1980s, personal savings could be used as capital for cross-investment in state enterprises, creating a kind of internal market within the state sector. Procedures were instituted allowing for the bankruptcy of inefficient state enterprises, and later the 1988 Companies Act created the beginnings of a stock exchange among state bonds. Joint ownership was encouraged in order to secure foreign investment in state enterprises (Ray 1990).

Had it been allowed to develop its potential, the NEM might have offered a model of socialist pluralism – the agricultural sector after all *was* left with considerable autonomy, scope for diversification into non-agricultural products and flexible pricing. As a result it became the most productive and efficient sector in the Soviet bloc (Adam 1987; Swain 1987). But many of the original aims of the NEM were limited between 1972 and 1975 amid official criticism of declining socialist morality, lack of discipline and petty-bourgeois attitudes. Similarly, the reforms in the DDR in the 1960s ran aground on opposition from the Central Committee, which eventually secured

Ulbricht's dismissal at the XI Plenum in 1965 (Kopstein 1994). The Liberman reforms in the Soviet Union ended after the Czech débâcle in 1968, which itself alerted reformers to the limits that would be imposed by the political power structure.

Marketized state socialism posed new problems, such as determining the reward for labour, capital generation in the absence of investment markets and drawing a boundary between plan and market (Nove 1988:xix). Further, dual systems created opportunities for leakage of resources from the regulated state sector to the commodified and more lucrative market sector. In the Hungarian case, the profitability of enterprises was limited by formal price regulations and CMEA; although the NEM gave enterprises freedom to widen their range of activities, use multiple channels and take risks, their operating environment remained a sellers' market. The foreign trade pattern was determined by the CMEA, and production decisions were influenced by the input process, therefore there was a lack of alternative sources of supply. Further, the state kept full control of imports and exports, so the system remained insulated from world prices and soft budget constraints remained (Bauer 1978; Nove 1991). Plan bargaining was replaced by regulation bargaining in which bonuses and privileges were awarded to managers for extra output. This created its own cyclical pattern in which pressure from enterprises still inflated investment inputs while personal consumption was financed through foreign borrowing (Swain 1992:124ff.).

A general conclusion from the fate of market socialism in Soviet systems is that the selection and institutionalization of potential learning capacities was subject to the balance of power relations within the polity. The implementation of decentralized and market-oriented models was always politically contentious because it challenged the right of the Party to determine production priorities and to dispose of the surplus product. None the less, the existence of alternative models gave the system room for manoeuvre and experiment at the limits of its organizational structure, especially in Hungary, which after 1956 was given greater latitude for experiment than elsewhere in the bloc. But in the Soviet Union, too, there were covert and subterranean shifts, not only at the level of official policy, but within cultural enclaves such as the Akademgorodok in Novosibirsk which was given relative intellectual freedom during the 1970s. Here social scientists such as Tatyana Zaslavskaya and Abel Agenbegyan, future architects of early perestroika, survived Brezhnev's attacks on sociology to develop a comprehensive critique and programme for reform of the system. The crucial question here, which will be examined in the next chapter, was whether the system could expand its capacity for flexible differentiation without undermining the authority of the Party – a circle that became increasingly hard to square.

LATENT INTEGRATION

Beneath these chronic rationality problems, then, there were steering mechanisms nestling in networks hidden in informal spheres of social space which, in due course, were to be crucial to the subsequent pattern of transition to post-socialism. Within Soviet systems rationality problems were offset less by formal strategies of crisis management than by an increasingly tolerated parallel or 'second' society alongside the 'official' economy. This was perhaps because

> [i]deologically integrated societies strive to politicize society and confine differentiation of the political system from the rest of society to the level of roles, rather than to expand it to a differentiation of values, norms and goals. Then differentiation of ideological–political behaviour and technical–bureaucratic administrative practice have to be secured latently. (Luhmann 1982:382n.)

Thus shortages resulting from the redistributive mechanisms were partially filled through informal networks, and by symbiotic exchanges between the informal sector and the state, based on patrimonial protection through mutual security and political corruption (Fehér 1982:66; Jowitt 1983).

In Soviet systems, unlike formal–rational bureaucracies, rule was not procedurally formalized but was rather 'control by exception' since regulations were departed from without formal revision (Fehér et al. 1984:175; Staniszkis 1992:11). Beneath the appearance of order (the rule of the Party, the planning mechanisms etc.) there was substantive disorder and dependence on adaptive responses of the socio-cultural system. Habermas (1976:75) identifies a crisis of the socio-cultural system when it changes in such a way that its output becomes dysfunctional. In capitalism, differentiation of public and private spheres within the lifeworld generates civil privatism (interest in the political system but low participation) and familial–vocational privatism (family-oriented pattern and concern with career status). However, in Soviet systems privatism was both functional and dysfunctional in different ways.

It was functional in that (i) the Party required limited mass participation or routinized participation at appropriate junctures; (ii) career orientation and deference to superiors created a pliant bureaucracy and people who do not 'ask too many questions'. Yet it was dysfunctional in that (i) the consumer orientation that accompanies familial privatism was hardly appropriate where there was a deficit of consumption goods; (ii) privatism established an orientation away from the public sphere of the Party; (iii) privatism facilitated the extension of horizontal networks of the informal and irregular economies in such a way that they distracted motivations from the state economy. Moreover, the turn to privatism, in the absence of a formal–legal framework in communist states, further eroded the limited legitimacy basis of the system by encouraging practices in conflict with the system's central values.[20] The very participation in irregular actions presupposed resistance to the system and tended to encourage cynicism, apathy and a negative work ethic in official life (Bugajski and Pollack 1989:187).

The second society had three dimensions: (i) plan bargaining, strategies referred to above consisting of horizontal networks among enterprises known as *na levo*, literally 'on the left', or illegally; (ii) an informal economy, which was self-provisioning on the basis of non-monetary reciprocity, such as home-building to escape years of queuing for municipal housing; (iii) an irregular economy, selling goods and services parallel to the official economy. The boundary between tolerated and illegal economic activity was indistinct and fluid, which permitted a vast network of transactions that contributed to consumer satisfaction, and provided an outlet for anti-system sentiments and activities.

First, horizontal integration or 'doing the plan' (*delat' plan*) was exemplified by plan bargaining, the defensive actions of enterprise

---

20 Even cautious people, said Berliner (1952), are often compelled to act contrary to certain state instructions in order to comply with others. As a consequence, the law will lose some of its moral force.

directors who protected their bonus-earning capacity by under-reporting their productive potential (Jessop et al. 1993; Kaminski 1991; McIntyre 1988:89). This created horizontal integration and local power bases, which Nove (1991:85) calls 'feudal principalities', long chains of barter in which enterprises traded excess resources and insti-tutionalized illegal or semi-legal means of plan fulfilment (Dallago 1990; Katsenelinboigen 1977).

Anticipatory competition and the chronic shortage of labour and materials had consequences such as deploying labour to process raw materials and re-tool equipment in-house. This made labour co-operation indispensable to plan fulfilment and permitted selective bargaining with enterprise managers. Between the ministries, central plan and enterprises there was an absence of clear criteria of productive capacity, and exchanges took the form of lobbying, reciprocity, clientelism, informal relations and the 'invisible handshake', which permitted the formation of sectoral interests and a kind of 'spontaneous decentralization' as the real mechanism regulating resource allocation was the power play of negotiations among ministries, sectors and enterprises.

Second, in the irregular economy (Dallago 1990:12)[21] goals and means were at variance with official practices which generated a motivation crisis as households diverted labour away from the state economy into parallel circuits of money and services. An irregular economy has a number of imperfections, such as high transaction costs, difficulties of communication, slow circulation of information and 'taxation' in the form of bribes to corrupt officials, and is likely to flourish only in the context of acute rationality problems. Timofeev explains that the

> [w]orkers cannot earn enough to buy meat through the back door, buy shoes from a speculator and give bribes when necessary to obtain essential goods. Therefore he [sic] has to work overtime ... or look for extra work on the side, or steal, or spend time growing vegetables in his own garden ... Neither could the professional politicians maintain the system's stabil-ity without purchasing unplanned black-market labour. (Timofeev 1985: 150–51)

---

21 Following Dallago (1990) the monetized second economy will be called 'irregular', and non-monetary exchanges, 'informal'.

The informal and state economies became so interpenetrated and symbiotic that it was difficult to separate them empirically. So, for example, legitimate private producers would exceed limitations on private accumulation and siphon off inputs such as fodder, fertilizer or transport from the state sector (Grossman 1977). Hankiss (1991:310) points out that the terms 'official' and 'second' societies do not refer to two groups of people, but to two dimensions of social existence governed by different organizational principles that were none the less dependent upon one another, in that the second society provided a degree of flexibility not permitted by the rigidity of the planning mechanisms. Moreover, planners relied on the ability of people to provision themselves via informal channels. Davies (1988) describes how increased prices combined with scarcity of welfare resources were absorbed by local communities through the 'self-management of austerity'. These transactive networks stimulated the management of internal affairs but generally on a short-term basis, in pursuit of windfall profits and through part-time work. However, this possibility of 'exit' was the basis of bargaining with the firm and could be formalized into semi-autonomous units, as in the Hungarian NEM.

Third, there were informal networks based on reciprocity and bargaining and mutual exchange (Misztal 1993). These were horizontal links and personal relationships that grew into extensive social networks of the second society and which offset shortages and planning deficiencies through mutual assistance, reciprocal labour exchanges, barter of scarce commodities and, eventually, petty commodity production.[22] Endre Sik (1988) has shown how households exchanged labour on a non-market basis, for example in rural house-building which is labour intensive and requires a high degree of organization while draining the income-generating capacities of the household. In Hungary in 1982, the average completion time for such dwellings was 19 months, and involved a wide range of informal

---

22 Since a great number of these exchanges were non-monetary it is difficult to esti-
mate the size of the informal sector, even if reliable data were available. A report to
the Central Committee of the CPSU in 1987 estimated that 1.5 billion rubles a year
were tied up in the second economy (White 1992b:118) (i.e. 0.2 per cent of GNP)
but this was a gross underestimation. Grossman (1977) estimated *legal* private
activity in the Soviet Union as accounting for 31 per cent of value added in
agriculture; 32 per cent in housing and 5 per cent in services, amounting to 10 per
cent of GDP overall, and suggested that the illegal and semi-legal sectors would
have been larger.

exchanges. All social strata and 85 per cent of households used reciprocal exchange of labour (REL) for social purposes, 34 per cent for services, and five per cent for house building, although 80 per cent of those who self-built used REL. These were motivated by shortage of services and welfare, the high price of labour in the second economy, and the working capacity of the family being too small to fulfil all its tasks (Szelenyi 1988).

These three types of latent integration in turn had paradoxical effects at a societal level. The state and irregular economies were symbiotic to a degree, but in the longer term, the latter corroded the former. The second society had dysfunctional consequences for the state sector, draining it of resources both directly (through theft, moonlighting etc.) and indirectly, by siphoning off motivational inputs, as attitudes towards the official economy became increasingly cynical and apathetic. The latter contrasted with relations of trust, reciprocity and self-interest in the second economy (Bugajski and Pollack 1989:187).[23] Moreover these defensive reactions, rational enough in a chronic shortage economy (Kornai 1986), themselves exacerbated the kinds of shortages and dysfunctions referred to above, that is, hoarding, falsifying data and storming. As households, stimulated by second-economy rewards, reduced the supply of labour and motivation to the official economy, so they became increasingly dependent on REL to satisfy consumption needs. Thus the purchasing power of wages declined further, with the result that more labour still was deployed in the self-provisioning, informal economies (Pine 1992; Stark 1992b).

However, the household was not the black box that much analysis of irregular economies often implies, but a subsystem of power, money and influence, and in particular was a gendered space whose production of use values was presupposed by the state economies. The irregular and informal economies were dependent on the deployment of women as unpaid carers and low-wage workers, as Davies (1988) points out in his study of 'Hungarcity' where women were highly represented in second-economy activities. Likewise, Elson (1988) argues that the 'success' of informal economies, smallholder production, or reciprocal labour exchanges in state socialism were dependent on

23 However, Sampson (1985–86) warns against romanticizing social relations in the informal sector, which could be as conflictual and exploitative as those in bureaucratic apparatuses.

women's labour, in a context of patriarchal relations, generally combined with first-economy employment. Informal economies are dependent on the uncosted production of use values and an unequal division of earnings, which in turn presuppose a power structure within which labour and goods are allocated in the informal economy. In the Soviet Union twelve million worked exclusively on personal plots, of whom three-quarters were women (Timofeev 1985) and this high participation of women in the second society confirmed their domestic 'private' status (Pine 1992:66). Within a patriarchal power structure, women's labour operates as a form of flexible cushioning against the chronic shortages of the state sector and in the process generates the 'dual burden' of subordination through both paid and domestic labour.[24]

In place of cultural modernity, Soviet systems generated traditionalistic pre-modern adaptations and latent integration via informal networks which consolidated a culture of privatism, further illustrating the unintended consequences of centralized planning. Sampson (1985–86) describes the informal sector as a 'de-bureaucratized' social space, characterized by relationships of mutual obligation and patronage, which not only survived well within 'the interstices of bureaucratic organization' but also assisted the latter to function. The key features of this were mechanical solidarity; informal networks ('shock absorbers' in private agriculture and intensified domestic exploitation of women); dissolving anonymity by eroding institutionalized trust; horizontal integration based on the particularism of family, friendship, or ethnic group (Stark 1992b). In this society, symbiotic yet separate from the state, traditions of conservatism, religion and national identity could be preserved, despite the 'modernizing' efforts of the regime (e.g. Schöpflin 1991). These were to become a source of anti-state public mobilization in the future.

The relationships between official and second societies are shown in Figure 5.5, where I suggest that the second society takes on each of the four functions of the official society, establishing boundaries Aa, Gg, Ii and Ll. At the Aa boundary, resources (time, materials, money)

---

24 This in part explains the low wage cycle whereby, despite high rates of women's labour market participation compared with most Western countries (over 70 per cent in the USSR in 1980 compared with 32 per cent in the USA) Soviet women were concentrated in low wage sectors such as textiles, service industries and unskilled factory work.

OFFICIAL SOCIETY

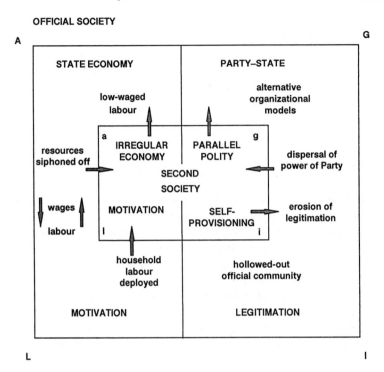

Figure 5.5 Official and second societies

are siphoned off the official economy in exchange for low wage labour in the state sector that presupposed subsidies to households' income from access to irregular economy employment. At the Gg boundary a parallel polity existed through circulation of unofficial publications in samizdat, informal meetings and underground groups. In so far as this was tolerated (even in enclaves, as indicated above), it involved some dispersal of power from the Party in return for alternative organizational models. This boundary, though, was subject to high levels of conflict. At the Ii boundary, legitimation via redistributive mechanisms in the official society (see Chapter 4) was eroded especially as this was subject to budget cuts, such as the 1987 Hungarian Stabilization Programme, which increased dependence on self-provisioning adaptations such as REL. At the Ll boundary, motivations are withdrawn from the state sector and given over to informal activities such as moonlighting, a practice which is inscribed into latent learning through socialization, since from an early age one learnt to distrust the official authorities. However, the very informality, traditionalism and privatism of the second society was to influence the eventual transition to post-communism in significant ways.

CRISIS TENDENCIES IN STATE SOCIALISM

The central crisis tendencies in the state socialist system arose because the political subsystem absorbed complexity from the economy and the Party became the arbiter of needs which it had no reliable way of assessing (Swain 1992:69). The scale, scope and complexity of planning encountered the constraint of inadequate time to process the information that would have been required to adjust output to social needs. Thus plans became increasingly complex and subject to arbitrary changes instead of developing open, variable and differentiated systems of decision-making. Increasing the selectivity of the system (e.g. stimulating innovation, isolating disturbances, simplifying decisions) would have required increased differentiation of and within economic and social organizations. However, this avenue, as we shall see in the next chapter, was blocked by the sovereign power of the Party which, unable to pluralize the system openly, came to rely less on formal administrative–command structures than on interdepartmental co-ordination and latent practices that were at variance with the publicly stated goals and ideology of the system.

Drawing on the above discussion, I would propose that one can identify four sites of crisis articulation. First, steering crises were manifest in cyclical over-investment and an uneven growth pattern tending towards cumulative self-obstruction (cf. Offe 1976). Second, a rationality deficit unfolded with the exhaustion of the Stalinist growth model and the emergence of informal decentralization which resulted in a weakening of central control, inflationary overhang, a growing contradiction between the expansion of chronological planning horizons and the actual forecasting capacity of planners. The preference given to heavy industry – a direct consequence of the power relations inscribed into the mode of domination – resulted in chronic consumer shortages, which for workers created the right to purchase but not to consume (Birman 1980; Jessop et al. 1993; Voslensky 1984). Third, this created conditions for a motivation crisis – apathy, illness, ritualism, withdrawal of labour from the state sector – such that increased wages were little incentive to increased productivity. Fourth, the more rationality and motivational problems accumulated, the less effective was the reservoir of integrative symbolism associated with the vanguard role of the Party. A destabilization of the official political culture was marked by competing norms – traditional values, market instrumentality, Western liberalism and social democracy – which began to inform the parallel polity. None the less, these systems continued to function and generate sufficient motivations to cohere and reproduce themselves. This was because the tendency towards steering crisis was not automatically amplified into a social identity crisis, and for many decades the system proved adept at self-regulation through crisis displacement. So long as crisis tendencies could be privatized and absorbed through informal networks the mode of domination remained relatively secure. However, beneath the apparent order of Soviet systems in the 1960s and 1970s, the cadre status system was already in transition towards a class system with a particular Soviet character.

6. The Legal Revolution

This chapter examines the intersection of systemic crises with crises of social integration which motivated but also constrained perestroika, the 'legal revolution'. I suggested in Chapter 5 that Soviet systems encountered problems of over-complexity which were resolved through a combination of latent regulation, depoliticization and varying the balance of plan and market, but always in a context that suggested their interim character. State socialism's regulatory systems (bureaucracy, informal networks, markets and local democratization) always contained a tendency towards crisis because of their chronic inability to co-ordinate increasingly complex interactions (a deficit of power) which led to the uncontrolled growth of informal regulators that finally escaped central control and drifted towards destruction.

During the 1960s and 1970s, Soviet systems encountered limits to the possibility of co-ordinating increasing levels of complexity through partially differentiated sovereign power. De-Stalinization had attempted to combine depoliticization of some aspects of everyday life without relinquishing the vanguard role of the Party, which had limited options for opening up new avenues of legitimation, especially in Central Europe where the Party had always rested on weak normative foundations. The manifestation of chronic organizational problems in the post-Stalin period, such as cyclical investment crises, growing debt problems and dependence on Western financial institutions were rooted in the over-extension of the state combined with the inability of the Party to relinquish control over the surplus product.

Decentralizing reforms, in response to the chronic dysfunctions discussed in Chapter 5, faced the dilemma that sooner or later the dictatorship of the Party would be called into question, especially by cadres themselves. Thus, during the 1980s there was considerable debate over the likely eventual outcome of reform in Soviet systems. While for many, such as Fehér et al. (1984:297), Soviet societies would prove ultimately incapable of reform, other commentators (e.g. Lewin 1988; Walker 1988) saw in perestroika and glasnost the potential for a genuine political and social renewal. In view of the eventual failure of perestroika one might feel that Fehér et al. have been proved right. However, perestroika arguably enjoyed a kind of success, in that despite widespread fears that it would prove to be as transitory as earlier periods of reform, notably Khrushchev's de-Stalinization, it was successfully institutionalized in the Soviet system, albeit with unintended consequences. One of these, I will argue in this and the following chapter, was that although perestroika failed to preserve the communist political system, it was instrumental in empowering the nomenklatura as new economic and political agents.

The central problem with perestroika was that the idea of the socialist law-based state (*sotsialisticheskoe pravovoe gosudarstvo*)[1] entailed a formalization of state rationality which actually exacerbated the decomposition of the system by undermining the *raison d'être* of the nomenklatura. Perestroika and glasnost had to cope with the legacy of the revolutionary foundations of a system not governed by statutory norms which left the executive with freedom from legality (Federowicz 1994:34; Fehér et al. 1984:175; Staniszkis 1992:11). This should be remembered in view of the widespread assumption that state socialist bureaucracies represented the epitome of rationalization. Bryan Turner (1994:123), for example, argues that 'Weber's fears about the stultifying consequences of bureaucratic regulation also appear to have borne fruit in the ... communist countries', and it was noted above (pp.2 and 45) that similar views were expressed by Bauman. But the vanguard principle was resistant to the very process of formal rationalization (which was central to Weber's understanding of the modern bureaucracy) and attempts to convert the Party's rule into a *Rechtsstaat* were actually a catalyst for its disintegration.[2]

---

1 According to one definition, the essence of the legal state is that its organs serve society and are not above it and that non-formal groups are included in legislative bodies such as the Supreme Soviet (view presented by Soviet social scientists in Varna, Bulgaria, 1988). This does, however, fall short of multi-party pluralism and citizen rights.

2 This should cause us to revise received views about the 'iron cage' of bureaucratization which arise from Weber's analysis, since formal rationalization and the ethical autonomy it presupposes might be forces for emancipation rather than confinement (for more on this see Ray and Reed 1994:158–97).

To understand the evolution and disintegration of communism, the following hypotheses will be considered. First, the identity of the social order was threatened by a situation of unstable equilibrium which resulted in the routinization of organizational charisma expressed particularly in the so-called post-Stalinist 'new deals' that followed upheavals in the mid-1950s. Second, increasing reliance on informal regulators (discussed in Chapter 5) weakened the authority of the Party and facilitated the emergence of nomenklatura property rights. Third, the decomposition of corporatist structures was both exacerbated by and in part resulted from links with the global economy via debt. Fourth, the collapse of corporatism was accompanied by both a consolidation of nomenklatura property rights and a technocratic ethos among the political élite that increasingly distanced itself from Leninist principles. Thus the decomposition of corporatist structures was attended by the recomposition of new power relations that placed their stamp on system building. Let us examine these in more detail.

FROM CHARISMA TO CORPORATISM

Any system, as Alexandr Yakovlev (1993:84) observes, has a threshold of complexity beyond which it becomes unstable and unpredictable. In the post-Stalin period, organizational differentiation involved the proliferation of technical and administrative specialists and the consequent division between cadres and masses in addition to increasing inequalities in access to benefits of the private sector (Szelenyi 1988). Cultural differentiation involved an increasing diversity of values and styles of life along with regulated but increasing pluralism in the arts (as socialist realism waned) and science, which under Khrushchev gained autonomy from direct Party control (Breslauer 1976). These were accompanied by the formation of decentred and role-distanced personalities oriented to the private domain of 'authentic interactions' against the hollow public world of coerced acquiescence (Havel 1988). An implication of Hankiss's (1991) account of the Hungarian second economy is that latent integration presupposed differentiated personalities, geared to 'private' exchanges with expressive and diffuse role expectations in intimate relationships and networks of reciprocity, and instrumental-specific roles in second-economy dealings.

Social differentiation in turn closely connects with the routinization of charisma (Weber 1978 II:1121–3), since it presupposes formal rule-following exchanges between subsystems. Increasing social differentiation, however, posed serious problems of identity for the social order, especially for the self-legitimation of the ruling cadres. This was partly because the goal of communism was a radically de-differentiated society, even if a technical division of labour is accepted as necessary in the transitional period. Such divisions could not be acknowledged as permanent without weakening the identity and cohesion of the élite, which might explain the apparent paradox that the bureaucracy was a continuous object of criticism even though it continued to expand until the fall of communism (Federowicz 1994; Lewis 1994). On the other hand, problems of post-Stalinist organization (discussed in Chapter 5) increased the need for further and explicit devolution of power, since by the 1970s the Party confronted an increasingly informally regulated society over which it reigned but did not govern (Yakovlev 1993:110).

These problems became visible in the aftermath of Stalin's death and the New Course initiated by Malenkov,[3] when a wave of violent upheavals spread across the central European people's democracies (DDR, Czechoslovakia, Hungary, Poland) and more sporadically the USSR,[4] which were to have important effects on subsequent forms

---

3 In the Soviet Union the New Course liberalized industrial planning quotas, increased agricultural procurement prices (70 per cent of national income was accumulated through producer prices), extended infrastructure into Siberia and Kazakhstan, gave increased priority to consumer goods and reduced Party control over cultural expression (Aganbegyan 1988:50ff.). This was in part a reaction to problems of collectivization and central planning and an awareness among sections of the élite of the extent of popular resentment at the regimes especially in the PDs (Kecskemeti 1969). In part, too, the nomenklatura had lived in fear during the purges so the end of arbitrary mass terror signalled an 'unwritten mutual security pact' (Kolakowski 1987:455). For Phelps et al. (1993) the partial decentralization of economic power that followed the New Course weakened the vertical integration of enterprises creating confusion over property rights that was later to facilitate insider privatization.

4 In 1956 oppositional intellectuals such as L.N. Krasnopevtsev (professor and secretary of the History Faculty Komsomol) organized protests at the invasion of Hungary and leafleted Moscow's working-class areas calling for public trials for

of crisis management. The different ways in which these events unfolded illustrated how the self-legitimation of cadre élites, reflected in their internal coherence and identity, was a crucial determinant of the ability of the system to withstand high levels of disorder. Where the New Course took the form of a gradual policy reorientation under a unified leadership (such as occurred in Bulgaria) the regime escaped a system-threatening crisis (Stillman and Bass 1955). Where serious and violent conflicts did occur, but in the absence of élite divisions, they were contained, albeit with severe repression. In Berlin and Leipzig (June 1953), for example, thousands went on strike and occupied government offices in protest at increased agricultural and industrial delivery targets. Although this episode ended with forty-two summary executions and 25,000 arrests, the delivery quotas were withdrawn (Lewis 1994:150ff.; Kecskemeti 1969:123). Again, in Czechoslovakia, strikes and violent protests in the Moravská Ostrava mining area of Plzen (where 5,000 workers occupied the town hall and demanded free elections) were contained and the Party élite remained publicly unified.

However, system-threatening crises arose in 1956 in Poland with the Poznan revolt, and with the October Hungarian uprising. In each case the local élite was divided, especially in Hungary where the reformist supporters of Imre Nagy and the Stalinist supporters of Rákosi took their struggle to the workers, who in the event proved more interested in getting the Soviets out altogether than in conflicts over the New Course (Kecskemeti 1969). Further, the extent of the purges in Hungary, combined with their renunciation during Nagy's first period as premier in 1953, provoked a crisis of self-legitimacy among the Hungarian communist intelligentsia.[5] This became evident in the Writers' Group in 1953–54 and in 1956 in the Petöfi Circle,

---

Stalinistcrimes. The group which he established received six to ten years in prison under the anti-Soviet propaganda law.

5 Imre Nagy's New Course switched emphasis from accumulation to consumption, redirected funds away from industry to agriculture, and increased wages. Heavy industry fell from 41.3 to 30.6 per cent of total investment in 1953–54 and light agriculture rose from 13.7 to 24 per cent (Swain 1992:85–6). The abandonment of this strategy with Rákosi's return to power in 1955 further intensified the intra-élite struggle that precipitated the uprising.

where Party intellectuals such as Lukács and Aczél defied the AVO (secret police) and campaigned for democratization and freedom of expression. The uprising and its tragic denouement was the result of mass opposition stimulated by this crisis of self-legitimation. In Poland, in the wake of Poznań, the Party was beginning to dissolve as thousands of workers left, while workers' committees and mass rallies called for the return of Gomułka as first secretary.[6] The success of these demands and the subsequent 'Polish October' conferred popular legitimacy on Gomułka's programme for an independent 'Polish road'. In the following years the initial promise of pluralistic self-managed socialism was lost as the Polish United Workers' Party (PZPR) rebuilt its leading role (Ascherson 1988:153–8; Nove 1991:153). But the success of Polish resistance to Stalinism established a pattern of workers' revolt that was to reappear during the following decades to an extent unprecedented in the bloc. Further, the sense of disenchantment (*rozczarowanie*) that followed the later Gomułka period, through to his removal in 1970, was symptomatic of the inability of post-1956 governments to consolidate any new social settlement for very long. This was to have serious consequences for the integration of the Soviet system in subsequent decades as Poland became the weakest link in the state socialist chain.

During the communist period, then, an unstable equilibrium was interrupted by a cycle of outburst, repression, concession and stabilization (Connor 1988; Lewis 1994:150ff.).[7] According to several writers, social stability was achieved during the 1970s and early 1980s through social contracts that integrated strategically significant forces in a neo-corporatist variant of the class societies with which they were in competition (Jowitt 1978). According to this view, the resolution of each system crisis left in place a new (though fragile)

---

6 Though largely escaping violent purges, in common with other peoples' democracies, the 'Muscovite' leaders in Poland, such as Bierut, Minc and Berman, who had spent the war in the USSR rather than in the anti-Nazi resistance, displaced the 'national communists' such as Gomułka, in the late 1940s. Gomułka had been expelled from the Party and imprisoned in 1948.

7 Indeed, a cycle of revolt–repression–concession could be said to have characterized communist systems from their beginning when war communism and the suppression of the Kronstadt uprising in March 1921 were followed by the NEP.

political settlement which expanded the flexibility and learning capacities of the social system through an uneven drift towards increased decentralization. Neo-corporatist structures, such as unity fronts, official trade unions and collective farms, were consolidated into a new consensus based on increased personal consumption and welfare (Evans 1986). Linda Cook (1992 and 1994) describes the Brezhnev period as founded on a 'tacit social contract' between the state and workers which, according to Bunce (1983), was a 'new mode of interest intermediation' seeking to minimize conflict and maximize productivity by incorporating dominant economic and political interests directly into the policy process, while cultivating the support of the masses through an expanding welfare state. Similarly, Zaslavsky (1982) writes of an 'organized consensus' based on recruitment of skilled workers to the closed cities (where residence was restricted to scientific and highly skilled cadres), and the accumulation of power and patronage by leaders in the republics. The importance of national integration through patronage is also taken up by Graham Smith (1991) who writes of a centre–periphery corporatism within the Soviet Union, in which the autonomy of local élites was exchanged for loyalty to Moscow and local governments could retain revenue for distribution along clientelist networks.[8] Indeed, political clientelism provided a basis for both extending state control over resource allocation and creating dependent constituencies. Meanwhile, officials in the bureaucracy devised means of allocating resources which strengthened their ties with particular locales, especially in the republics. Within local power centres, according to Tarkowski (1981: 185) patrons are found at all levels of the hierarchical structure in the economic, political and administrative spheres, especially if the patron was born or used to work there.

These 'corporatist' accounts broadly follow Schmitter's (1979) analysis of interest intermediation in capitalist societies where constituent units, such as trade unions, employers' organizations and government bodies, are brought into consultation through the state and are granted representational monopolies within their respective areas,

---

8 The Soviet policy of building locally recruited bureaucracies in the republics was to backfire once the availability of resources from the centre diminished, since local apparatuses were regional centres of resistance to Moscow and often backed independence movements (Kagarlitsky 1990:60–61).

in exchange for observing controls on articulation of demands (Hausner and Wojtyna 1991). However, applying this somewhat problematic notion to Soviet societies needs qualifying, for at least three reasons.[9] First, corporatist theories tend to endow the state with the power to license, control and create integration, when in practice, as Jessop (1990:112) argues, 'the state' is the object of struggles among an ensemble of social relations within which it is deeply implicated. State power is what Jessop calls a 'mediated effect' of a balance of forces that create an unstable equilibrium of compromise. Second, whereas capitalist corporatism tended to politicize economic relations (especially the labour market) that had previously been regarded as matters of private contract, communist corporatism had the opposite effect of depoliticizing social relations that had previously been subordinated to central control. Third, whereas capitalist corporatism delimited the scope for bargaining, according to Nielsen (1993) the communist variant was unofficial and not explicitly limited. Cook (1994), however, suggests that a more explicit contract pertained and the Soviet leadership was constrained to satisfy material needs in order to legitimate its authority. Either way, corporatism might have ameliorated problems of over-complexity in Soviet societies during the 1960s and 1970s, but created longer-term legitimation problems which followed from the routinization of vanguard norms and of the exchanges between the Party and the people.

These points can be elaborated as follows. Regarding the emerging form of the post-Stalin state, it could be argued that Brezhnevite corporatism was the result of a struggle over strategies for minimizing social conflict, the outcome of which reflected the emerging societal power of the nomenklatura, power which became apparent in their successful ouster of Khrushchev. According to Breslauer (1976) and Hosking (1992) Khrushchev's rule was a failed attempt to found a new type of post-Stalinist legitimacy that involved appealing for mass loyalty through democratization and legality. Moreover, Khrushchev resisted routinization of the revolution, which was evident in his populism, illustrated by grandiose ventures such as the Virgin Lands

9 Space does not permit a detailed account of theories of corporatism in relation to capitalist societies, but for recent reviews see Jessop (1990:110–43) and Williamson (1989).

programme and the promise to build the basis of communism by 1980. Further, Khrushchev attempted to prevent the formation of a stable cadre stratum by

- announcing the end of the dictatorship of the proletariat, that the state was 'of the whole people';
- expanding the rights of soviets and mass organizations versus state officials;
- transferring some administrative functions to social organizations such as neighbourhood committees and comrades' courts;
- expanding Party membership (*privlecheniye*);
- campaigning in *Trud* in 1961–63 for factory trade union committees to protect workers against violations of health and safety and arbitrary powers of managers;
- introducing the *sovnarkhoz* regional economic boards, which reduced the power of central ministries and permitted more lateral integration.

Further, and especially unpopular with the political élite, there was a rapid circulation of personnel during the Khrushchev period which in part provoked the 1964 coup (Fehér 1986; Hill 1988; Hosking 1992: 334–5).[10]

Khrushchev's populism was not simply a strategy to preserve the existing order as Hewett (1988), for example, suggests. Rather, it weakened Party control by invoking democratization as a strategy of mass legitimation against nomenklatura privileges (Breslauer 1976). According to Jowitt (1978) Khrushchev attempted to use circulation of personnel and local democratization to resist the familialization of office holding. Although Hosking (1992:381) regards clientelism as more important than familialism *per se* as the organizing principle of Soviet society, a view that would be shared by Willerton (1987), these writers agree that the defeat of Khrushchev signalled the emergence of a consolidated status system. Even so, Khrushchev's decentralization posed new rationality problems, such as the *sovnarkozy* which,

---

10 Between 1956 and 1961 two-thirds of the Council of Ministers, Presidium and oblast secretaries and half of the Central Committee were replaced (Hosking 1992:376–7).

as economic sovereigns without the regulation of effective money, allocated resources arbitrarily (Wiles 1960:199).

Developed socialism restored centralized ministries and established the 'stability of cadres' while minimizing ideological conflicts.[11] Power circulated through clientelistic cadre networks, and where decentralization occurred it did so in a way that attested to the stability of Party rule (Rigby 1990b; Voslensky 1984). During the 1960s and 1970s, a status society (*ständische Herrschaft*) developed where rank was conferred and regulated via hierarchical career structures and the *propiska* (dwelling permit) that created strata spatially through mobility regulation (Zaslavsky 1982; Yakovlev 1993:71). Moreover, Brezhnevite 'corporatism' was instituted at the cost of further undermining the chiliastic legitimation of the Party in that an instrumental compact among interest groups was given higher priority than the goal of building communism.

The social contract operated on at least three levels. First, between the Party apparat and leadership, after the XXIII (1966) Congress when, under the slogan of 'trust the cadres', power was decentralized within the hierarchy – to ministries, oblast (province) and raion (district) levels (Hough 1976). Shlapentokh (1988) claims that a social contract between leadership and apparat lasted for twenty years after Khrushchev was ousted. Second, 'developed socialism' offered sectoral interests access to policy, limited political interference, delineated responsibilities and negotiated production targets (Bunce 1983). Power in the workplace was conceded to workers in the absence of effective control options (Ticktin 1992:116; Filtzer 1992a and b). Third, welfare benefits and the redistributive economy were extended with full employment, subsidized prices, and medical and child care facilities (Cook 1992 and 1994). Income inequalities were reduced as the ratio of the top to bottom decile earnings fell from 4.4 (1956) to 3.7 (1964) and 3.2 (1970) (Wiles 1974:48). Following the 1966 Plenum on agriculture, investment in the countryside increased

---

11 Khrushchev was accused of counterpoising the 'state of all the people' against the dictatorship of the proletariat and over-emphasizing homogeneity and consensus in society. Sixty-one per cent of Central Committee members present in 1961 were re-elected in 1971 as were 81 per cent of the 1966 cohort. Of members present in 1971, 89 per cent were still there in 1976 by which time 28 per cent were over 65 years old. Between 1966 and 1981 40 per cent of the membership remained constant (Hosking 1992:377).

from 14 per cent of total investment under Khrushchev to 20 per cent in 1973 (Hough 1976).

In return, the state demanded compliance, moderate demands and support for the prevailing distribution of power, status and economic resources. In this period of successful stabilization, redistribution of the surplus reduced conflict potential, which enhanced political stability, and increased the regime's legitimacy, which in turn reduced both bureaucratic and worker sabotage and increased motivational inputs. There was a continuation of the switch from ideology to performance as criteria for advancement in the bureaucracy and Party reflecting a tendency identified in Hough (1969). By the 1960s local Party organs, which Hough likens to French prefects, had acquired considerable latitude to deal with local officials, enterprise managers and government departments. They were not tightly locked into a command–action hierarchy which left scope for discretion and flexibility.

Elsewhere in the bloc, social contracts displayed a range of variation reflecting particular patterns of post-war development and national characteristics. In Hungary, Kádárism was the outcome of the 1956 uprising and the repression that followed. Combined with the 1962 amnesty, these 'well committed cruelties' demonstrated that the existing arrangements presupposed obedience (Fehér 1979).[12] Closely linked to the NEM (see above, pp.123–4) Kádárism, like the Brezhnevite social contract, operated on three levels:

- a compromise between the Soviet and Hungarian leaderships in which the latter accepted Soviet control of military and foreign security affairs in return for wider autonomy (compared with pre-1956);
- a compromise between the Hungarian leadership and the population, who exchanged acquiescence to HSWP rule for depoliticization, personal security, rising living standards and cultural liberalization (Fehér 1979; Lovas and Anderson 1982);
- a compromise between the leadership, Party apparatus and the state which preserved the nomenklatura principle in exchange

12 After the uprising, 2–3,000 people were executed and tens of thousands imprisoned. The term 'well committed cruelties' comes from Machiavelli.

for pragmatic policies and increased autonomy in economic and cultural life (Gomulka 1986:36).

According to Swain (1992:161) this was an intra-élite pact which extended to the public in their role as consumers and private subjects, but offered little to workers who were generally excluded from decision-making. As in the Soviet Union, moreover, long-range social mobility ended with the consolidation of self-reproducing intellectual stratum on the one hand and high immobility of disadvantaged groups on the other (Lane 1988; Matthews 1978; Swain 1992:191).

Kádárism is a good illustration of the tendency towards instrumental 'new deals' in this period since ideology and participation became less important than the hollowing out of Party life. Thus 'politics' for district Party committees often meant stimulating local morale in pursuit of particular economic policies (Horváth and Szakolczai 1992:65ff.). At the same time the Party's claim to legitimacy was negative – offering tolerance towards an informal life that began to take on its own systemic properties (Szenlenyi 1988).[13] Although economic performance compared well with countries of similar size and economic development (Swain 1992:117–19), the result of these arrangements was a weak Party and state bureaucracy which, under the sway of powerful organizations, over-committed resources that were increasingly financed by foreign debt (Szalai 1992).

Poland, on the other hand, was a case of permanent instability following failed attempts at instituting social contracts, and this was to have decisive consequences for the fate of the bloc as a whole (Lewis 1994:182; Tittenbrun 1993). After 1956, the PUWP could not establish sufficient authority to set price and wage levels, and this created a cobweb of persistent disequilibria (Nove 1991:156). Tittenbrun identifies four cycles of crisis and leadership change, each of which began with leadership promises to improve living standards and extend democratic participation. These were followed by a reassertion

---

13 First-economy incomes tended to equalize, with the ratio of highest–lowest deciles at 5.8 in 1962, 4.6 in 1967, 5.0 in 1972 and 3.8 in 1982 (Flakierski 1979; Swain 1992:191). However, by the 1980s second-economy incomes had become a significant stratifying variable (Szelenyi 1988).

of the control by the Party and curtailment of democracy, increasing social inequalities, price rises, forced investment in capital goods and a decline in the share of non-productive investments, and therefore a decline in the share of social consumption. Declining living standards in turn provoked protests, mass opposition and then further leadership change followed by a temporary peace which became more difficult each time.

Mass protest (strikes, riots, occupations) as ways of overturning government policy became inscribed into working-class consciousness in a way that was unique in the bloc (Koronski 1989; Lewis 1994). In 1971–73, following the Gdańsk riots, Gomulka was replaced by Gierek, who appealed to the shipyard workers to support a programme of better living conditions and revised targets. This, too, was an unstable compromise and in 1976 the government proposed new food prices, which, although withdrawn after further strikes, was followed by repression (Bromke 1976). In 1981, Jaruzelski's coup temporarily ended a further cycle of protest and perhaps thereby the opportunity was missed to enter into a corporatist settlement with Solidarity.[14]

The outcome of the first two post-Stalin decades across the bloc, then, was to create a patchwork of social contracts threatened by economic instability and social protest. Further, even where it was successful in securing social peace, the costs of corporatism were high and the system began to disintegrate during the mid-1970s. This was partly because increased agricultural productivity was slow and costly and the ratio of capital investment per unit increase in agricultural output grew rather than fell during 1965–75, reflecting the high cost of modernization and monoculture (Smith 1993:121). Meanwhile increases in personal income, combined with slow increases in consumer goods, caused inflation and encouraged money and motivations to leak into the informal economy. Therefore, as social complexity increased, the state was subject to increasingly diverse redistributive demands and scarcity of distributable resources, which prompted the formation of competing sectional interests and a

14 Whether Solidarity would have entered a power-sharing pact with the government in 1980–81 is not clear, but Walesa (1988:152) writes as though this was a possibility. He says, for example, 'so inflexible was the government that it failed to take advantage of the favourable climate that had developed during the strike negotiations. If our movement was to become the driving force of change ... we needed the government's support in the sharing of power'.

consequent fluctuation between consumption and investment. Moreover, flexibility and decentralization, combined with the absence of open accountability, created opportunities for the consolidation of sectional interests and local networks of corruption. Thus the sectoral anarchy or 'consultative corporatism' of this period created a de-centred polyarchal corporatist order (Flaherty 1988).

CUSTOMARY PROPERTY RIGHTS

Within this process of decomposition, however, there was at the same time a process of recomposition taking place, which brings us to the second issue here, the enfranchisement of the nomenklatura. The decomposition of repressive corporatism was accompanied by a process of value-differentiation within the system, which was consequent upon a process of routinization. This is outlined in Figure 6.1, which suggests four value clusters and potential lines of fracture in Soviet societies.

Class achievement–universalism cluster	Status–particularism achievement cluster
'Modernizing élites' responding to pressures from increased integration into global elites.	Traditionalistic routinization of charisma into syncretic organizational–familial status group.
Incentives, individualistic ethic.	Brezhnevite élites.
Market versus customary rights.	Customary rights tending towards marketization of office.
Universalistic–ascriptive cluster	**Ascriptive–particularistic cluster**
Vanguard ethic of leadership cadres.	Status-like attitudes among peasantry, working class and professionals.
Universalistic goal of communism embodied in status structure of society.	Legacy of corporatism.
	Role expectations embody proper pattern of adaptation.
National Bolshevism.	*Garantirovannost.*

Figure 6.1 Routinization and organizational charisma

Leninist organizational charisma (bottom left) survived among leadership cadres committed to the heroic myth of the vanguard and goals of organizational charisma, such as the Ferenc Munich Society in Hungary. However, during the Brezhnev years, the routinization of organizational charisma which followed in part from the stability of cadre positions created an ascriptive–particularistic value cluster which was essentially traditionalistic, signalling the formation of the gerontocracy into a familial status group. In the bottom right box, also as a result of the Brezhnevite social contract, we find a cluster of status-like attitudes among the peasantry, working class and professionals who were committed to the securing of prevailing institutional arrangements (Zaslavskaya 1984). However, in the top left box we see the rationalization of organizational charisma associated with reform communism defined in terms of increasing procedural formality (the legal state) and an achievement motivation (incentives, wage differentials, marketization), the realization of which was to require an assault on each of the three other value positions. For this group, moreover, aware of the technological and organizational gap between the Soviet system and developed capitalism, and unable to renew the charismatic values of Leninism as an alternative, the West tended to be viewed as offering an exemplary developmental model. One result of the consolidation of the status principle in the Brezhnev period was a decline in the Bolshevik performance ethics of social mobility (of the *vydvizhentsy*), and the universalistic goal of future communism. The routinization of developed socialism into an ascriptive performance ethic (expectations of a good Party member, respect of the clientelist system, collaboration in falsifying data, etc.) meant that the chiliastic goal of communism was replaced by the ritualistic goal of keeping one's office. Of course, no individual or faction fits neatly into any one of these value clusters, but they help clarify the terrain of the ideological struggle that ensued in the attempt to replace Brezhnevite corporatism with a less status- and more 'class-based' social settlement. Further, each form was capable of transmutation in diverse directions. Thus the vanguard ethic reappeared in nationalism and the red–brown alliances that appeared after the fall of communism, whereas reform communism gravitated in different measure towards social democracy or monetarism.

However, this is not to say that the Brezhnev period was characterized only by 'stagnation'. On the contrary, it saw the submerged formation of alternative proto-systems in what Starr (1988) described as a period of ferment. Although the Liberman reforms were curtailed after 1968, other experiments, often in specific enterprises, continued through the 1970s, as they did in the DDR and Hungary.[15] The increased professional autonomy accorded to technocrats combined with the lessons of their experience in the Khrushchev years, created a professionalized generation of the *shestidesyantniki* (1960s liberals) who conducted a debate throughout the 1970s, for example in *Dengi i kredit* (Money and Credit) over means of increasing productive efficiency. These developed strategies for reducing the inflexibility of Gosplan, but also challenged many assumptions of the redistributive economy. In 1980, these debates spilled into the public domain with a piece in *Pravda* (27 December 1980) by Gavrill Popov (economist at Moscow University and again later a member of the New Team), which advocated wages cuts, work incentives and planned unemployment, albeit tied to redeployment schemes with a guaranteed minimum wage. Similarly in Eastern Europe in the mid-1980s, younger members of the Party intelligentsia regarded expanding markets and democratic pluralism as crisis solutions, though they often acknowledged that this would break tacit understandings with the workers.[16]

The most significant development during this period, though, was the transformation of the nomenklatura from dependence on the Party to dominance over the Party. Naishul (1993) describes this as the formation of administrative property rights among the managerial nomenklatura, which began in the 1960s when horizontal informal networks emerged in the post-Stalinist economy and when enterprise directors gained de facto rights of disposal over state assets under

15 For example, at the Tula Chemical plant the wage fund was frozen in 1967 and the plant was given a five-year target plus financial autonomy. Over the first five years, average wages had increased by 45 per cent, although 1,300 workers (one-third of the workforce) had been made redundant. Over ten years output rose by 170 per cent and productivity by 240 per cent and the share of wages as a proportion of production costs fell from fourteen to five per cent. Such schemes were extended to 1,000 enterprises in the 1970s and by 1980 all heavy industry was self-sufficient and responsible for its debts (Walker 1988:41; Aganbegyan in *Trud* 12 December 1982).

16 This observation is based on interviews conducted by the author with members of the Research Bureau of the HSWP in October 1985 and September 1988, and in the Research Bureau of the Bulgarian Communist Party in Sofia, September 1988.

their control. These exchanges were regulated by customary law which also allowed the illegal sale of state offices in the Soviet Union for hundreds of thousands of roubles, a practice which Zemtsov (1976) suggests continued throughout the 1970s despite exemplary corruption trials. In Azerbaidjan in the early 1970s, the post of raion procurator cost 30,000 roubles, police chief 50,000 and raion Party committee first secretary 200,000. Similarly, Yakovlev (1993:113) describes 'regional mafioso networks at all levels' by the 1970s, opposed to the Party that could still expose them, in uneasy alliance with professionals for whom the Party was irrelevant.

Rather than view this simply as corruption or 'kleptocracy' (Andreski 1970) this process could be seen as part of a culture of illegality from which new types of social relations were emerging. This was similar to the situation described by Weber, where patrimonial office was treated as a personal affair and political office considered as personal property to be exploited by contributions and fees (Weber 1978 II:1029). Power was discretionary and office regarded as a personal right not (as in a formal bureaucratic state) derived from impersonal occupational specialization. Thus the formal organizational monism of Brezhnevite ideology served as a legitimating fiction which masked the fragmentation of the Soviet economy into sectoral anarchy. As with the erosion of earlier forms of patrimonial bureaucracy, trade in benefices was the product of an advancing money economy and the growing tendency to invest wealth in sources of fee incomes (Weber 1978 II:1036). However, appropriating benefices curtails governmental power and vitiates attempts at rationalizing the administration through the introduction of a well-disciplined bureaucracy. Thus Gorbachev's goal of the legal state ran counter not only to organizational charisma but also to the developmental tendency of the social system.

Post-Stalinist regulatory strategies tended to work against each other, since legitimation relied less on mass mobilization around consumatory–charismatic values and more on instrumental exchanges between society and the Party, such as raising living standards, increasing the supply of deficit consumer goods and expanding personal freedom. Yet consumer growth was inhibited by the persistence of a structural bias within plan bargaining that favoured the military and capital goods sector, while increasing personal freedom and decreasing surveillance reduced the risk of participating in informal social activities. The hollowing out of the Party indicated by the acquisition of private benefices militated against the formalization of a rational–legal state, which would have inhibited the conversion of political status into economic class position, in that open communications within a public sphere would have placed the process under scrutiny and potentially, therefore, regulation. Conflicts over the institutionalization of administrative property rights were to become a central issue in perestroika and post-communism.

Post-Stalinist strategies, then, increased the short-term stability of the system at the cost of weakening the legitimacy of the Party. Not only had social contracts substituted instrumental exchanges for substantive values, but this routinization of charismatic legitimacy resulted not so much in a formalized state as in a decaying patrimonial disorganized state governed by the familial principle of rule by right. Perestroika was then to face the dilemma that the more the political élite attempted to rationalize the system by reducing political regulation, the more social integration relied upon informal negotiations and second-society activity which effectively obstructed the overt goals of perestroika and accelerated the system's disintegration. It was in this context that the economic empowerment of the nomenklatura took place.

STATE CRISIS AND GLOBAL LINKAGE

By the close of the Brezhnev period a crisis of social integration was emerging, partly conditioned by, and partly conditioning, the disintegration of the corporatist settlement. In order to meet their ideological commitments and maintain a minimal base of legitimacy, socialist states offered a wide range of social services at little direct cost, which imposed a heavy burden on state budgets. Being an 'owner' rather than 'tax' state (Jessop 1993), fiscal revenues in socialist states were dependent on surpluses generated from enterprises. But soft budget constraints, low productivity and leakage of resources into the irregular economy all reduced available surpluses (Campbell 1992). Marketization generally served to exacerbate this problem, though, by expanding the opportunities for and legitimation of irregular activity. Thus a chronic deficit of regulation undermined the Soviet order from within as increasing dependence on latent integration led to an explosion of informal regulators; these were amplified into a kind of positive feedback, since an increase in the value of the control parameter (latent integration) caused its further growth, leading to a total dislocation of the system (Federowicz 1994:27).

Perestroika and reform communism elsewhere in the bloc addressed this systemic impasse, but were confronted with the effects of increasing integration into world circuits of capital during the 1970s. Debt left Soviet economies open to the consequence of a global recession of which they had initially been beneficiaries. The first oil shock (1973) caused a fall in aggregate demand in the capitalist economies but left finance markets awash with petrodollars, and the prospect of lending to stable centrally-planned economies was attractive. Thus the 1970s saw a massive flow of capital towards low- and middle-income states, and 'practically unlimited credit lines for productive or unproductive investments as well as joint ventures and other forms of assistance in setting up production facilities' (Arrighi 1991). This expansion in global credit included the communist states, who moved in quickly to fund consumer expansion and technology imports by assuming financial obligations that were among the heaviest in the world (Zloch-Christy 1987:174).

However, this involved investment in industrial projects with long gestation periods and during the mid-1970s diminishing world markets for Soviet bloc goods combined with reduced capital and trade flows (Zloch-Christy 1987:76). Endogenous systemic difficulties were then compounded by exogenous problems of debt, the failure of détente and a renewal of the arms race in the early 1980s. Increasing proportions of foreign currency earnings from Soviet oil and gas exports were being used to pay for grain imports, heavily subsidized trade within the CMEA (Bunce 1983) and imports of Western technology. By the mid-1970s East–West transactions were highly asymmetrical with mounting debts to the West and trade imbalances such that by 1981 the current account East–West trade deficit was $6.2 billion, the debt to the West was $88.1 billion and the ratio of debt to hard currency earnings was 145 per cent. By 1985–86, the USSR's foreign debt stood at $24 billion (Carlo 1989) and the CMEA as a whole, at $93 billion (Zloch-Christy 1987:49).

In Hungary, an import-led economic growth strategy combined with external shocks exacerbated a deteriorating trade balance (see

Chart 6.1). Products of Central Development Programmes (promoting key sectors such as natural gas, petrochemicals and light construction)

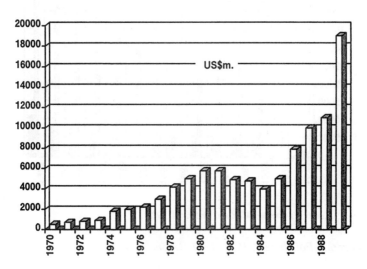

Sources: Swain (1992:147) and Bönker (1993).

Chart 6.1. Hungarian debt, 1970–1989

relied on Western technology, which represented 27 per cent of machine investment in the 1970s, and was financed by Western banks. This enabled domestically consumed national income to rise faster than gross material product between 1971 and 1979 (Zloch-Christy 1987: 77–8).

Thus corporatist legitimation strategies placed contradictory demands on the Soviet-type societies, and increasing indebtedness ran counter to goals of full employment, diversification, reducing shortages and increasing international competitiveness. Debt-financed social consumption and investment masked latent problems that became apparent during the 1980s when the regulation deficit was amplified into a crisis that threatened the identity of the systems. This can be illustrated with reference to Poland's convertible currency external debt against hard currency earnings during 1971–91 (see Chart 6.2). Initially (in the 1970s) about 20 per cent of the credit was used for imports of Western technology; about 65 per cent for imports

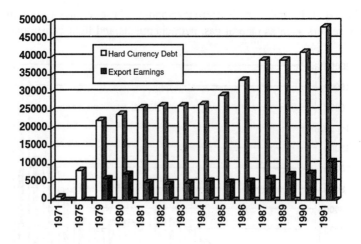

Source: Antowska-Bartosiewicz and Malecki (1992)

Chart 6.2 Polish debt, 1971–1991 (US$m.)

of partly-manufactured goods and about 15 per cent for imports of consumer goods especially food (Antowska-Bartosiewicz and Małecki 1992). However, high international interest rates and slow repayment meant that increasing amounts of debt were spent on accumulated interest payments. By the mid-1970s, 40 per cent of export earnings were spent on debt repayment and by 1979 this reached 100 per cent, necessitating further loans and creating a typical debt spiral.

By the early 1980s, foreign lenders were insisting on austerity programmes as part of adjustment packages, which involved cuts in inventory investment, imports and consumption. This left the Soviet Union with the burden of financing corporatism in the peoples' democracies, as its hard currency subsidies rose to $6.2 billion in 1981, the value of rouble credits to $3 billion by the end of the 1970s, and Soviet trade subsidies to $79.5 billion. Austerity created additional problems for state socialism since it was difficult to expand the production of exportables while reducing investment when cuts in social consumption were already provoking protests. Further, austerity programmes such as the Hungarian stabilization programme of 1977–78 increased dependence on informal private sources of welfare and hence increased differentiation between official and second societies (Batt 1991). Persistent shortages of health care and medical personnel in Poland, for example, resulted in 40 per cent of patients paying informally for medical services that were notionally free (Tittenbrun 1993:114ff.). Similar reports came from Hungary (Csaszi and Kullberg 1985; Hoós 1993; Szalai 1986) and the Soviet Union (Brucan 1986). Finally, austerity programmes were proposed by governments, which, because of their chronic legitimacy deficit, they generally lacked the authorization to implement (Commisso 1990; Gomulka 1986:227–50).

Thus the dual effects of the global recession and long-run endogenous steering problems were apparent by the early 1980s. Soviet growth rates from official data for all major indices (national income, gross industrial product, gross agricultural product, labour productivity and real per capita income) fell from an average of 8.86 between 1951 and 1955 to 2.76 between 1981 and 1985 (see Chart 6.3). At the same time, average growth for all CMEA countries fell between 1951 and 1987 from 9.47 per cent to 3.27 per cent (see Chart 6.4). As a

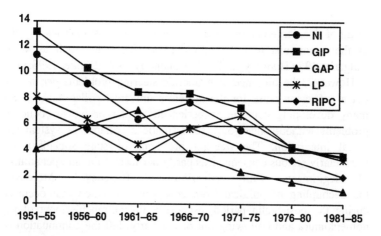

NI = national income
GAP = gross agricultural product
RIPC = rate of increase in production

GIP = gross industrial product
LP = labour productivity
Average rates from official data

Chart 6.3 Soviet Growth 1951–1985

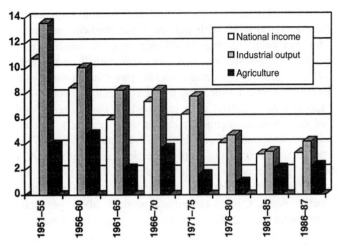

Source Tittenbrun (1993: 231).

Chart 6.4 CMEA average annual growth, 1951–1987

result of this, large external debt was one of the most onerous legacies of the communist regimes with debt service ratios such as 48 in Bulgaria, 49 in Hungary, and 76 in Poland by 1989 (Bönker 1993:17).

However, the presence of economic steering problems *per se* was not a sufficient cause for the system's universal collapse. After all, many developing countries experienced similar or worse economic problems without undergoing so dramatic a collapse of system and social integration. The steering problems of state socialism had particularly serious consequences partly because of the interpenetration of legitimacy with redistributive efficiency.[17] Moreover, the decoupling of political from economic regulation that occurred during the post-Stalin period, especially the enfranchisement of the nomenklatura and hollowing out of the Party, left the continuation of the existing institutional order of decreasing importance for the reproduction of the mode of domination.

17 Unlike the Newly Industrialized Countries of East Asia, credits to state socialist countries were not used for outward oriented development but for consumption, which reflected the latter's priority for redistributive legitimacy.

EXIT ROUTES – THE WITHERING AWAY OF THE PARTY

In Chapter 5 it was suggested that the outcome of crisis management might depend on a number of factors, including the availability of legitimation resources and structural constraints on goal preferences for crisis intervention.[18] Both of these had a significant role to play in the exit from communism initiated by perestroika. Before examining these, however, in view of the controversy that surrounded it, the nature of perestroika should be outlined.[19]

The Gorbachev administration inherited the unresolved steering crisis caused by the chronic overload of government administrative capacity (Flaherty 1988). However, the frequent claim that perestroika and glasnost were merely élite strategies aimed at perpetuating the existing system through limited reforms is over-simple. These were not simply reactive strategies of crisis management, but constituted a new state project initiated by the rising cohort within the political apparat, keen to address the long-term systemic problems discussed above. The New Team were (either by intention or by the logic of events) both in-system reformers and outsiders. On the one hand, they were insiders, career communists who had been socialized into the rules and values of the system. Gorbachev, Ryzhkov, Ligachev, Chebrikov, Yeltsin and Zaikov had risen via the usual career channels of the Party, and had KGB connections through links with Andropov's faction in the Central Committee. As an insider movement, perestroika was an attempt to implement strategies that had evolved (but not been dominant) among the Party intelligentsia during the 1960s and 1970s. On the other hand, as Gooding (1990) and Sakwa (1990:368) argue, the New Team were more than in-system reformers in that having evolved in response to external and internal crises, perestroika underwent dramatic transformation, especially after the XXVII Congress, where the system as a whole was subject to criticism.

18 Others were depth of steering crisis (outlined above), experience of earlier adaptation (e.g. second economy) and congruence between perceived and actual rationality crises.

19 The account in this section refers mostly to the Soviet Union because it was the system crisis there which released the crisis potentials across the bloc.

With the advent of perestroika and glasnost, the political system became self-reflexive in that the steering mechanisms became objects of analysis and intervention by the polity, which itself underwent internal differentiation, thereby creating new possibilities for dealing with internal and environmental complexity. For this reason it would be wrong to reduce perestroika and glasnost to representative movements of particular interests or factions, such as the bureaucracy, KGB, intelligentsia or whoever. From a system-theoretical perspective, the implications of perestroika are of wider significance than whether it resulted in the survival of either particular individuals or institutional forms.

However, for many writers, perestroika was a strategy of systemic management intended only to protect the identity of the system and its mode of accumulation. Like other communist reform initiatives, according to this view, it was doomed to fail because it ran counter to the rationality of the system (Gerner and Hedlund 1989). Fehér and Arato (eds) (1989) argued that Gorbachev faced a 'trilemma', in that reform would either be too limited (geared to the transformation of only one mechanism of co-ordination without challenging the system's principle of identity) or it would be 'radical reform'. The latter, however, was blocked in two directions. First, confronted by the opposition of conservatives, Gorbachev attempted to build a constituency among intellectuals, but this was an insufficient basis for a social historical movement.[20] Second, radical reform would have required the reconstitution of civil society and the change of the agent of reform from 'above' to 'below', to eliminate the primacy of discretionary power of the Party (Fehér and Arato, eds 1989:7). Only the former was compatible with the goal function of the system which would either successfully obstruct reform or provoke a state of revolution (Fehér et al. 1984:286). Thus the whole programme amounted to 'no more than' changes in personnel in the Politburo and bureaucracy; cultural and human rights (but without a legal–rational foundation); micro-democracy, for example, in local soviets or the workplace (but leaving administrative structures unchanged); limited

20 It is true that Gorbachev did attempt to co-opt intellectuals into the reform movement but to put it this way suggests that they were outside the reform initiative, when many were its inspiration (Sakwa 1990:74).

legalization of private enterprise and co-operatives (Fehér and Arato, eds 1989).

However much such analyses appear to have been vindicated by the actual turn of events, they are flawed to the extent that they interpret perestroika only as a system-preserving strategy, when it was actually an assault on both Brezhnevite corporatism and nomenklatura privileges. Moreover, four central objectives of perestroika illustrate that this was more than just a strategy of crisis management. First, it aimed to seriously restructure the redistributive economy, which was reinterpreted as a state paternalist system of *garantirovannost* sapping initiative and efficiency (Cook 1992; Flaherty 1988; Zaslavskaya 1984). Rising real incomes would be set against fewer entitlements and reduced subsidies, meritocratic distribution and increases in inequality, the effects of which would none the less be mitigated by social welfare, unemployment benefit and retraining opportunities (Gorbachev 1986; Hauslohner 1989). Second, decentralization and horizontal integration of enterprises would replace command structures and end the 'petty tutelage of enterprises by ministries and departments' (Gorbachev 1986). Co-operatives and joint ventures would be encouraged, while prejudice concerning 'commodity–money regulations' would be overcome within a 'regulated market economy' (Aganbegyan 1988; Gorbachev 1986). Third, widening the base of participation, combined with political rights and personal liberties, was linked to an attack on unelected nomenklatura positions and privilege (Flaherty 1988; Yakovlev 1993:103; Gorbachev 1986; Whetten 1989:39). The emphasis of this shifted after 1989 towards more radical democratization and the formal rational–legal state (Gooding 1990; Goldman 1991). Fourth, according to Yakovlev's reflections on the process in which he was a key player, perestroika furthered the routinization of organizational charisma by instituting a thorough disenchantment of what was left of the CPSU's mythological aura (Yakovlev 1993:114).

In these terms, perestroika was successful in changing the political culture and left a legacy of civil movements, increased complexity, internal differentiation and increased risks of disorder. It expanded opportunities for public debate, advanced the ideal of democracy, created a climate of reform which included the belief among professional élites of the inevitability of marketization, and made visible the underlying factions within the CPSU along the lines set out in Figure 6.1.[21] Perestroika was clearly unsuccessful in preserving the institutional form of the Soviet Union or the Communist Party, but in this regard, it arguably failed not so much because of resistance from the nomenklatura, so much as from its inability either to break the legacy of the Brezhnevite social contract or to create an alternative hegemonic alliance. One reason for this was the increasing discrepancy between perestroika and available legitimating resources.

It is true that early perestroika was grounded in the organizational learning capacities of the system. There was arguably a continuity from Khrushchev's *sovnarkhoz*, Kosygin's Liberman-inspired 1965 reforms, the industrial association reforms (1973) and the principles of self-management embodied in the 1987 Law on Enterprises.[22] Again, in agriculture, Gorbachev's ideas of *kollektivny podryad* (collective contract) and later (1988) *arendnyi podryad* (lease contract) have their origins in Khrushchev's rural wage reform and the link system. Gorbachev's initial concept of perestroika stressed discipline (e.g. the anti-alcohol campaign) and a return to Leninist norms (*Pravda* and *Izvestiya* 26 February 1986), and it did not contemplate a multi-party system or relaxation of control in the regions (White 1990). Early perestroika thus remained within the universalistic–ascriptive cluster, which served as a cultural resource for an attack on status particularism that had emerged under Brezhnev. None the less, problems such as poor quality consumer goods were to be resolved bureaucratically through the State Quality Control Board, rather than through decentralization or market steering (Smith 1993:103).[23]

This early phase, which might be called authoritarian perestroika, was essentially a strategy of centralization, efficiency and acceleration (*uskorenie*) begun by Andropov with the goal of 'stepping up intensification of production, accelerating effectiveness, raising labour productivity and increasing output (*Pravda* 28 November 1982).[24]

---

21 This is not to mention its effect in international relations where the new Soviet initiatives were largely responsible for ending the Cold War.
22 The State Enterprise Law created self-regulating enterprises with Councils of Labour co-operatives (STK) that elected directors.
23 The effect of *Gospriemka* was to increase supply bottlenecks and antagonize workers who lost bonuses.
24 True, Gorbachev's vision was quite different from Andropov's in that it sought a

This was located within the dominant values of the system and involved emphasis on the Party's vanguard ethos in the call to furthering socialism, mobilization and discipline. For example, under the heading 'Workers Pledge Sanctions Against Violators', *Izvestiya* (29 December 1982) devoted a page to all-Union calls from factory associations for labour discipline, and *Pravda* followed in similar vein the next day.[25] Moreover, Zemstov sees in the increasing merger of Party and KGB authorities (Andropov was KGB chairman, 1967–82) a process of 'de-partyization' in which the Party became redundant to the reproduction of the nomenklatura. This is illustrated in the way Andropov began to circumvent official structures (such as Gosplan), for example by commissioning Zaslavskaya's report (1984) which opened the assault on Brezhnev's apparat.[26]

However, after the 1986 Congress Gorbachev brought the systemic crisis into public awareness, and further weakened the system's normative and substantive legitimacy in a succession of hesitant strategies of democratization and marketization. This could be described as regulated market perestroika, which involved cultural liberalization, allowing a plethora of informal groups and reform proposals to surface under the banner of socialist renewal. Gorbachev condemned 'investment bulimia', reflecting entrenched departmental interests which obstructed the transfer of investments from heavy to flexible high technology industries (*Partinaya zhizn* 13/ 1986:10–11).

democratic regeneration of state socialism, but early perestroika began with Andropov's frame of reference.

25 For example the Moscow Electric Lamp factory association called for 'penalties for botchers, absentees, drunkards and violators of public order' and the Sergo Ordzhonikidze machine tool plant called for violators to be demoted, refused summer vacations or moved down the list for improved housing (*Izvestiya*, 29 December 1982).

26 In 1983 Andropov commissioned the Novosibirsk Institute of Economics and Organization of Industrial Production to produce a critical analysis of the entire system of economic management. In her report, Zaslavskaya (1984) attacked the rigidity of the planning system, corruption, inflexible work practices and the inhibition of market forces, and identified middle-ranking bureaucrats, planners and enterprise managers as the most likely opponents of reform, since they would defend their privileges. Signalling an end to any pretence to uphold egalitarian values she argued that the social mechanism of economic development at present operating in the USSR creates the type of worker who fails to correspond not only to the strategic aims of developed socialist society, but also to the technological requirements of contemporary production.

Further, perestroika sought to release cultural reserves that could overcome the deficit of motivations. This required transforming existing institutional and normative practices especially the status expectations which, according to Lisichkin, created an 'archaic leveling consciousness which had enfeebled the working class' (*Literaturnaya gazeta* 24 June 1987). Reformist academics were encouraged to develop exemplary organizational models, largely drawn from market socialism and the principle of self-management, which were reflected in the 1987 State Enterprise Law.

As perestroika evolved into a self-reflexive process, however, the new leadership had relatively few cultural resources upon which to draw. Hence, Gorbachev tended to invoke the NEP as a historical model of socialism, but after seven decades of communist rule, such a temporary expedient measure was a rather weak claim to legitimacy. In plenums, the Supreme Soviet and regional conferences in 1987, speakers addressed problems of enterprise underfunding and the prospect of regional depression that would follow unemployment (Cook 1992). At the same time, formalization of the system would have involved the replacement of substantive Leninist vanguard ethics by a formal procedural ethics which would have left the Party's leading role without justification. In practice, in any event, renegotiation of the social contract in favour of incentive-driven strategies of increasing labour productivity met with resistance (Filtzer 1992a).

None the less, frequent attacks were made on the nomenklatura in the name of defending 'socialist property', which was an allusion to the appropriation of state property via customary property rights. Zaslavskaya repeatedly criticized the culture of laxity, irresponsibility, over-staffing, and weak production incentives in the economy, which generated social injustice. She reinterpreted social justice in terms of rewards allocated according to ability, and ending co-operation among stratum and sectoral interests to gain resources in the bureaucratic system (e.g. *Sovetskaya Rossiya* 7 January 1986; *Sovetskaya kultura* 23 January 1986). Both of these attacked two crucial aspects of the Brezhnevite settlement – sectoral bargaining and weak control of the labour process. Further, a common theme in the press during 1986 was that there existed 'an immobile, inert and viscous Party–administrative stratum' between the Central Committee and the working class, as a worker, 'Ivanov' from a Tula production association, put it (*Pravda* 13 February 1986). This echoed Yeltsin's speech to the XXVII Congress which again condemned bureaucratic excesses, social injustice caused by bureaucratic privileges and an 'inert stratum of timeservers within Party membership cadres whose special benefits violate democratic principles' (*Pravda* 27 February 1986).

Indeed, the Party reformists' strategy was increasingly restricted by structural constraints. It was not clear how the 'regulated market' would deal with the de facto property rights of the nomenklatura. Gorbachev promised both to remove unearned income derived from access to public property and to overcome prejudice concerning commodity–money relations. In practice, though, extending the latter tended to give more latitude to the former, which was to dog all subsequent efforts at market reform. Further, market-regulated perestroika gave rise to unintended dislocations. For example, a supply crisis arose because, confronted by price deregulation and high inflation, suppliers imposed conditions on deliveries such as advanced payment, or on the contrary trade via barter rather than money (Filtzer 1991). These problems were not the result of an irrational inertia, but of actor-rational decisions within a set of social relationships still embedded in the corporatist settlement.

In this context the pursuit of full marketization while large monopolies with a long history of distorting the system remained in place was utopian. In fact, the original model of perestroika as self-management was abandoned in favour of a market utopian[27] programme of transition to capitalism. The 1990 Enterprises Act stripped the Councils of Labour Co-operatives (STKs) of their power, and directors began converting enterprises under their control into joint-stock companies of which they were increasingly in a position to become owners. By mid-1989 radical proposals appeared amid a full-blown crisis in which the political élite had little self-legitimacy or coherence. The Abalkin Plan (1989), which proposed stabilization through a mixed economy, gradual price liberalization and break-up of the state monopolies, was presented by Prime Minister Ryzhkov. By

---

27 The term 'market utopia' comes from Karl Polanyi, who used it to describe a belief in the market as guarantor of the greatest possible freedom, assuming the constraints on sustainable production in a world of scarcity creating co-operation without coercion (Polanyi 1944:84; Glasman 1994).

March 1990 this had collapsed during a major dispute over sequencing, that is whether privatization should precede price reform or vice versa. In May 1990 under Yeltsin's chairmanship of the Supreme Soviet, the Shatalin '500 Days' plan for full marketization and extensive privatization by 1995 was proposed. Opposition in the Supreme Soviet was extensive and Gorbachev's support for Shatalin wavered. After the Red Army occupied Red Square in October, a proposal for a referendum on a market economy was postponed. Meanwhile, the crisis had spilled out of control with hyperinflation, loss of confidence in the rouble, ethnic unrest and growing disintegration of the USSR. Gorbachev began to abandon the market reform constituency within the Congress of People's Deputies and Supreme Soviet and courted those (such as Kryuchkov, Yanaev, Pavlov, Yazov and Pugo) who were to stage the attempted coup in August 1991 (Goldman 1991:240).

During 1985–91, then, central power weakened under Gorbachev and personal–informal relations of mutual assistance grew, along with horizontal links among enterprises which became feudal principalities within republics (Kagarlitsky 1990:61; Nove 1991:81). This outcome was an unintended consequence of the 'weak state' (van Atta 1989–90) that could not rely on the loyalty of its officials, partly because a culture of illegality had arisen as a consequence of planning irrationalities, but also because the principle of élite legitimation (instrumental and consumatory) conflicted with the attempt to mobilize mass support for perestroika and the project of legalization. Power struggles over reform reached dénouement in August 1991, when, as in 1968, the old (military–heavy industrial) nomenklatura could see that pluralization of the system threatened the end for its self-reproduction within a network of bureaucratic privilege.

MONEY AND POWER

State socialism involved rule through visible structures of political intervention combined with informal regulators and therefore carried a higher de-legitimation risk than capitalist orders that rule through the invisible mechanisms of the market. Unlike money (see Chapter 2 *passim*) where an expansion in its supply (credit) heightens the internal complexity of the system, the superimposition of power has de-differentiating consequences. Crises then arise from self-blocking mechanisms in planning, where rational action orientations (e.g. enterprises hoarding inventories) have dysfunctional effects. Rather than reducing complexity then, the intrusion of bureaucratic steering into the lifeworld provided a visible focus for resistance. Thus economic disputes could very easily turn political and call the rule of the Party into question, especially where the social settlement was weak, as in Poland.

The collapse of communism, then, resulted from the interlocking of informal regulators within the status system that had become dependent on a particular kind of corporatism. Maintenance of this system had been achieved at the cost of integration into global financial circuits via debt, which placed even heavier pressures on already weak and internationally uncompetitive economies. The austerity that resulted from structural adjustment packages further undermined the ability of redistributive mechanisms to perform integrative and legitimating functions. This in turn increased the role of informal regulators and allowed the system to enter free-fall, as the boundaries between official and second societies eroded, with the result that the latter ceased to serve to offset crisis tendencies.

Reform communism in the late 1980s dealt with a system that had not in the past permitted manifest differentiation within either the economy (in the form of market steering) or the cultural system (as differentiation of value spheres) partly because these would have required a transition from substantive to formal ethics. Perestroika in its later stages did initiate a transition in this direction but was unable to tap into sufficiently strong cultural reserves of legitimacy – largely because of the form of routinization that communism had undergone during the period of Brezhnevite repressive corporatism. The legal state was to retain a substantive principle of legitimation (*sotsialisticheskoe* as well as *pravovoe*) but confronted the problem that while there was no institutional basis for formal legality, the system of social guarantees was becoming unviable too. Thus reform leaders, such as Gorbachev, found their social constituencies either fragmenting into defence of the old order or pushing beyond the confines of the system towards post-socialist forms of co-ordination.

Notwithstanding the severity of these system problems, however, we still need to address the question posed by the Czech sociologist

Mozny (1991): 'proc tak snadno?' (why so easy?) The remarkable rapidity with which crisis overtook Soviet societies was matched only by the willingness (with well-known exceptions) of their ruling élites to bow to historical necessity. The answer to this question might be found by examining how the decomposition of communism was also a process of systemic recomposition involving the survival of significant aspects of the *ancien régime*'s culture and economy. This should not surprise us at all, since contrary to the hopes of market utopians – both communist and post-communist – market regulators do not descend *ex novo* from the political system but develop from existing institutions and patterns of co-operation. This point will be developed in the following chapters.

7. The Rectifying Revolutions?

What was the significance of the anti-communist revolutions of 1989 and towards what organizational futures do they point? At the time they were variously compared with the classical revolutions of 1789 and 1848, and with the counter-cultural movements of 1968, but as the contours of the post-revolutionary orders take shape, some commentators are wondering whether they actually happened at all. With much of the optimism of 1989 now extinguished, there is talk of 'recommunization' as post-communist parties are democratically returned to power in many countries in Eastern Europe and the former Soviet Union, and as the former political élite, the nomenklatura, converts political capital into economic power, to become central players in newly privatized enterprises. In addition, fears for future political and economic security are fuelled by recession, nationalist and ethnic conflicts, and the spectre of Yugoslavia, which might still lie in the future for some post-communist societies.

These uncertainties about the real significance of 1989 raise important questions about actual paths of transformation and their relationship with the organizational forms of Western modernity, towards which these societies are supposedly travelling.[1] In particular, as the privatization process advances, rather more slowly than many hoped it would, what kind of capitalism is taking shape? Is a new order emerging here at all, or is a disordered and poorly regulated adventure capitalism part of what Robert Kaplan (1994) has called 'the coming anarchy', a 'jagged-glass pattern of city-states, shanty-states, nebulous and anarchic regionalisms'? These issues are discussed in this and the following two chapters.

Parts of this chapter have appeared in *Organization* 2 (3–4) 1995. I am grateful to Sage Publications for permission to include the material here.
1 Following increasingly common usage, the term 'transformation' is preferred here to 'transition' which has the teleological connotation that post-communist societies are treading a pre-determined path.

DIVERSE MODERNITIES

One of the problems with Luhmann's account of functional differentiation and with Habermas's theory of communicative discourse is that
they mistakenly assume an immanent tendency towards single
organizational forms in modern societies. The USA, Britain, Scandi-
navia and Japan are all functionally differentiated societies but with
particular cultural patterns and balances between the economy, polity,
welfare rights, modes of state regulation and so forth. Moreover, as
Runciman (1995) says,

> capitalism as a mode of production is compatible with a number of different
> modes of both persuasion and coercion. Although there is undoubtedly
> some sort of 'elective affinity' between a capitalist mode of production, a
> liberal mode of persuasion and a democratic mode of coercion, ... it is
> possible to conceive of a capitalist mode of production combined with a
> theocratic mode of persuasion (... Iran) or a socialist mode of coercion
> (... China).

Not an original point perhaps, but one relevant to understanding the
transition away from state socialism. The developmental potential of
one form of politocratic status organization has been exhausted but no
clear socio-cultural alternative has yet emerged, thus it is too early to
speak of either new convergence or the 'triumph' of capitalism. In any
event, what is crucial to social evolution is the way in which mutant or
recombinant practices emerge and what sequence of events causes
them to survive. One cannot infer likely outcomes from plans or the
purposes of reformers in post-communist governments, since from the
perspective of systemic development these are random inputs from the
political subsystem that will have effects, certainly, but often ones that
are unintended. The former mode of domination became unviable in
the wake of exogenous and endogenous crisis tendencies which gave
increased scope to informal regulators in the second society. However,
a context of uncertain regulation during the transformation might be
favourable for the recomposition of *ständische* ownership and
authoritarian state clientelism. Thus the prospect that liberal capitalism
will result from emerging socio-political orders is by no means self-
evident.

Post-communist societies are not, of course, developing towards a single organizational future, and divergent aspects of these possibilities are manifest in different places. Overall though, the future stability and progress of the region will depend on the emergence of differentiated institutional structures, especially of distribution and ownership, which command legitimacy. However, these will not emerge as optimal social forms as a result of a spontaneous process of adaptation, but will depend instead on configurations of power expressed through the state and market. The stabilization of socially differentiated structures, I will argue, will be dependent on the extent to which they are embedded within normative regulation that permits extensive impersonal social action, which in turn requires the institutionalization of systemic trust.

Property relations, emerging in the privatization process, are the focus of fateful struggles for control of the post-communist transformation. In the course of these conflicts though, identities are formed through a powerful dialectic of past and present, in which the Soviet experience and the capitalist future both provide partial models for emulation. Andras Sajo (1994) comments that 'one gets the feeling that, despite differences, ... all the post-communist countries of eastern and central Europe are desperate to resist radical change to a private, property-based market system and its unpleasant social consequences'. If this is so, then perhaps we should ask what it tells us about the nature of social transformation, the interests at stake and the paths to modernity being forged.

RECTIFYING REVOLUTIONS?

Habermas has depicted the Eastern European revolutions of 1989 as 'rectifying revolutions' (*die nachholende Revolution*) that 'overcome distance' with Western Europe. By contrast with the classical revolutions of modernity (the English, American, French and Russian), which were oriented towards the future, the anti-communist revolutions expressed a desire to connect up with the inheritance of bourgeois revolutions, taking their methods and standards entirely from the repertoire of the modern age. The democratic spirit of the West, he says, is catching up with the East (Habermas 1990 and 1994:62) where the guiding ideas were anti-statist and democratic, notably those of civil society, anti-political politics and the self-limiting revolution. Eisenstadt (1992), Arato (1994), Dahrendorf (1990) and others develop similar arguments, which resonate with the widely voiced notion of 'rejoining Europe', widespread among Eastern European intellectuals at the time.[2] Eisenstadt notes that, unlike earlier revolutions, the millennial, charismatic and utopian elements were missing from 1989 – the market economy was never going to attain sanctification comparable to the 'Rights of Man'. Again, Timothy Garton Ash (1990:154–6) concluded that 1989 offered no really new ideas, but a restatement of 'old truths and tested models', of liberal democracy and the European Community 'as the only really existing common European home'.

The idea that revolutions face towards both the past and the future is hardly new, though, and was expressed by Marx's observation in the *Eighteenth Brumaire*, that,

> just when they seemed engaged in revolutionizing themselves ... they anxiously conjure up the spirits of the past ... to present the new scene of world history in ... time-honoured disguise and borrowed language. (Marx 1978:300)

This judgement might well apply to the resuscitation of the ghost of 'civil society' that briefly haunted the capitals of Central and Eastern Europe at the end of the 1980s. In rather more negative vein than Habermas, Borucha-Arctowa (1994) argues that, indeed, unlike the French and American revolutions, those in Eastern Europe were 'backward-looking', marked by a 'fear of innovation' and 'desire to return to lost traditions'. These were in important ways restorationist, counter-revolutions, undoing the order of 1917 and redressing old wrongs, such as the Yalta settlement that had divided Europe into two blocs.[3] Restitution has been expressed both symbolically, for example

---

2 For example, the address of the new Czech Foreign Minister to the Charter 77 conference, May 1990, 'Going Back to Europe' which spoke of rejoining the pluralistic Europe of democratic states based on the development of civilization over the past 2,000 years which 'the past forty years have not been able to kill off'.

3 In January 1985, for example, the Polish underground papers, *WSN*, *Wyzwolenie* and *Niepodłość* carried the statement that 'We declare that we regard the treacherous decisions of Yalta as invalid and completely reject them ... as an expression of the illegal and anti-democratic dominance of great powers over smaller states'. At the same time, papers such as the Ukrainian *Nowa Koalicja* campaigned for a joint Polish–Ukrainian rejection of Yalta.

returning to pre-Soviet street names, and practically, in some privatization laws that have sought to restore property (especially in agriculture) to pre-1948 owners or their heirs.[4]

None the less, Habermas's notion of the rectifying revolutions has a different emphasis, and links up with his critique of post-modernism, to the effect that modernity's emancipatory potential, far from exhausted, remains unfulfilled. Indeed, 1989 offers Europe a 'second chance' to realize the idea of a communicative civil society in both East and West, but this time free from 'Eurocentric narcissistic self-absorption' (1994:72). Further, Habermas does not (to my knowledge) say, but would be entitled to do so, that the collapse of communism illustrates the power of communicative discourse. Bureaucrats bereft of legitimacy, who in Habermas's terms could not provide good reasons for the continuation of the system, faced the choice of capitulation or 'non-normatively authorized commands', that is, violence. However, the latter option had in the past required self-confidence and belief in the legitimacy of the system, at least among those to whom orders to shoot and arrest were given. Since by 1989 Soviet bureaucrats by and large possessed neither, capitulation was the only option left open to them.

Even so, the notion of overcoming distance needs interrogating, especially since, without careful qualification, it could replicate older modernization theories and the problems associated with them. In particular, are post-communist societies to recapitulate stages and features of Western modernity or do they generate a modernity of new type? On this level, Habermas's foundational concept of modernity, elaborated in the theory of communicative discourse, is rather a-historical and does not help much. Societal change always occurs in unique circumstances, and the availability of extant organizational models for emulation gives it an inescapably reflexive character, so one cannot self-consciously repeat phases of modernization that were once experienced unselfconsciously. The initial industrial revolution in Western Europe was a consequence of an accumulation of complex unplanned social changes, but once models of capitalist societies were up and running, modernity became a state to be achieved, the object of conscious reflection and deliberation. One could not then avoid the

4 For example: the Bulgarian Law on Co-operatives 1991; the 1991 Czech Law on Regulation of Ownership of the Land.

questions of consciously deliberating how and whether to follow one or another developmental path. Post-communist societies are confronted by a diversity of capitalist paths (the American, British, German, Scandinavian, South Korean etc.) none of which can be exactly replicated, while attempting to do so might result in yet another simulated modernity, this time of Western capitalism rather than socialism (Böröcz 1993).

Further, Habermas's notion of the 'democratic spirit of the West' suggests the progress of some Hegelian *Zeitgeist*, when in reality Western democratic systems were the outcome of struggles for extension and inclusion, especially by civil rights, labour and women's movements. In some ways, these critical issues of 'high modernity' (Giddens 1990) are confronted anew by post-communist societies. After all, an old-style working class is a central feature of the sociological landscape in 'the world's most advanced nineteenth century economy' (Chirot 1991:5). Thus conflicts over issues such as representation, collective organization, labour contracts and working conditions occupy centre stage in public life, to the extent that, according to David Ost (1995), 'the political future will be shaped in large part by the way labour's anger is mobilized'. This might appear to be replaying the drama of high modernity, yet present circumstances, conditioned by the Soviet experience, are actually quite novel. Working-class politics may be central, but the emancipatory language of socialism has been discredited by the communist past, and mass organizations tend instead to adopt the time-honoured disguises and borrowed languages of populism and nationalism. More will be said on this in Chapter 8.

Capitalism by design

Post-communist societies, then, confront problems of constructing capitalism reflexively, but in unique circumstances, for which no appropriate models are available (Offe 1991; Bryant and Mokrzycki (eds) 1994). Three issues are particularly important here.

First, there is the problem of the scale of envisaged privatization. The Polish privatization programme alone would be equivalent to all privatizations undertaken anywhere in the world, vastly surpassing those in UK in the 1980s (Delorme 1992). This is unprecedented and uncharted territory with some known but many unknown risks and a high probability of unintended consequences. Further, problems arise from legacies of the particular pattern of industrialization and social integration in Soviet societies:

- Declining production, large inventories and accelerating inflation, the 'transition recession', that has affected every post-communist society (Bakos 1994; EBRD 1994; Kazimierz 1993), have slowed down privatization. The scale of the recession is indicated in Figure 7.1, and even if some Central European countries (especially Poland) are showing signs of recovery, the full force of the crisis in employment may not yet have broken further east, in Russia and Ukraine.[5]
- Lack of physical infrastructure – buildings, roads, telephones, other communications in need of investment which are not profitable for private investors to undertake, while the state on the other hand experiences a fiscal crisis (Campbell 1992) which is exacerbated by the erosion of its revenue base as a consequence of privatization.
- Problems of competitive advantage. Lack of competitiveness impedes integration into the global economy which is exacerbated by the technology gap with the West and the attempt to duplicate its production base. The collapse of CMEA (see Figure 7.2) was swifter and more extensive than expected, while the end of the Russian soft currency trade provoked an energy crisis in non-energy producing countries (Jackson 1991).
- Lack of knowledge or experience with market systems and lack of institutional regulation, and the need to create tax law, corporate law, codes of practice, consumer protection, consumer information and currency regulation, which again require both institutional and normative changes.
- In addition to problems of obsolete plant and old technologies, and histories of planned unprofitability, enterprises often own cultural centres, housing, polyclinics, sports facilities, kinder-

---

5 Estimates of real GDP by the European Bank for Reconstruction and Development (EBRD) tend to be more optimistic than some others and the calculations depend in part on how the growth statistics of the communist period are interpreted. On this see Bratkowski (1993). Kazimierz's (1993) figures for example, suggest a deeper and longer-term recession in Central Europe than those of the EBRD.

a. *Percentage change in GDP for selected post-communist countries*

	1991	1992	1993	1994
Bulgaria	–12	–6	–4	0
Czech Republic	–14	–7	0	3
Hungary	–12	–4	–2	1
Poland	–8	2	4	5
Russia	–9	–19	–12	–12
Ukraine	–12	–17	–14	–20

b. *Rates of unemployment*

	1990	1991	1992	1993	1994
Bulgaria	1.5	11.1	15.3	16.4	16
Czech Republic	0.8	4.1	2.6	3.5	6
Hungary	2.5	8.0	12.3	12.1	11
Poland	6.1	11.8	13.6	15.7	na
Russia	0	0.1	0.8	1.1	na
Ukraine	0	0	0.3	0.4	na

Source: EBRD (1994).

Figure 7.1 Transition recession

gartens etc. that potential purchasers would not want (Filatotchev et al. 1992a and b).

Capital shortage and lack of capital markets. These are rather notional figures, but even if all the savings of the ex-USSR in 1990 (R.700bn) had been available for investment, this would only have amounted to about 25 per cent of the base-value and current assets (R.2700bn) (Fischer et al. 1992). In Poland, the 1985 asset value of the state sector was 28.3 billion zlotys, while bank deposits amounted to 1.3 billion. This problem is compounded by the reluctance of foreign investors to re-capitalize the industrial sectors (Biernat, 1994).

Trade within CMEA	Exports			Imports		
	1989	1990	1991	1989	1990	1991
Bulgaria	-10.6	-32.1	-37.3	-16.7	-24.8	-43.2
Hungary	-9.5	-21.4	-28.5	-14.4	-19.1	1.1
Poland	-2.5	14.9	-60.3	-5.7	1.6	-16.8
Czechoslovakia	-11.7	-27.4	-0.7	-6.9	-17.3	22.6

Source: Andreff (1992:38)

Exports to OECD	1990	1991	1992	1993
Bulgaria	26	27	28	78
Former Czechoslovakia	20	35	40	1
Hungary	29	17	9	-10
Poland	48	11	13	-2
USSR/CIS	24	2	-2	11

Imports from OECD	1990	1991	1992	1993
Bulgaria	-34	6	13	6
Former Czechoslovakia	35	29	72	2
Hungary	18	22	18	9
Poland	26	63	8	9
USSR/CIS	-3	5	-6	8

Source: EBRD (1994).

Figure 7.2 Foreign trade performance (growth in US$ percentage values)

Second, even approximately to recreate the conditions of Western European modernity involves creating not only an entrepreneurial class, but also novel forms of institutional regulation, consumption patterns, social values and modes of interest articulation. As communism disintegrated, it was widely believed among Eastern European social scientists that the second society would expand to fill the space opened by the retreating state and that previously informal social relations would become progressively institutionalized (e.g. J. Szalai 1989). Now, however, it is often argued that the requisite shifts in organizational and value patterns will be accomplished through imposition and example. In common with earlier modernization approaches, 'cultural inertia' is often identified as an obstacle to capitalist growth. For example, the Czech sociologists, Mares, Musil and Rausic (1994), argue that problems of modernization in Czechoslovakia include a discrepancy between popular values and the needs of a market economy, especially egalitarianism and belief in the right to work; the legacy of the patrimonial state based on clientelism and patronage; a reward system based on privilege; low confidence in money; lack of interpersonal trust. Witold Jakóbik (1993) condemns the 'inertia and passivity' of Polish workers, whose attitudes are a heritage of the planned economy and cannot be changed 'without the painful impact of new institutional solutions'. In similar vein, Mokrzycki (n.d.) claims that 'modernization is inherently a challenge to society' and that the idea that economic systems can be changed through negotiation and consensus 'runs counter to sociology and experience'. This may be true, but it implies that conflict and uncertainty lie ahead.

This view is reinforced if we ask, what will this modernization actually entail? Przeworski (1993:158) describes modernization as 'the process by which individuals become acculturated to market relations'. But what does this mean? It hardly means that people must learn to participate in consumer markets (as opposed, say, to relying on self-sufficiency) since they do that already. Indeed, we have seen that survival in the Soviet period required ingenuity, entrepreneurship and skill in a variety of formal and informal markets. It is more likely, as the above quotation from Jakóbik suggests, that this refers to employment markets and the transformation of organizational practices along lines familiar in the West as the 'enterprise culture' (Ray 1990). That is, the imposition of new behavioural standards, new technologies of surveillance, and the reshaping of employees' identities in terms of reduced dependency, increased 'flexibility' of organizational boundaries, internal competitiveness and individual accountability (Du Gay and Salaman 1992). These changes in organizational culture, which are discussed later in this chapter, are unlikely to win the consent of those to whom they are aimed, if they entail increased insecurity and falling living standards.

The third issue, which follows from this, is the problem of creating 'capitalism by democratic design' (Offe 1991). Attempting simultaneously to construct democracy and capitalism constitutes two subjects, citizens and market agents, whose interests do not coincide.[6] On the contrary, privatization and stabilization have generated rising inequalities, poverty and uncertainty which increase support for parties offering social protection and slower change, often of the authoritarian right (Cirtautas 1994). Recent data on levels of poverty in Poland, for example (see Figure 7.3), indicate the impact of the

	WORKERS	**MIXED**	**FARMERS**	**OAPs**
1985	18.5	21.2	30.3	34.9
1986	17.9	20.6	29.8	28.9
1987	24.1	23.9	31.9	26.9
1988	17.9	16.6	24.9	28.4
1989	13.7	12.3	22.3	26.4
1990	33.2	28.3	41.8	32.2
1991	38.1	21.2	39.4	33.0

Sources: E. and B. Czarny (1992), *From Plan to the Market: The Polish Experience 1990–91* (Warsaw: Friedrich Ebert Foundation); A. Pestoff, J. Hoós and V. Roxin (1993), *Institutional Changes in Basic Social Services in Central and East Europe during the Transition to Market Economies* (Cracow: Academy of Economics).

Figure 7.3   Social costs of the transition: percentage of families living at or below subsistence level

---

6 This is illustrated by opinion polls where respondents support privatization but oppose increasing inequalities, and consistently accord civil liberties lower priority than social security (e.g. *Polish General Social Surveys*, 1992–93:118–19).

transition recession on everyday life, especially on families of industrial workers whose standards have fallen steeply since 1989. Stable democracy requires a differentiated but inclusive social order which, regarding antagonistic interests as permanent, creates conditions for discontent to be articulated and negotiated. Yet the legitimacy of representative democracy is undermined by mass impoverishment and social insecurity, which engender powerless rage and alienation.

In view of these formidable obstacles, it is hardly surprising that, with the exception of former East Germany,[7] privatization of the industrial sector has proceeded slowly, and figures suggesting that private sectors in post-communist societies generate 40–50 per cent of employment (e.g. EBRD 1994) should be treated with caution. This is because there is a high degree of interpenetration between the state and 'private' sectors, which Kazimierz (1993) calls 'surface privatization', where satellite companies are set up as wholly-owned subsidiaries of state enterprises and assets are transferred to manager-proprietors. Moreover, post-communist economies are still by and large nationally owned, with very low levels of direct foreign investment (as a percentage of GDP, 1993): Bulgaria, 0.49; Czech Republic, 1.92; Slovakia, 1.46; Hungary, 6.03; Poland, 0.41; Russia, 0.63 (EBRD 1994:123).

Further, integration into the global economy has been slow and growth in trade with Organization for Economic Co-operation and Development (OECD) countries (Figure 7.2) has been uneven. After a burst in 1992–3 this has recently tailed off, with the exception of Bulgaria, which secured a free trade agreement with the European Free Trade Area (EFTA) and opened five free trade zones in 1993. However, the total flow of goods exported to the OECD from Eastern Europe and the former Soviet Union did not equal that from South Korea alone in 1993 (EBRD 1994:122). The post-communist region is therefore likely to remain marginal to the global economy, at least in

7 By the end of 1993, the Treuhandanstalt had sold 95 per cent of East German state-owned enterprises, although at such low prices that rather than cover the costs of restructuring as intended, privatization covered only 36 per cent of the Treuhand's own administrative costs. This privatization left 72 per cent of employees of liqui-dated enterprises redundant, unemployment at an estimated 30 per cent, and the new Länder, representing 19.4 per cent of the German population, producing only 7.8 per cent of its GDP. Social costs on this scale were only possible because of the absorption of East Germany into the Federal Republic (Roesler 1994) but have none the less created disorder, such as rising racial violence.

the immediate future, and dependent for growth on interregional co-operation (Jessop 1994). Further, given post-communist governments' understandable reluctance to face the political consequences of mass unemployment, they are likely to continue to protect and subsidize uncompetitive industries.

SHOCK THERAPY OR ORGANIC DEVELOPMENT?

Two theoretical approaches and development strategies can be discerned in debates about the pace and direction of the transformation. One stresses the urgency of rapid restructuring, or 'shock therapy', a position associated with the former Polish Minister of Finance, Leszek Balcerowicz, and the former Russian deputy prime minister, Yegor Gaidar. Balcerowicz argues that revolutions such as 1989 are followed by a short-lived period of 'extraordinary politics' in which there is high legitimacy for rapid transformation and learning, but time is scarce and this political capital rapidly returns to 'normal' levels when people lapse back into their former habits and expectations. Only if enterprises are confronted by an environment of market-clearing prices, foreign competition and clear ownership structures will they behave efficiently, and the worse the economic situation, the more effective will be the 'cold turkey' strategy (Balcerowicz 1993). The model of organizational change underlying this view is that markets and private corporations adapt flexibly to environmental challenges, and consequently, once freed from state control, tend towards optimal organizational forms and behaviour. This assumes in fact the kind of optimal convergence model that was discussed in Chapter 4.

This approach is vigorously opposed by advocates of gradualist organic development, often drawing on Polanyi's notion of embed-dedness and the constructive role of the state in economic development (e.g. 1944). Indeed, a great deal of socio-historical political economy emphasizes, in opposition to economic formalism, that market exchanges are embedded in supportive but constraining social, organizational, institutional and normative frameworks. Bryant and Mokrzycki (eds) (1994) and Skapska (1994) stress how economic systems emerge organically from particular historical and cultural contexts, and, in Durkheimian fashion, point to the non-contractual elements of contract that are ignored by neoliberals. Not unlike Habermas, Bryant (1994) warns against shock therapy that changes everything at once, which, even if rapidly abandoned, engenders a sense of powerlessness leading to susceptibility to authoritarian populism. Similarly, Hans van Zon (1993) questions the neoliberal assumption that free markets and parliamentary democracy are natural and optimal states, since they both depend on trust, stability and institutional regulation which have to be carefully developed.

It was noted in Chapter 2 that sociological theory has often assumed that the dislocation of solidary bonds and community identities results in pathologies, such as criminality and support for extremist political movements. Habermas, for example, warns that the 'reckless penetration by Western modes of production, into the interior of cultures already undermined by bureaucratic modernization, will destroy cultural milieus and reserves of meaning'. This way threatens anomie, civil war and chaos and 'regression into pasts of nationalism and ethnocentric fantasies' (1994:75). This is the consequence of the colonization of the lifeworld by systems of money and power that disrupt cultural reproduction and frames of meaning.

However, the relationship between culture and market exchanges is perhaps more complex than this implies. Habermas's argument, for example, suggests that culture is both positive (not to be destroyed) but alternatively negative, threatening to regress into the wrong paths. Habermas tends to stress how cultural frames of meaning generate learning capacities and secure identities which, if disturbed, generate pathologies.[8] However, large-scale disorder or even small-scale criminality, results not from atomized individuals but from coalitions of combatants, impossible without prior relations and networks. That is, they presuppose the existence of communities and shared frames of meaning.

This point is taken up by theories of embedded networks, which attempt to avoid both the undersocialized conception of actors in neoliberal theory, and overemphasis on culture as a determining agent. In these terms, stable networks are viewed not so much as 'frictional drag' impeding competitive markets, but as constitutive of

8 It is, of course, questionable whether describing social conflicts as 'pathologies' adds anything to the analysis, and may serve to obscure the underlying issues and interests at stake.

economic behaviour (Granovetter 1992:53). This is presumably what Habermas (1989:194) means when he refers to the importance of 'institutionally anchoring' mechanisms of system integration in the lifeworld. However, this approach only partly addresses the relationship between markets and culture, because the notion of 'embeddedness' is somewhat loose (Sayer 1995:ch. 4) and different types of markets can be 'embedded' in different ways. This can be illustrated by contrasting two ideal typical market situations. One, similar to Okun's (1981) notion of consumer market prices, might be described as 'embedded', while another, like Okun's auction-market prices as 'disembedded' (see Figure 7.4). The former envisages economic exchanges as embedded in community networks, which constrain the circulation of money and thereby reduce risk. Rules tend to be situationally specific and govern behaviour within well-established networks, where trust is dependent on face-to-face interactions or reputations, and generalized or systemic trust (Luhmann 1982) is low. In this model, credit tends to be limited by mutual obligations rather than mediated impersonally by banks. By contrast, in 'disembedded' systems of exchange, ties of community are progressively replaced by impersonal, arm's length connections and money acts as a symbolic store of value and a steering medium. There is a high degree of risk and fluidity (rapid entry and exit), and behaviour is governed by abstract rules and high levels of institutionalized, systemic trust. Here credit expands via a well-developed banking system and, as Luhmann puts it, money becomes self-expanding and reflexive.[9] These two types correspond to Giddens's (1990:80) distinction between *facework* and *faceless* commitments. The former involve trust in relations sustained by social connections; the latter involve faith in abstract systems such as professional expertise or symbolic tokens.

These two models of exchange are polarized here for the sake of clarity. Even so, it is apparent that both are actually 'embedded' but in different ways. As a number of studies have emphasized, apparently fluid and anonymous markets are actually dependent on situated networks and tacit knowledge. For example, the theme of a great deal

9 That is, '[W]e can apply the mechanism of money to itself, paying for money itself with the interest due after obtaining it on credit ... [With] the possibility of exchanging the possibility of exchange, wider possibilities of guiding behaviour through economic calculation can be put into effect' Luhmann (1982:208).

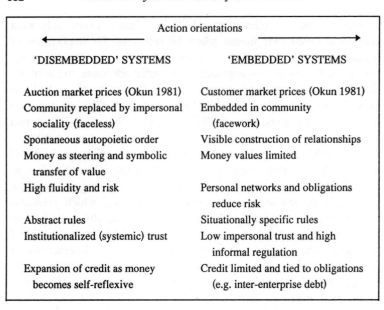

Figure 7.4 Models of 'disembedded' and 'embedded' systems

of Granovetter's work is that order in markets is achieved through the presence of stable networks, and Eccles and Crane (1988) argue that banks mediate the flow of equity between investors through fluid and informal networks. Moreover, recent studies of Russian entrepreneurs in eight regions suggest that these models should be viewed not so much as distinct social spaces, but as action orientations that can appear in combination, depending on the particular partners to transactions. The *Report by the Expert Appraisal Institute of the Russian Union of Industrialists and Entrepreneurs* (Yasin (ed.) 1992) found that:

- informal structures and contacts were crucial to business conduct;
- direct ties became the basic form of supply with 60 per cent using contract for less than half their needs, bartering for raw materials (which avoids VAT, at 28 per cent);
- marketing was done via direct ties and prices were regulated by informal commitments;
- a three-tier system of pricing involved charging the lowest prices

to traditional customers, higher prices of 100–150 per cent to new partners, and higher rates still to foreign firms and state enterprises;[10]

- in-house banks were used for reciprocal support and there were high levels of inter-firm debt.[11]

In other words, both types of behaviour ('disembedded' and 'embedded') can be present within the same institutional settings depending on what types of networks are activated in particular exchanges.[12]

However, the concept of embeddedness in itself neither accounts for those networks nor offers much insight into what effects commercial transactions have on them. Simply contrasting dis-embedding with re-embedding practices (as Giddens does, for example) is inadequate, because in differentiated social orders various kinds of embeddedness will appear in combination. Giddens describes professional expert systems as 'disembedding' mechanisms, since their knowledge is esoteric and removed from the immediacy of everyday contexts (1990:28). Yet expert systems are actually highly embedded markets for skilled services, inscribed within professional codes of conduct, regulatory systems and juridical practices. They become disembedded, surely, when they escape normative and juridical regulation, and unsuspecting clients are at the mercy of unscrupulous practitioners in the absence of institutionalized trust. This issue is relevant to problems of developing systems of market regulation in post-communist societies. To understand the form of modernity emerging here, we need to appreciate under what conditions personal-ized trust and reputation might be replaced by systemic trust. This, I would argue, is dependent on the development of forms of institu-

10 High prices to state enterprises may have been related to the process of insider deal-ing, which is discussed below.
11 According to Rostowski (1993) inter-enterprise debt was equivalent to about 50 per cent of all transactions in Russia in 1992 with the consequence not only of increas-ing the money supply but of embedding credit in systems of mutual obligation.
12 Similarly, Kharkhordin and Gerber (1994) identify two different value orientations among new Russian entrepreneurs, one 'ethical', the other 'anti-ethical'. The latter views the market as an ethically void negation of socialism permitting the maximization of personal utility, which corresponds to the model of fluid, rapid entry and exit markets. The former views market exchanges as bound by ethical restraints, established reciprocal networks and *kollektiv* value orientation, which is consistent with the embedded market model.

tional regulation that command both acquiescence and legitimacy, since property rights require normative and legal justification (Pedersen 1993).

The pattern in much of the post-communist world is to rely extensively on informal, facework connections, reflecting a lack of impersonal trust, which is a consequence of weak regulation and the problematic role of the state. This is so in at least three senses. First, the line of demarcation between the state and the private sector is fuzzy, which weakens the potential role of state agencies as regulators. This is illustrated in the study of St. Petersburg firms (Webster and Charap 1993:58) which showed a high degree of interpenetration between the state and newly private sectors. Most firms purchased or leased equipment from the state, in 77 per cent of cases via personal connections, while labour markets were heavily dependent on state resources. Only one-third of firms had permanent employees, one-third sub-contracted for labour to state enterprises, and one-third of firms were actually leaseholders within the state sector, which meant that both management and workers were part state, part private employees.

Second, in post-communist societies, the historical legitimacy of the state is weak, and this further weakens its potential as a regulator of emergent capitalism (Szalai 1991). This is apparent in areas of tax and corporate law where decades of illicit dealing, falsification of records, informal arrangements with other enterprises, complex manoeuvres with state planners, not to mention the extensive 'grey economy', leave a legacy of reluctance to comply with officialdom (Winiecki 1994; Jarosz 1993). This is especially so where illicit dealing – perhaps equivalent to 20–30 per cent of official economic activity – was not only a matter of personal survival within an irrational system, but was often perceived too as 'principled' resistance to an oppressive regime (Bugajski and Pollack 1989:99–100; Kornai 1990a:90).

Third, and of considerable importance here, the state is not generally the sole effective owner of what are apparently state assets (Bauman 1979). On the contrary, there are various 'stakeholders' in public assets since managers and workers exercise a degree of de facto ownership, which is combined in Russia with the claims of local soviets and branch ministries (Phelps et al. 1993:14). Institutional regulation and inter-firm governance, then, is dependent on the resolution of power struggles between competing claims, which will resolve issues of control of resources, boundary disputes, defining the state's role and licensing, as well as self-regulation.

One consequence of these ambiguities is that institutional outcomes are contingent and subject to reversal, depending upon the shifting balance of power among key actors. This is relevant to analyses that emphasize 'path dependency' as an alternative to evolutionary models of progress towards optimality. David Stark (1992a) argues that present forms of asset conversion can be related to the range of options circumscribed by earlier paths of development, in particular the 'path of extrication from state socialism'. Hence, unification in Germany resulted in colonization and centralized privatization through the Treuhandanstalt, which extended West German systems of governance into former socialist enterprises. Capitulation and the collapse of communist institutions in Czechoslovakia resulted in voucher privatization, because the new élite had confidence in the market and was untrammelled by agreements with the former communist authorities. Electoral competition in Hungary produced the conservative Hungarian Democratic Forum government, unsure of the market and keen to control the privatization process, which proceeded slowly through the centralized State Property Agency (SPA). After the Round Table compromise in Poland, leaders were unsure of the legitimacy of market values among the population, especially given the long syndicalist tradition of Solidarity. The result was a decentralized and again slow process of privatization which emphasized citizen vouchers to increase the popularity of private ownership among a sceptical population. In each case, however, as we shall see below, those best placed to become new owners by virtue of their 'positional property' were the former nomenklatura (Stark 1990).

Rather than gravitate towards the same equilibrium, then, 'in real time and history future development is affected by the past' and especially by the way certain organizational forms get 'locked in' (Kwasnicki 1992). However, path dependency is an elastic concept that could refer to the effects of a conjunctural crisis (as with Stark's account of modes of extrication from communism), or the development of reform communism in the 1980s (as does Wojtyna 1993), or presumably to a process of *longue durée* rooted in the Austro-Hungarian period or the second serfdom, which inhibited the growth of capitalism in Eastern Europe. At each stage of development, outcomes could have been different from what they were, depending on the particular balance of power among key actors, so a theory of the transformation needs to account for the pattern of selectivity – why particular organizational forms become dominant in the process in question.

STRUGGLES OVER PRIVATIZATION

Modernization approaches to post-communist development tend to over-simplify the process of system-formation and often view capitalism as the outcome of cultural innovations carried by 'thrifty entrepreneurs' as Kornai (1990a:50) puts it. Yet new social classes do not precede the development of capitalism but are its result, and come into existence via the institutionalization of property relations. The question of ownership has to be resolved before markets acquire stability and can be effectively regulated. Elsewhere (Ray 1993:ch. 5; 1994) I have argued that a decisive conflict over the fate of the transition is bound up with nomenklatura privatization, in which the crucial questions are which actors control the privatization process (and hence the process of accumulation), and how it is controlled, that is, what forms of institutional, legal and cultural regulation are emerging? The process variously known as 'insider', 'spontaneous' or 'nomenklatura' privatization refers to members of the former ruling stratum who acquire ownership of privatized enterprises. Spontaneous privatization enables former managers to become owners of productive resources in a situation where economic restructuring is subject to little regulation (Kowalik 1991; Hausner 1992; Levitas and Strzalkowski 1990; Mandel 1991; Ray 1994; Simoneti 1993; Staniszkis 1991).

Peter Rutland (1994), however, objects to the term 'nomenklatura privatization' on two grounds. First, he argues that the nomenklatura was a specific bureaucratic device used by the Communist Party to control appointments to key positions, but officials currently acquiring state assets may or may not be drawn from the old communist nomenklatura, as opposed to other élites, such as academic, KGB and Komsomol. Second, the nomenklatura system has broken down and there is no 'mafia' controlling appointments which are no longer subject to a central bureaucratic élite, which has lost its cohesion. The first point is valid in that not all new manager-entrepreneurs are necessarily from the old nomenklatura, but it is odd to imply that KGB, Komsomol and even academic élites (in some institutions) were excluded from the nomenklatura system.[13] The second point is literally true (the system does not function any more) but, as Tarkowski argues, new economic relations are dependent on connections formed in the past:

> Thanks to early retirement, police officers, Party apparatchniks, and officials in state administration may leave their careers in the prime of their lives and go on to establish industrial enterprises, shops, brokerage agencies etc. They do not of course break their former connections or friendships; in fact, they usually count on the support and protection of former colleagues. These types of symbiotic relations developed ... on a wide scale in the 1970s. Today they are ripe for expansion. (1989:59)

Political clientelism and patrimonial relations that characterized the Soviet system are to some extent reproduced within the current privatization process, creating a renewed political capitalism. The term 'nomenklatura privatization', then, refers to the process by which the former political–bureaucratic élite (and the social practices on which they were dependent) transform political capital into economic power, which has the potential to be re-converted into political influence.

Nomenklatura privatization is not a uniform process and it takes a variety of forms. These include the legal purchase of state enterprises by former managers (whose investment capital may have been accumulated illegally) and the acquisition of state property by virtue of current position and privileges. The central issue here is the conversion of political capital acquired from the former system into economic capital in the present. Specific types of nomenklatura privatization include practices that Stark (1993) calls 'recombinant capitalism' where the line between private and state activity is fuzzy. These include:

- The use of unused capacity in state enterprises by a nomenklatura

---

13 Elite academic institutions such as the Institute of World Economy and International Relations in Moscow or the Sofia Academy of Social Sciences and Management were subject to the nomenklatura system.

company consisting of the state enterprise's management who 'sell' themselves capacity (e.g. cargo space on Gdańsk containers) at a high price (Skapska 1994).

- Hollowing out – the selective leasing of the most efficient departments of state enterprises to private companies in which people associated with the managerial staff have shares, while throwing costs on to the state enterprise.[14]

- The bankruptcy of state enterprises (perhaps engineered by additional taxes) which are then transferred from the Treasury to nomenklatura owners at low cost via heavily discounted shares (Tittenbrun 1993:190).

- Interlocking directorships that tie the new private sector to the state economy and continue practices of political clientelism in which informal connections are crucial, while limiting the entry of foreign capital (Böröcz 1993).

- Organizational ownership, where assets are owned by political parties, trade unions and social organizations, such as the Association of Polish Students, which had an extensive network of travel offices, publishing houses and service co-operatives (such activities accounting for one-sixth of activity of the traditional private sector in Poland). Here functionaries of the organization would purchase property from the state and change themselves into a company, distributing the shares among themselves (Staniszkis 1991).

There are many examples of this process. It was reported in October 1990 that 250,000 foreign currency or convertible roubles were moved from the Leningrad Soviet executive committee's account into Lentok (a private firm) as joint-enterprise capital. On instructions from the mayor, the account was then moved to the Russian Ballet fund, in Switzerland. Among the small entrepreneurs backing Lentok, one-fifth were powerful founders – administrative bodies, who supplied them with buildings and state funds for capitalization. Members of Soviet executives were frequently setting up small firms, funded by the city (*Izvestiya* 10 October 1990). In Poland, *Tygodnik Solidarność*

---

14 For example, the Moscow Ventilator Factory was leased and bought out at an arbitrary price of R.6.5m. in 1990, the major corporate customer, Svetlana, providing an interest-free loan in return for future supplies at a reduced price.

(8 September 1989) claimed that the Mazowiecki government's reforms 'will please the communists because they will not damage the foundations of the system'. Throughout the state industrial sector, it continued, private partnerships created by members of the nomenklatura were springing up, which 'prey on the ineffectual state, ... benefiting from personal contacts previously developed ... and reaping colossal gains without improving the country's economic situation'.

Nomenklatura privatization is controversial, and a number of privatization programmes have attempted to arrest it, through, for example, centralization, as with Hungary's SPA, or the more decentralized Polish tripartite strategy of corporatization, liquidation and citizens' vouchers.[15] Nomenklatura privatization is viewed by its critics (e.g. Tarkowski 1989 and 1990) as perpetuating old structures of domination and establishing an unfair distribution of the benefits of the transformation. The Piyasheva–Selunin Group[16] have claimed that since the bulk of the population have no savings, the real buyers of state enterprises will still be commercial organizations set up by the former nomenklatura, a process they describe as 'a special, socialist form of corruption, one that ... surpasses all Sicilian models'. (*Smena* 28 April 1992). Gorbachev has argued that property should be turned over to producers free of charge as an alternative to nomenklatura privatization (*Komsomolskaya pravda* 29 May 1992), a proposal denounced by Anatoly Chubais (architect of the government programme) as 'the latest resurgence of the Bolshevik mentality' (*Izvestiya* 26 February 1992).[17]

15 The most successful example of voucher privatization has been that in the Czech Republic, where each resident citizen over 18 in October 1991 was eligible to purchase a voucher booklet for Kčs 35 ($1.20) to register for Kčs 1,000 worth or vouchers (about 25 per cent of the average monthly wage). By early 1992, 79 per cent of those eligible had registered. Two-thirds of all investors have invested all their points in intermediaries, including joint-stock companies, and banks such as the Czech Savings Bank, Austrian Creditanstalt and Harvard Capital and Consulting. A total of 4,377 intermediaries controlled 40 per cent of all voucher points by the end of 1993.

16 L. Piyasheva (Deputy General Director, Moscow Mayor's Office); Members of Moscow Economic Council: A. Isayev (Dir. Institute of Economics Planning and Management of the Aircraft Industry), V. Selyunin (economist and public affairs writer), G. Lisichkin (economist), S. Khokhlov (adviser to Research Centre on Private Law), S. Alekseev (member of the Russian Academy) and B. Pinsker (surgeon).

17 Gorbachev's critique of Yeltsin's privatization programme drew the accusation from the latter 'aggravating political tension – in essence, ... constituting a

It is true, as Andrew Arato (1994:102) points out, that the 'survival of old élites' is not the main issue, since this equates a sociological category with a structure, and old élites can survive to play a new historical role. None the less, nomenklatura privatization does have an impact on organizational practices, since it erodes the law and delays legislative reforms, as legal loopholes are exploited as a source of profit. It presupposes a weak framework of civil law and (as will be seen shortly) repression of institutional public spheres through which competing interests might be articulated. It strengthens the monopoly tendencies in the state sector, because the companies built around the former monopolies continue to enjoy monopolistic power via the interlocking satellite companies mentioned above. It exacerbates the weakness of capital markets since owners from the nomenklatura rarely invest their own money but capitalize power arising from political connections. High levels of inter-enterprise debt undermine the anti-inflationary effect of the privatization of the state sector by increasing the money supply and weakening the potential regulatory powers of other bodies such as banks (Rostowski 1993). The transfer of value to the new private sector (effectively a state subsidy) has accelerated the accumulation possibilities for cadre capital but weakened the state's resource base, contributing to the fiscal crisis and high budgetary deficits. Finally, scandals surrounding nomenklatura privatization (combined with shock therapy austerity) compromise the idea of privatization in the public's mind and encourage support for populist politics (Hausner 1992).[18]

Two principles of ownership are vying with one another in formulating privatization strategies. Restitution laws, such as those in the Czech Republic, are supported by the view that property is a natural right and legitimately allocated according to a principle of justice, grounded in historical proprietorship. According to this view, communist nationalizations were illegitimate and justice demands that property be restored to pre-1948 owners or their descendants. By

---

destabilization of the social and political situation in the country' (*Izvestiya* 3 June 1992) and in October 1992 Gorbachev's freedom of movement was temporarily curtailed.

18 Some would see the recent success of post-communists in elections throughout the region in this light, although this is complicated by the frequently close association between post-communist parties and cadre-capitalists, such that the former could be viewed as the new political establishment.

contrast, a technocratic concept of legitimate proprietorship ties claims to allocative efficiency, suggesting that appropriate owners are those who will use their assets most efficiently and creatively. The latter view tends to accept the post-communist status quo as a *fait accompli* and accepts nomenklatura privatization so long as the new owners act like entrepreneurs. Neither view is entirely separable from the other in practice and each can be deployed to justify a desired outcome.

The latter view does lead some members of the former opposition, such as Jadwiga Staniszkis (1991) and Elemer Hankiss (1990), to consider nomenklatura privatization as a natural and even desirable process. Perhaps, given their experience, information, connections and financial resources, it is argued, the former nomenklatura are well placed to run enterprises in a situation where capital and buyers are scarce and there are political objections to the extensive entry of foreign capital (Skapska 1994).[19] This is the view of the Russian Minister for Privatization, Anatoly Chubais, who, arguing against broad-based employee ownership schemes and voucher privatization, said that 'entrepreneurs are a specific socio-psychological type who will not be found by distributing capital collectively' (*Izvestiya* 26 February 1992). Similarly, Boris Rumer (1991) argues that nomenklatura privatization represents the formation of an accumulating capitalist class and it would be a mistake to underestimate their business acumen. It may be true that 'a peculiar economic system' is developing (Sutela 1994) but one adapted to the constraints of a unique situation. Similarly, Malkov (1992) distinguishes the 'conspicuous rationality' of Western market economies from the 'disguised rationality' of Russian economic agents, whose behaviour is intelligible from the standpoint of Russian cultural traditions of collectivism. Moreover, it has been argued that nomenklatura privatization exemplifies the process of embedded organic economic development, arising from administrative property rights developed among the managerial nomenklatura under the command economy. It has been seen how

19 It is too early to say quite what the longer term implications of this type of privatization might be. Levitas and Stralkowski (1990) question whether it represents the formation of a *grande bourgeoisie* since state assets are being appropriated mainly for consumption. However, Kryshtanovskaya (n.20 below) suggests that among new entrepreneurs 85 per cent reinvested profits and lived frugally and only 15 per cent reported using profits for consumption. On the other hand, many from the former nomenklatura 'lived comfortably' but were not economically active.

during years of informal negotiation required to meet planning targets, networks and rules of barter developed tacit acknowledgement that enterprise property could be regarded as personal assets to be hoarded, traded and used for personal gain, which some writers suggest are customary property rights (Naishul 1993). This process may have broader legitimacy, since Stephen Holmes (1994) claims that 'seeing old élites ... cling to positions of political and economic influence may actually provide psychological reassurance to those who are disoriented by the devastating discontinuities in their lives'.

This may be so, but another aspect significant of this process is the interconnection between the collapse of impersonal, systemic trust and the growth of criminality. Even if there is no longer a meta-phorical nomenklatura mafia (Rutland 1994) it is often claimed that nomenklatura privatization has links with an actual 'mafia' of organized criminality in general (e.g. Webster and Charap 1993:58). The 'mafia' has been described as a growing fusion of the bureauc-racy, economic administrators and 'affairists' of the private sector, who create shortages through monopoly structures, and illicitly transfer state resources and funds into private hands (*Komsomolskaya pravda*, 12 December 1990).[20] Varese (1994) argues that mafia-type organi-zations in Russia are a response to lack of trust and consequentially high demand for protection following the break-up of state ownership of the economy. Economic reforms from 1986 onwards created a dramatic surge in small property ownership, with new enterprises increasing from 20,000 to 82,000 between 1992 and 1993. This was not matched by clear property rights legislation, but rather by a variety of laws, statutes, decrees and presidential edicts that were often contradictory and unenforced. The failure of the authorities to

20 In a recent study of the life-styles of the Russian 'new rich' 40 per cent of new entrepreneurs admitted to illegal behaviour in the past (especially the 'black market') and 25 per cent to present criminal connections (Olga Kryshtanovskaya, of the Institute of Applied Politics, in *Izvestiya*, 7 September 1994). Claims that nomenklatura privatization involve 'mafia' or underworld connections in which elements of the former CPSU are implicated have been made in Russia for some time: see, for example, stories about 'the nomenklatura élite and the shadow economy', *Izvestiya* (16 February 1990); 'the plunder of the nomenklatura', *Komsomolskaya pravda* (10 April 1990); 'most new entrepreneurs are resourceful and corrupt' (*Literaturnaya gazeta* 17 April 1991). Even so, not all accounts are negative. *Literaturnaya gazeta* (17 April 1991) ran a story on 'new young marketers like Vladimr Kadannikov (General Director of the Volga Automotive Plant, Togliatti) who are opposed to the corruption of the past'.

control serious crime, which increased in Russia by 32 per cent in 1989 alone, further undermined trust among citizens (Varese 1994). Meanwhile, the army and police were demoralized by redundancies of around 40–50,000 a year. The state lost its monopoly of force as arms leaked on to the informal economy and criminal gangs (often ex-police and army) offered private protection for new businesses. Within a short period, then, the new commercial sector was heavily penetrated by mafia networks, and among these barons lies the nucleus of a new patrimonial capitalism. Thus Jacques Nagels (1993) refers to *sauvage* capitalism in the former USSR facilitating primitive accumulation and the formation of multiple centre–periphery relations in a general process of 'third-worldization'.

Alternative stakeholders

It has been seen, though, that nomenklatura privatization can be interpreted as the transformation of customary property rights into *de jure* rights (Suhij and Lepekhin 1993) and an optimal solution to problems of divesting antiquated enterprises. However, these accounts overlook the process of conflict under way between the competing claims of different stakeholders. Spontaneous privatization institutionalizes embedded customary property rights selectively, and only as a result of struggles that determine which claims are given priority. The eventual crystallization of property relations and regulatory regimes is likely to reflect the outcome of these conflicts, since as the Russian economist, Sergei Kugushev argues, the process will be legally regulated only after it has become established (*Komsomolskaya pravda* 6 February 1991).

One of the main alternative contenders for customary property rights are employees whose proprietary rights were expressed in a number of ways (Clarke et al. 1994; Glasman 1994; Panków 1993; Fields 1991). These included:

- the syndicalist tradition in Poland, apparent in the workers' councils movements in 1945 and 1956, and Solidarity 1979–80, especially the programme of *Samorządna Rzeczpospolita* (Self-Governing Republic) (Kowalik 1994; Wolnicki 1989);
- ad hoc agreements with managers to meet plan targets gave workers informal control of the labour process in a context of

low labour mobility (Clarke et al. 1994; Filtzer 1992a; Ticktin 1992);

- legislative acknowledgement of workers' proprietary rights in late communism, for example, in the 1981 Polish Workers' Self-Government Act, the 1987 Soviet Law on State Enterprises, the 1984 Hungarian Law on Enterprise Councils and the 1986 Bulgarian Labour Code, each of which gave extensive powers to labour co-operatives;
- voucher privatization or preferential option schemes that offer employees a stake in the privatized enterprise.

As an example of the latter, the Russian voucher privatization scheme acknowledged the de facto ownership rights of management–worker collectives in that:

- workers receive 25 per cent of shares without voting rights, 10 per cent of proceeds of privatization and a 30 per cent discount on a further 10 per cent at 1991 values;
- workers and managers may buy 51 per cent of shares at 1.7 times their book value;
- a subset of workers and managers with capital of 50 million roubles and 200 employees may buy 20 per cent of the shares at 30 per cent discount and a further 20 per cent a year later.

However, the ensuing struggle for control of the workplace is symptomatic of conflicts that will structure the social organizational of post-communist societies. In some cases, employees' councils did exercise decision-making powers in the early stages of privatization. The Russian employees' vouchers scheme meant that divesting assets to labour collectives was quite common (Clarke et al. 1994). In 69 per cent of Polish enterprises privatized through liquidation and 13 per cent of State Treasury companies, a majority of enterprise workers decided on the privatization strategy (Panków 1993:124ff.). Further, in the early stages, in 25 per cent of liquidated firms (and 15 per cent of Treasury firms) top management personnel were replaced at the instigation of workers' councils. In Hungary, the Trade Union Council (SzOT, later MSOSz) instigated workplace activism in the 1980s, and Enterprise Councils were heavily involved in the privatization process (Hughes 1994; Patkay 1993). According to Panków (1993:134) this represented the 'enfranchisement of an industrial middle class' of skilled workers, supervising employees and specialists, who predominated on workers' councils.

However, there is considerable evidence that privatization is followed by a rapid shift of power from workers' councils to centralized and hierarchical management structures. Calling this Russia's 'managerial revolution', Clarke et al. (1994) claim that workers' savings were needed for the employee buy-outs, and inducements to subscription were often backed up by an implied threat that those without shares would be the first to be made redundant in the future. Once privatized, management would restructure lines of control, widen income differentials, and offer to buy workers' shares for cash with the result that ownership rapidly becomes concentrated. David Mandel (1991) reported acute conflicts between Russian managers and self-management councils, manifest in the wave of strikes and occupations across Soviet industry during 1990–91. Suhij and Lepekhin (1993:40) argue that despite the attempt to organize social partnership at a national level in Russia through the Trilateral Commission of government, trade unions and entrepreneurs, there are very few agreements at local levels, where directors of state enterprises and private employers 'are trying to avoid collective agreements retaining freedom of action unlimited from the employees' side'.

In Poland, similarly, commercialization of enterprises was followed by a reassertion of the power by the central authorities (Dąbrowski 1993; Kowalik, 1994:183). Panków (1993:193) found that the position of enterprise managers in the power structure was consolidated while workers' legal entitlements to participation were neglected. His evidence suggests that employee consultation on major issues in enterprises fell from 60 per cent in the first quarter of 1990, to 52 per cent in the third quarter, to 28 per cent by October 1991, and in only 10 per cent of enterprises was employee influence 'compatible with the statute'. This situation was congruent with the political hostility towards workers' councils during the Mazowiecki and Suchocka governments.

One consequence of this was increased social polarization, the implications of which went beyond the realm of industrial relations. Traditions of worker proprietorship that had increasingly been legitimated in late communism created the possibility for building tripartite agreements between employers' councils, government and managers, perhaps along the lines of the German social market (Glasman 1994). This would offer an alternative model of embeddedness to those in neoliberal theories of Western capitalism and the newly emerging form of political capitalism in post-communist societies. Arguably, widespread employee participation would have created the conditions for new forms of interest intermediation and perhaps increased the potential for consensual transformation towards a decentralized system (e.g. Biernat 1994; Wolnichi 1989). However, exclusion of workers from the 'Great Transformation', combined with social insecurity and falling living standards, gave rise to expressions of demoralization and anxiety. According to Jarosz (1993) Polish opinion polls reveal the 'revival of a polarized vision of society' reminiscent of the communist period, and disillusion with a revolution that had been appropriated by a new élite ('we are supposed to have democracy but we have got capitalism'). Moreover, the decline in worker participation in enterprise governance has coincided with increased resistance to restructuring which suggests that this is less a consequence of 'inertial attitudes' so much as the structure of organizational power. As Crozier and Friedberg (1977:334) observe, in relation to French institutional restructuring in the 1970s, 'members of an organization are not really attached in a passive or limited way to their routine habits ... [but are] ready to change them very quickly if they are able to find their own interest in the games suggested to them'.

Increasing social polarization, combined with poorly regulated adventure capitalism, does not bode well for the future stability of democracy in post-communist societies. The problem of managing 'capitalism by democratic design' appears here from two sides. First, there is the danger that active resistance to privatization, in response to the erosion of employee participation, will encourage those among new political élites who talk ominously about the need for a period of Chilean-style dictatorship to establish a market economy.[21] Second, mass disillusion with the post-communist transformation could

---

21 Such as Lt.-Gen. Aleksandr Lebed, suggested as a future replacement for Defence Minister Pavel Grachev, who calls for a Pinochet-style dictatorship in order to create a law-abiding capitalistic ethos. Lebed retired from the army in May 1995, possibly to pursue a political creer. Some, however, such as Gaidar and journalists at *Izvestiya*, claim that a Pinochet-style government has already come to power in Russia since the Security Council functions as an extra-constitutional junta. For more on this see Chapter 8.

engender the kind of nostalgia for the past that concerns Habermas and others, especially if mobilized by authoritarian populist social movements (Hausner 1992; van Zon 1992). This risk is likely to increase if the recently elected post-communist parties of the left leave frustrated expectations that welfare and social security can be maintained along with marketization and privatization (Chan 1995).

MODERNITY REVISITED?

Complex societies are unable to remain integrated unless action is co-ordinated through anonymous steering mechanisms. However, the market is crisis-prone and creates disparities that, if unchecked, regress to chaotic and barbaric conditions. Thus social integration is dependent upon markets being socialized within normative and institutional forms of regulation and interest articulation. The foregoing discussion has identified two dimensions of economy–society relationships, embedded and disembedded, but it has also suggested that regulatory norms can be arranged on a continuum between familial-particularistic and universalistic civic ethics. By 'familial-particularistic' I have in mind the notion of 'amoral familism' described by Tarkowska and Tarkowski (1991) and Hankiss (1990). By 1989, according to these writers, a highly privatized society had emerged in state socialism, which Marody (1991) characterizes in terms of the ethic of 'defend your own and take what you can'. Similarly, Szelenyi (1988:215) doubted whether the new 'socialist entrepreneurs' in his study would embody the dual status of *citoyen* and bourgeois, finding 'little civic consciousness' in the Hungarian new *petite bourgeoisie* who 'may be forced to rip off the system (and their customers) as often and quickly as possible'. Amoral familism, it is argued, is a consequence of second-economy networks which created a traditionalistic ethical dualism in which moral principles were binding among primary groups but not towards strangers. Tarkowska and Tarkowski (1991) describe this as 'the uglier side of the second economy', creating aggression, social pathology and an 'unfriendly society'. This is consistent with the culture of facework commitments described, here, where social space is contracted to the immediate locale and privileging informal (embedded) over formal ties.

These two dimensions, embedded–disembedded and particularistic–universalistic, reflect the differentiation of value clusters described in Chapter 6. If they are combined, we can tentatively identify different types of socio-economic orders defined in terms of which combination of elements predominates. This is shown in Figure 7.5.

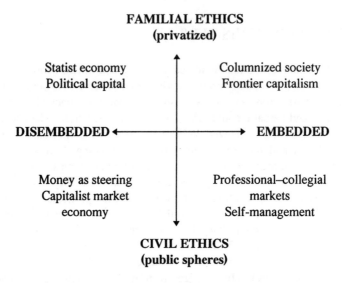

FAMILIAL ETHICS
(privatized)

Statist economy
Political capital

Columnized society
Frontier capitalism

DISEMBEDDED ◄——————————► **EMBEDDED**

Money as steering
Capitalist market
economy

Professional–collegial
markets
Self-management

CIVIL ETHICS
(public spheres)

Figure 7.5 Dimensions of embedded and disembedded systems

Western capitalism presupposes impersonal steering media within a plurality of forms of regulation balanced through juridical and financial institutions such as banks, insurance companies and stock markets with clear lines of ownership. On the other hand, Soviet-type economies embodied impersonal systems of political capitalism that presupposed weak regulation by autonomous civic bodies which was (as we have seen) consistent with familial-privatized ethics, resulting in a particularistic, clientelistic order. In the example of nomenklatura privatization above, political capitalism is giving way to fragmented and embedded structures of 'mafia' or adventurer capitalism again weakly regulated and consistent with a particularistic-familial ethos and low systemic trust. The tendency of latent forms of integration in the second economy was to weaken the state and create what Alexander (1984) describes as a columnized society of parallel and antagonistic groups. I have suggested, though, that there existed at least the potential for an alternative, collegial form of embedded economic system based on decentralized self-management in which production and distribution were subject to participatory regulation.

However, the dominant model of modernization in post-communist societies involves dismantling not only the decaying edifice of Soviet industrialism, but also precisely those indigenous expressions of working-class articulation – self-governing councils – through which resistance and identity were often defined during the communist period. Although post-communist societies have the potential to develop collegial forms of economic governance, the implication of multisided struggles for the fate of the transformation is to weaken the possibility of an inclusive and participatory democracy.

If post-communist societies do, as Habermas suggests, recapitulate the dilemmas of modernization encountered by Western societies, they do so in changed circumstances in which outcomes will reflect local configurations of culture and society. Therefore it is perhaps premature to speak of 'overcoming distance', and still less of creating a new European communicative civil society. This is not to say, however, that the latter should be discarded as a potentiality, since what is at stake in these conflicts is whether the disintegration of one repressive organizational regime will be lead to its replacement by a more open and representative form of modernity. This will be discussed in the following chapter.

8. Civil Society and Citizenship in the New Europe

This chapter discusses the types of political orders emerging from communism, problems of democratization and the formation of citizenship rights. According to classical sociology, democratic revolutions facilitate the process of social differentiation between the polity and societal community (Parsons 1971:79) which is a period of strain (Alexander 1978/1990). A theme in this and the following chapter is that whether social strain is resolved by increased social differentiation or by de-differentiation and reconstitution of status societies depends in large measure on the way in which the state is embedded in the institutional orders of civil society. This in turn is dependent on an ensemble of interrelations between economy, community and culture. Replacing the Party, which according to some accounts was still operating moderately effectively at a local level, with marketized and functionally differentiated systems of co-ordination creates great potential for disruption (White et al. 1993:222). These dangers are often expressed in the following terms, if not always as dramatically. Open society, says Brown (1994:10) needs 'experience, institutions, procedures, the rule of law, civil society and civil vigilance ... without which it becomes an open sewer into which pours the human detritus of national hatreds; antisemitism; dictatorship; populism; sham parliamentary life or none at all; lawlessness, intolerance, Orwellian newspeak and porno culture'!

Yet other writers see in the collapse of communism grounds for reviving theories of convergence. Alexander (1995), for example, argues that modernization theory stipulated that great civilizations would converge towards the institutional and cultural configurations of Western society. Certainly, he continues, 'we are witnessing something very much like this process today'. This view is found elsewhere, among those who, like Ash, see in post-communism a return to old truths and tested models, and the final triumph of capitalism and liberal democracy (e.g. Fukuyama 1992), reflected in a rather more sophisticated way in Habermas's notion of the rectifying revolutions (see Chapter 7). Again, for Bauman (1992) post-communism represented a different kind of convergence, but a convergence none the less, with the post-modern culture of narcissistic self-enjoyment and instant gratification. More recently though, Bauman (1994) has described post-communism as a state of 'liminality', a wasteland, the outcome of which is indeterminate.

By contrast with both convergence and apocalyptic visions, exponents of a 'third way' between Soviet socialism and Western capitalism (Alexander and Skapska (eds) 1994; Konrad 1984; Krizan 1987; Szelenyi 1990) see in the rhetoric and methods of anti-communist revolutions the potential for a new politics of self-management, the limitation of state authority, and power sharing within pluralistic societies.[1] This view places the concept of 'civil society' at the centre of concerns with self-government, activism and privacy, separation from the state, human rights, free economic initiatives, and the definitions of the social itself (Keane (ed.) 1988).

CIVIL SOCIETY AND SOCIAL DIFFERENTIATION

During the last phase of communism the idea of 'civil society' was prominent in the rhetoric of the anti-communist social movements. Civil society was first widely used by eighteenth-century political philosophers (such as Locke, Ferguson and Hegel) to describe the new commercial social order, the rise of public opinion, representative government, civic freedoms, plurality and 'civility'. After the concept had passed into disuse, it resurfaced in Gramsci's work where it referred to non-corporeal forms of class rule, an ideological space between state and economy. Latterly the term has depicted a social order in which people were dominated neither by the state nor by smaller ritual-based communities, but rather lived in a plurality of

---

1 Actually Alexander and Skapska (1994:xv–xvii) describe their preferred future as the 'fourth way' in which the reconstitution of the market benefits the entire population, is concerned with workplace democratization, and avoids illegitimate forms of exclusion and socio-economic domination.

institutions (Gellner 1994:99–100). This revival of civil society theory
has been encouraged by the collapse of communism and its use by
writers such as Vajda (1988), Konrad (1984) and Fehér and Heller
(1986) to capture the essence of dissident politics. Theorists such as
Rödel, Frankenburg and Dubiel (1989), Arato (1981) and Cohen and
Arato (1992) excavated the concept of civil society during the disintegration of state socialism, combining ideas of radical civic republicanism with Habermas's procedural discourse ethics. The central idea of
new civil society theorizing is that of identifying a social space for
public discussion, of voluntary citizens' associations, which is neither
narrowly economic and merged with the market, nor an adjunct to the
state. This reworks Hegel's concept of civil society, which was understood as a system of needs, private law, and police and corporations, to
capture the notion of new structures of public discussion, a *Zivil-
gesellschaft* rather than *bürgerliche Gesellschaft* (bourgeois society).
Again, with Eastern Europe in mind, Sztompka (1993:73) argues that
civil society is the key to closing the chasm between public and private
realms, involving:

- pluralism of voluntary associations, interest groups, political
  organizations and local communities;
- markets and representative democracy as institutional arrangements linking public and personal choices;
- active and informed citizens;

Cohen and Arato (1992) further argue that the new public spheres
in Eastern Europe could provide a model for a more general idea of
civil society that is appropriate in the West too, which suggests that
rather than Habermas's one-way (eastward) movement of the spirit
of the West, the emergence of a new Europe will involve mutual
learning and experimentation. For Arato (1981) the seeds of new civil
society germinated in *samizdat*, self-defence movements such as the
Workers' Defence Committee (KOR), the idea of self-managing
democracy and permanent rights theory (Fehér and Heller 1986).
Social movements such as Solidarity aimed to limit the state, or by-
pass it altogether through alternative networks, but not to seize it as an
instrument of coercion, and in this sense they were quite different from
earlier and more traditional revolutionary movements (Pelczynski

1988).[2] Thus the notion of self-government transcends the liberal dichotomy of public–private (like Habermas's *Öffentlichkeit*) by bringing rational democratic procedures into everyday life, through extrapolating the networks and practices of intellectuals in the parallel polity (Vajda, Kis, interview with Gorlice 1986).

Indeed, the anti-communist revolutions were 'revolutions of the intellectuals' (Ash 1990:136) that propelled into power literary and academic figures such as Havel, Bronisław Geremek, Tadeusz Mazowiecki, Zhelyu Zhelev, for whom the language of public discourse was congenial. This coincided with a relatively brief carnival of reclaiming the public sphere. During this time civil society was represented by the very public presence of masses of people in areas previously supervised by the Party (such as the Lantern Theatres in Prague, December 1989), the catharsis of speaking publicly what had previously been said only privately, open mass religious observance, ecological and nationalist demonstrations, independent trade unions, new publishing houses and public opinion polls. These all appeared under the sign of 'civil society' but this remained a largely untheorized metaphor for autonomous social action. During the collapse of communism, meanings of the term were highly fluid, matching the revolutionary political currents in which a multiplicity of issues would be compressed into single protests or collective action.[3] This very breadth of possible meanings though, was a source of ambiguity, giving 'civil society' a nebulous and undifferentiated character (Ely 1992). Accounts such as Rödel et al. (1989) share Habermas's tendency to de-institutionalize the concept of the public sphere into the domain of potential (but always counter-factual) communicative ethics.

Moreover, the position changed rapidly after the fall of communism. Intellectuals of the *limen*, the unstructured threshold, Bauman

---

2 It is important to stress that the early Solidarity programme of *podmiotowość* (self-management) was a radical alternative to Western democracy as well as to Soviet-type socialism. The democratization of the economy was part of a differentiation of the social order into autonomous subsystems of economy, law, politics, religion and science managed along the lines of professional self-government (Glasman 1994).

3 One example from many: the mass demonstration in Budapest in September 1988 against the proposed Gabakovo-Nagymóros dam across the Danube basin was also a demonstration for democratization, freedom of the press, multi-partyism, and nationalist issues such as the rights of Hungarians in Transylvania (author's observation).

notes with irony (1994:23), hope again for a historical subject that will not appear. This time, though, instead of the proletariat, the putative historical agent is the bourgeoisie, but when the new entrepreneurs fail to appear, post-communist governments find themselves suppressing popular needs in the interests of building a new order. Indeed, much of this civil society enthusiasm has already dissipated in the wake of the political demobilization of society. The crisis of socialism arose from an atrophy of the former political system, and, with the exception of Poland, the bursts of mass action were relatively brief, as in Moscow after the attempted coup in 1991, the fighting in Bucharest in December 1989, or the breach of the Berlin Wall. Moreover, even in Poland, activist notions of the self-governing republic were relatively short-lived. Ost (1990) notes that the concept of 'citizen' in Poland underwent several transformations. The 'revolutionary subject of the Gdańsk soviet', became the parliamentary delegate of the Gdańsk Accords of 1981, although during martial law the notion of permanently open democracy returned again for a while. However, during the 1980s there was a radical questioning of Solidarity's syndicalist past, and the ideal citizen as entrepreneur came to replace the parliamentary delegate as Kuroń apologized for his past 'communist sympathies'.[4] Hausner and Nielsen (1992) write of the 'protracted death agony' of state socialism leading to a systemic vacuum, in which the *ancien régime* disintegrated in such a way that new social forces failed to emerge. They refer to the social disembedding of market reforms, shock therapy as a 'revolution from above' combined with the disappearance of mass-based social movements. Solidarity membership, which was about 10 million at the time of its defeat in 1981, had fallen to two million when the PUWP lost power 1989–90 (Walicki 1991b). Kostov (1993:224) argues a similar case for Bulgaria, and evidence of the de-activation and privatization of post-communist societies has been seen in the low levels of participation in elections, especially local ones.[5]

4 This transition is apparent in Michnik (1986) whose early essays in his *Letters from Prison* (e.g. 'Maggots and Angels') are written from the standpoint of self-managed socialism, but the collection ends (in 'Conversations in the Citadel') with a positive evaluation of the pre-war National Democrat, Roman Dmowski, to 'discover the values hidden beneath the thick layers of insult, resentment and falsehood' (1986:330).

5 Actually, the evidence here is mixed. Bauman (1994:28) claims that in 1991 90 per

The binary opposition of civil society and the state could be described as a political code (in the sense discussed in Chapter 2), a rhetorical counter to the sovereignty of the Party over society which, since the political system was imploding, had become fictional, invoking another fiction, the sovereign 'people' as a monolithic collective subject. This is suggested by Szacki (1991) who argues that successful social mobilization probably requires illusions such as this, although others regard the language of civil society as dangerous, since by rejecting formal politics and the state, it obstructs further pluralism and social differentiation (Lewis 1994:264). Lewis sees, in its informality and antipathy to acknowledging divergent interests, the possibility of dogmatic moralizing politics and a failure to guarantee rights. Mazowiecki, for example, regarded interest-based politics as a legacy of the communist past, rather than central to a stable democracy (Ost 1995). Civic Forum held out against becoming a political party, but broke up in February 1991 into hostile factions. Similarly, Solidarity as a political force decomposed in bitter factionalism and public animosities (Lewis 1994:264). Again, although there is a high level of political activity in Bulgaria, the political culture is deeply polarized along fractures that often coincide with ethnic, urban–rural and generational cleavages, such that, according to one author, 'even the initial structures of civil society' are absent (Nikolov 1993:143). The social movement organizations that appeared in later communism were perhaps what Weber called *Schicksalsgemeinschaften* (communities of fate), retaining little cohesion once their common enemy was vanquished.

Systems theory is similarly sceptical of civil society theorizing, on the grounds that it does not address social differentiation in complex societies. Luhmann (1982:153) argues that citizens confront different authorities via a series of roles – taxpayers, proponents of resolutions, voters, writers of letters to editors, supporters interest groups and so on – that are divided according to the requirements of the political

cent of Poles did not attend a single political meeting or belong to any political party. In Hungary the participation rate in local elections in 1990–91 was 10–15 per cent, but by 1994 had risen to 43 per cent (*East European Constitutional Review* 4,1:13). In Bulgaria, with a traditionally high level of political participation in mass organizations, participation in the 1990 election was 91 per cent and in 1991, 87 per cent (Nikolov 1993:142). In the 1993 elections to the Russian Duma, participation was 50 per cent.

system. However, 'civil society' rests on a dualism of the public realm of the state and the private realm of voluntary associations, which does not address the modern ensemble of functionally differentiated roles that has no cohesion or unifying principles.[6] Moreover, unconstrained communication of the kind supposedly envisaged by Habermas, or the permanently open democracy of civil societarians, would be chaos (Luhmann 1982:287–8). Again, Alexander (1995) argues that civil society provides a 'semiotic field' for conflicts contrasting idealized qualities of rationalism and trust with irrationality, conformism and deceit.

Offe and Preuss (1991:166) point out three difficulties with broad concepts of democratic participation. First, regionalist and gender issues illustrate the thorny problems of defining the appropriate universe of participation, of answering the questions, who is affected and who can legitimately participate? Second, the issue in modern democracies is often one of protecting minority rights (which is also a crucial issue in post-communism) rather than broadening the participation base. Third, the quality of outcomes is not demonstrably improved by broadening rights to co-determination, because particular rather than collective interests often prevail. Kymlicka and Norman (1994) argue similarly that civil society theorists demand too much of voluntary associations, expecting them to be schools of citizenship, when their values might often be more akin to 'not in my back yard' parochialism.

Where do these observations leave the idea of civil society? It is true that civil society theories appeared more appropriate when broad anti-communist coalitions defined a common enemy than when post-communist governments confronted the more mundane tasks of reconstruction, when, as Chapter 7 indicated, divergent interests are articulated. Moreover, especially in cases of negotiated transition to post-communism, such as Poland, the political code of 'state versus society' was difficult to sustain. Bauman (1994:18) comments that two apparent adversaries, Michnik and Jaruzelski were 'integral (though mutually opposite) partners of the same historical discourse' and only together could they dismantle communism. In fact, rather

---

6 Civil societarians are not oblivious to this, and for Gellner (1994:99–100) 'modularity', that is, the capacity to combine associations and institutions without these being total and underwritten by ritual, is central to the idea. Even so, this does not address the question of what it is that gives civil society cohesion or the interpenetration of state and society in complex systems.

than juxtapose state and society, late communism saw complex ideological interpenetrations of government and opposition, which Hankiss (1990) calls the 'grand coalition'. The secularization of the communist leadership, the replacement of Marxist–Leninist values by more pragmatic and technocratic ones, which began in Poland under Gierek, intensified during the Jaruzelski period. In his 1982 May Day speech ('The Philosophy of Revolution') Bronisław Łągowski argued that under Solidarity collective control of individuals would prove more penetrating than ever, whereas democracy was premised on limitation of the state. In 1986 the Prime Minister, Prof. Zbigniew Messner, argued (in his 'Thesis Concerning the Second Stage of Reform') that the market economy, independent banking and the profit motive were central to social development. In the Round Table negotiations, Rakowski sought a deal with Solidarity in order to proceed with reforms, which resulted in the June 1989 elections and Mazowiecki's coalition government, committed to stabilization and rapid privatization (Walicki 1991b).[7] In view of this, the state–society dichotomy, central to civil society theories, has been exaggerated since both are internally differentiated and interdependent.

Even so, the functional differentiation of citizenship roles referred to by Luhmann presupposes two processes. First, one of inclusion and value generalization in which subjects become citizens within a modern state, within which various exchanges are regulated (ideal-typically) by constitutionally guaranteed rights. Second, citizenship expresses an abstract relation to the state, defined by procedural rather than substantive rights and legitimacy claims. The pursuit of interests arising from the system of needs (in the classical formulation of civil society) takes place within a framework of procedural rationality, grounded in rights. In this sense, the diffuse concept of 'civil society' can be abstracted and formalized into the concept of citizenship, which acknowledges the complex interpenetration of state and society

---

7 The universal commitment to market strategies among European post-communist governments (which had been anticipated during the later Jaruzelski period) was influenced, of course, by the pressures of foreign debt and loan conditionality imposed by Western lenders, notably the World Bank and IMF (Glasman 1994; Frank 1991). It is true that although Wałęsa's faction of Solidarity entered the anti-crisis pact with the government in 1987, this was controversial and he was accused of betrayal by Gwiazda's Workers' Group and of increasing the exploitation of the workers by Jan Lipski, one of the founders of KOR.

that occurs in socially differentiated orders. Citizenship rights allow substantive differences of interests, roles, values and membership of voluntary associations to be articulated through a putative community of 'equals' (Rueschemeyer 1986:151)

Citizenship rights and formal procedures rather than a homogeneous civil society are central to the process of democratization. Ost (1995) argues that political democracy requires inclusiveness and acknowledging the permanence of difference. That is it not about eliminating conflicts and social anger, but rather about organizing antagonisms in such a way that particular groups are not treated as enemies because of what they may think or believe, or because they are members of a different ethnic group. Thus successful democratic systems permit the circulation of power as an impersonal medium, via certain normative structures that are impersonal and universalistic rather than particularistic, and acknowledges that bargaining occurs among different groups all of whom have citizenship rights. Thus citizenship is an impersonal but normatively and institutionally embedded concept, which facilitates the restraint of corporate and state power, which is the precondition of voluntary association. Institutionalized exclusions, on the other hand, threaten to sabotage democratic processes and the co-ordination of social differentiation. These include making ethnicity a basis for citizenship, attacks on women's rights, privileging particular faiths (such as 'the Catholic state of the Polish nation') and denying access to social citizenship through impoverishment, lack of representation, contract violations and poor safety standards.

Citizenship rights, then, are the symbolic basis for exchanges in differentiated social systems, formal codes that are interchangeable between specific contexts and roles, such as those of employee, consumer, spouse, client, welfare recipient and voter. The existence of civil society, in these terms, does not just require the presence of non-state organizations (which would apply to Lebanon in the 1980s) but an acceptance of rules of behaviour by both government authorities and citizens that self-limit their mutual claims (Heller 1988; White et al. 1993:226–9). However, the self-limitation of power does not arise spontaneously from the process of functional differentiation (as Luhmann suggests, 1982:214) but implies a procedural threshold sustained by the diffusion of power through the social system. Moreover, sovereignty and deliberative democracy do not depend on the existence of homogeneous communities but anonymously interlocked subjects and flows of communication (Habermas 1992). This can only occur, as Offe and Preuss (1991:161) argue, when power is embedded (*vergesellschaftet*) in social norms and networks, local and diverse public spheres. In this context Sciulli's (1992) response to Weber's dilemma (see Chapter 2) is relevant. The drift towards authoritarianism, which is endemic in large corporate and governmental organizations, is restrained through collegial associations which (following Leon Fuller) he develops into a more empirical approach than Habermas. Not unlike Durkheim (who actually gets scant mention) Sciulli (1992:240) insists that power is restrained through the diffusion of collegial formations that:

- are permanently organized and supported by sanctions;
- impose invariant restraints by their presence in countless sectors of civil society and government;
- create a social infrastructure within which there is a lived anticipation among power-holders that those within the relevant network will scrutinize their decisions and the justifications proffered for these.

Examples of these micro-public spheres are found in courts, legislatures, universities, corporations, professional associations, worker collectives, and so on, where power is accountable to sanctions embedded in social networks. This idea of civil society presupposes a critical and democratic culture operating in the institutional life of society rather than in the political system alone.

CITIZENSHIP AND SOCIAL MOVEMENTS: COMPARATIVE PERSPECTIVES

Sciulli offers a focused and empirical approach to civil society and citizenship since the presence or absence, effectiveness or ineffectiveness of collegial associations can be ascertained and compared in different settings. However, the idea of civil society is still open to Marx's objection that formal rights merely obscure substantive inequalities, an issue that has been taken up in recent feminist theories of civil society (e.g. Pateman 1988). This is a critical issue for the post-communist transformation, since the establishment of formal rights occurs simultaneously with the emergence of new inequalities and the consolidation of old ones. How, then, can the comparative presence or absence of rights and inclusive structures be explained?

Social movements have played a crucial role in expanding the scope and nature of citizenship rights, constituting the 'driving force behind the fully fledged status for citizens' (Habermas 1992). Marshall (1950/1992), whose work influenced Parsons's (1971) theory of value generalization, saw citizenship as the evolution of social institutions that would balance the market, through the progressive expansion of entitlements. This occurred in three stages. First in the seventeenth century, the abolition of censorship, the right to a fair trial and habeas corpus, established political citizenship. Second, the extension of suffrage, from the enfranchisement of leaseholders in the 1832 Reform Act and to universal suffrage early in the twentieth century, established political citizenship. Third, the development of the welfare state in the mid-twentieth century established social citizenship in which membership of the national community entailed rights to health and social security. Including the dimension of social citizenship means, as Kymlicka and Norman (1994) point out, that the idea of citizenship is extended to the whole ensemble of state–society relationships, the understanding of which will involve analysis both of its historical development and of the balance of social forces that constitute the boundaries of membership[8].

Marshall was aware of the role of social movements, 'the struggle to win those rights' (1992:25), in the process, but this was not a central concern of his analysis. Yet the role of social movements has been crucial to the expansion of citizenship. The achievement of women's suffrage in the UK was the outcome of forty-eight years of campaigning from 1866 to 1914. Social citizenship followed the political empowerment of the working class in post-war capitalist societies (Bottomore 1992; Giddens 1982; Offe 1980; Turner 1990, 1992, 1994). Further, as Turner argues, the types of citizenship rights which

---

8 This is not actually, as Habermas (1992) suggests, a linear progression, because Marshall points out that, with the expansion of civil contracts and political rights in the nineteenth century, ancient social rights (such as wage subsidies and outdoor relief) sank to vanishing point (1992:17). This has relevance to the fate of welfare rights in post-communist societies.

become institutionalized depended on particular configurations of social movements, the state, and the relative strength of public and private spheres. He develops a four-fold typology of radical, liberal, passive and authoritarian forms of citizenship, which is shown in Figure 8.1. Radical republican citizenship, exemplified by France, is the result of revolution from below, popular sovereignty and an active public sphere. In the USA, by contrast, the thrust of revolutionary protest from below was constrained by a strong emphasis on privacy and localism, which resulted in liberal pluralism and rights devolved to local institutions. A third case is represented by England, where the Glorious Revolution of 1688 was a revolution from above, which established parliamentary power over the sovereign but constituted citizens as passive subjects. Finally, the absence of bourgeois revolution in Germany resulted in a weak public sphere dominated by a strong aristocratic state in which popular sovereignty was limited to plebiscitary approval of leaders (the *Führerprinzip*) and the private realm was regarded as a place of refuge from the state.

	BELOW	**ABOVE**	
	Revolutionary contexts e.g. France	Passive democracy e.g. England	**PUBLIC SPACE**
	Liberal pluralism e.g. USA	Plebiscitary democracy e.g. Germany	**PRIVATE SPACE**

Source: Turner (1990).

Figure 8.1 Citizenship and social movements

Since the state, revolution and public–private dichotomy are actually interconnected variables, this could be seen as a model of different ways in which the state is embedded in the institutional orders of civil society. As polar types, revolution from above entrenches the power of the state over civil society and leaves the structure of pre-revolutionary society relatively unchanged, whereas revolution from below establishes space for the activity of civil society and allows a new social system to develop. The strength of the public sphere defines the limits of social movement activity, which in turn affects the extent of public debate and draws upon cultural resources and traditions of political activity. This systemic approach may offer a useful general framework in which to examine the emergence of post-communist civil society, where it would be artificial to apply Turner's model too literally. Turner envisages a seminal, revolutionary passage to modernity which sets the contours of subsequent citizenship rights, whereas the transition to post-communism is in flux, and is in part (as was noted in Chapter 7) a self-conscious restitution of an imagined earlier path of development. The development of socially differentiated pluralistic orders out of a system of status domination entails risks, which are shown in Figure 8.2. In particular, the crisis of Soviet societies generates a high degree of complexity of options while the traditional instruments of power are marginalized. The state lacks legitimacy and, as was seen in Chapter 7, is competing with other power centres to establish its authority, while in many cases new political parties have tenuous organic links with those they claim to represent. Cirtautas (1994) argues that there has been a general failure in post-communist states to establish satisfactory political institutions with competences clearly defined and regulated by the rule of law. Liberal politicians, she says, have opted for parliamentary activity rather than building social constituencies and have attempted to create liberalism by fiat. James Hughes (1994) argues that in post-communist Russia there are political factions, but a deficit of political organizations to channel cleavages in society. Ost (1995) paints a similar picture for Poland, as do Szelenyi and Szelenyi (1991) for Hungary.

From this it might be argued that there is a high risk of regression to authoritarianism, in the absence of a differentiation of power within the polity and among other institutional orders of society. In terms of the framework outlined above, we would expect the chances of avoiding authoritarianism to increase where the public sphere is strong and social movements are active in creating the parameters of the state and economy. However, the balance of power between

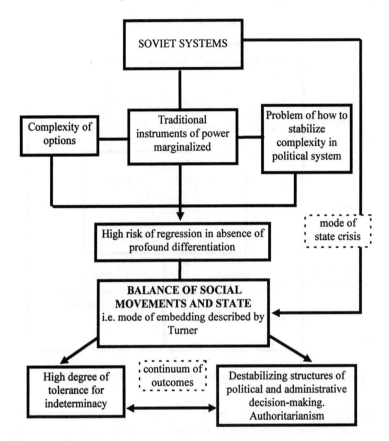

Figure 8.2 Model of potential transition paths

social movement organizations and the state will be conditioned by the pattern of extrication from state socialism and the nature of the crisis. A set of possible outcomes and cases is shown in Figure 8.3; it is presented tentatively, since these are still early days in post-communist development. This should be read in conjunction with Figure 8.4 which summarizes the major developments in social citizenship in Central and Eastern Europe, albeit one that is rapidly changing.

No existing post-communist system entirely satisfies the radical republican model although in some respects the Czech Republic

SOCIAL MOVEMENTS

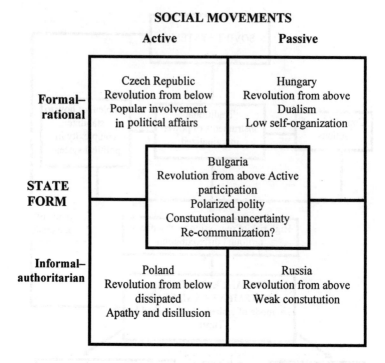

Figure 8.3   States, social movements and types of citizenship

approximates to it. Here the velvet revolution was not really a revolution from below since is was pushed less by internal opposition, which was weak and confined to intellectuals, than by the domino effect of uprisings elsewhere (Adam 1993; Miszlivetz 1991). Even so, the dismantling of communist power was more rapid there than elsewhere in Central Eastern Europe, and the Charter 77 tradition of organized intellectual dissent provided a model for the development of a new civil society. Some regard the Czech transition as the most successful in the region to date (e.g. Rutland 1992–3). In terms of citizenship rights it is argued that:

- the system is actually one of tri-partite social democratic corporatism, providing a means of interest intermediation between government, unions and employers, despite Prime Minister Klaus's monetarist rhetoric (Rutland 1992–3);

- some aspects of the former system of social security are maintained (Castle-Kanerova 1992);
- there is a strong emphasis on constructing a legal state with active participation in public issues (Bayard 1992–3);
- workers' rights and labour contracts are legally binding and provide for compulsory arbitration in disputes, during which time employers cannot hire replacement workers (Rutland 1992–3);
- unemployment has been kept relatively low, with an emphasis on re-training, and unemployment benefit is set at 60 per cent of the previous year's earnings (Castle-Kanerova 1992);
- the extensive take-up of voucher privatization (see Chapter 7) demonstrates public confidence in the system and active citizen participation.

However, against this view of the Czech Republic it could be pointed out that:

- there are frequent allegations of discrimination against minorities, especially the Roma, many of whom have been effectively excluded from citizenship by legislation recently upheld in the Constitutional Court, and criminal courts have been lenient in cases of racially motivated killings (*East European Constitutional Review* (*EECR*) 1995, 4,1:8–9);
- as elsewhere, the social costs of the transition have been high, which creates economic disfranchisement (Adam 1993; Mares et al. 1994) and welfare is being restructured (see Figure 8.4);
- the labour laws still fall short of ILO recommendations and exclude co-determination through employee councils (Rutland 1992–3);
- rapid housing privatization has been accompanied by extensive 'tenant relocation' using unscrupulous methods, especially in prime real estate sites (*Prague Post*, November 1993);
- public confidence in voucher privatization was weakened in 1994 by corruption cases, involving the Director of the Coupon Privatization Centre (*ibid.*).

Czech post-communist development, then, illustrates how transformation risks have the potential to be resolved in a way that increases social differentiation and citizenship rights, although social movement activity and institutionalized rights remain fragile. Difficulties of creating public spheres are compounded by the lack of an agreed political language of rights, reinforced by weak civic cultures, combined with hegemonic institutions such as the Church.

In the Polish case, a revolution from below arose as a result of the PUWP's failure to stabilize a post-Stalin settlement, combined with a strong pre-communist Catholic syndicalism. After 1989, though, the revolution from below was curtailed by the radical monetarism of the first Solidarity government, which eviscerated public political life and weakened participatory citizenship, as in the case of employee co-determination discussed in Chapter 7. A Constitutional Tribunal is currently drafting a new constitution which will be debated by the National Assembly (Senate and Sejm) and then put to a referendum. A critical issue here will be the role of the Church, in particular whether agreement can be reached with the Sejm over a proposed Concordat with Rome that would give the Church special constitutional status in the 'Polish State of the Catholic Nation'. This is resisted by the largely secular, left-of-centre Sejm.[9] A crucial issue here, in addition to the constitutional role of the Church, is that of abortion rights, which were greatly curtailed by 1990 legislation (Fuszara 1993). Parliament's attempt to pass new legislation in 1993, which would have restored the relatively liberal legislation of 1956, was vetoed by the President, who claimed moral and populist rather than constitutional authority. The Church, the Solidarity Labour Union and Lech Wałęsa have intimated that, failing an agreement on the Concordat and the inclusion of a clause protecting 'human life from the moment of conception', they will urge rejection of the new constitution (*EECR* 1995 4,1:18–20).

The institutionalization of citizenship rights and active public spheres is dependent on clear constitutional boundaries between

---

9 The 1993 general elections left the Democratic Left Alliance and the Polish Peasant Party, both successors to the ruling parties of the former régime, together with 303 of the 463 seats in the Sejm and 35 per cent of the popular vote. The present government is a coalition of these parties and two former Solidarity parties, the Democratic Union and Labour Union.

Bulgaria	Social security financed by 40 per cent tax on wages and transfers from the state budget. Cuts in entitlement 1992. Unemployment benefit 80 per cent of previous year's earnings. Private medicine encouraged and state services reduced. Reproductive rights: no change.
Czech Republic	Tax reform 1993 transformed social security funding from general taxation to insurance-based system. Social security contributions are 37 per cent of wage sum for employers and 13 per cent for employees. Rapid housing privatization and 'tenant relocation' reportedly often involves forcible methods. Unemployment benefit is 60 per cent of past earnings but increases with voluntary workfare. Reproductive rights: restrictive constitutional amendment.
Hungary	Little change since 1988, but new reforms of social security planned for 1995–6. Eligibility for unemployment benefits reduced. Extensive housing privatization since 1988. Homelessness rising. Reproductive rights: 1992 Act allows abortion if woman 'in crisis'.
Poland	Payroll tax to finance Social Insurance Fund increased from 38 per cent in 1989 to 45 per cent in 1992. Unemployment benefit 30 per cent average wages. Rents and house prices unregulated and often equivalent to West. Homelessness rising. Health spending cut 25 per cent in 1989–91. Reproductive rights: 1990 Act very restrictive.
Russia	Social security contributions 40 per cent wage sum. Unemployment reportedly low. Homelessness rising. Cost accounting in health services and shortages of medicines, but universal provision remains. Drastic increase in inequality. Ten per cent of population lives below subsistence. Reproductive rights: no change.

Sources: Deacon et al. (eds) (1992); EBRD (1994); *Prague Post* (December 1993); Pestoff et al. (1993); Ringen and Wallace (eds) (1993).

Figure 8.4 Social citizenship in post-communist societies

spheres of competence. However, the continuing conflict between parliament and the President suggests that differentiation of powers is not yet stable, and a populist style of politics could still become dominant in the future. For example, in 1994 Wałęsa dismissed two members of the National Radio and Television Council (Marek Markiewicz and Maciej Illowiecki) despite a Supreme Administrative Court ruling that he had no power to do so. Conflict flared again over the President's dismissal of the Defence Minister (Piotr Kolod- ziejczych) and rejection of the PM's nominated successor, Login Pastusiak, who had been critical of NATO and the USA. These events prompted a resolution from the Sejm appealing for an end to presi- dential actions that 'threatened the neutrality of the military and media' (*EECR* 4,1:18–20). Thus, despite a long activist tradition in Poland, post-communist apathy and difficulties establishing the boundaries of state intervention in civil society leave longer-term outcomes uncertain.

In Hungary the absence of a revolution from below was partly a result of the strength of Kádárism, which was itself a post- revolutionary settlement of sorts that allowed the expansion of a limited civil society. The lack of mass involvement in the régime change has given rise to the notion that what occurred was a *rendszerváltás* (exchange of systems) rather than revolution (Arato 1994:100). None the less, perhaps because of this gradual evolution, Hungary is avoiding some of the constitutional difficulties experienced in Poland. The May 1994 elections replaced the right-of-centre coalition led by the Hungarian Democratic Forum with a parliament in which the Hungarian Socialist Party (HSP) had 209 out of the 368 seats. Although they could have ruled alone, the HSP entered into a coalition with the liberal Alliance of Free Democrats (AFD) which won 70 seats, thus enlarging the consensual basis for reform. The HSP further agreed to take only ten seats on the 27-member parliamentary committee convened to draft a new constitution, a further ten going to opposition parties, five to the AFD, and the remaining two to non- party experts.[10] That the ruling party has limited its own parliamentary

---

10 Their Hungarian names are: Magyar Demokrata Forum (Hungarian Democratic Forum); Magyar Szocialista Párt (Hungarian Socialist Party); Magyar Szabad- demokraták Szövetsége (Alliance of Free Democrats).

power in these ways, combined with the fact that the new constitution is to be submitted to popular ratification, suggests that the Hungarian system is evolving towards effective procedural formalism (Racz and Kukorelli 1995).

Emergent public spheres are in part dependent on the ability of social movement actors to mobilize legitimating norms in such a way as to widen the parameters for representation. Comparing the Danube protest from the mid-1980s with the taxi drivers' blockade of Budapest in October 1990 over increased fuel prices, Szabó (1994) argues that the latter was more successful than the former in increasing the plurality of power in the political system. Both disputes were the focus of broad anti-government sentiments, in the former case for nationalist and democratic demands, in the latter, in protest at the social costs of the transition. The Danube protest against the proposed Nagymőros dam had mobilized large demonstrations (such as 30,000 people in Budapest in September 1988) but remained fragmented and confined to intellectual and alternative life-style circles. The taxi drivers, however, were able to frame their protest via the mass media, in terms of both the mythology of citizens' self-defence against the state (thus drawing upon culturally inscribed forms of political action) and the democratic norms of the then new HDF coalition government. Thus when the latter initially responded in an authoritarian fashion, calling on the police and army, negative media coverage threatened to de-legitimate the new administration. The taxi drivers' protest was successful in reducing fuel prices because it went beyond the 'state versus society' rhetoric of earlier movements and mobilized multiple actors and alliances in civil society. This had the result, according to Szabó, that the scope for pluralistic articulation of interests in the political system was widened.

According to some accounts, then (e.g. Arato 1994), Hungary now has a dynamic and active public sphere with stable political parties. However, a number of studies refer to the way in which parliamentary sovereignty combined with an absence of interest intermediation involving, for example, trade unions and local citizens' groups, creates a weak civil society and passive citizens (Körösényi 1991). As Szabó acknowledges, both the Danube and taxi drivers' protests were short-lived. Moreover, Szalai (1992) found a 'dualized society' in which one part become active citizens in a new welfare capitalism, the other finding no solutions in the new situation. As elsewhere in the region, those forced into economic marginality are excluded from full citizenship by the social costs of the transformation, which are likely to worsen as welfare is reorganized and universal benefits curtailed.

Russia is probably the clearest example here of a revolution from above and attendant risk of an authoritarian reversal, illustrated both by the support for Zhirinovsky's Liberal Democrats in the 1993 Duma elections (receiving 22.8 per cent of constituency votes) and by the invasion of Chechnya in 1994. Pashkin (1994:85) argues that it is unlikely that constitutional control will prove very effective in Russia where a meek Constitutional Court, preoccupied with its self-preservation, will obediently approve unlawful acts. The weakness of Russia's public sphere is evident in the power struggle between the president, parliament and regions in which politics remains personalistic and pre-constitutional (Lessig 1994). James Hughes (1994) argues that the failure of Russian democracy is the failure to manage relations with the regions and an economic policy that takes no account of local socio-economic structures. At the same time, according to Vyacheslav Nikonov, political parties do not form policy, neither do they campaign, nor link up civil society and the state (*Nezavisimaya gazeta* 7 August 1992).

The Constitutional Court was suspended between 17 October 1993 (following Yeltsin's *ukaz*) and Autumn 1994, during which time Federation politics proceeded according to unwritten laws, and the status of each political subject was dependent on de facto bargaining with the centre (EECR 1994, 3,4:19; J. Hughes 1994). That the state began to act in an increasingly peremptory manner was illustrated by the Presidential Decree on 'Measures to Protect Citizens Against Banditry and Organized Crime' (14 June 1994) which increased police powers of detention and search without warrants, and permitted phone tapping and arbitrary methods of gathering information. These appear to have violated several constitutional provisions[11] but the

---

11 For example, Article 23.1 states that 'Each person has the right to inviolability of his private life and individual and family privacy'; Article 23.2 that 'Each person has the right to privacy of correspondence, telephone conversations and postal, telegraph and other communications'; Article 25 that 'Dwellings are inviolable' and may not be entered 'except on the basis of judicial decision'; Article 22.2 that 'Arrest, taking into custody ... are permitted only by judicial decision. An individual may not be detained for a period of more than 48 hours without a judicial decision.'

absence of a Constitutional Court left no authority empowered to challenge the President.

The Constitutional Court was reconvened in October 1994, but complexity and inflexibility of procedures hamper its work, and its independence from the President – who has the power to abolish it – remains uncertain. The supplementation of judges' salaries by perks (such as an apartment in central Moscow rather than one in the suburbs) provides the President's office with a potential tool of patronage, as does the reduction of tenure from life to twelve years for new justices. The terms of reference of the new Constitutional Court include few regulations concerning procedural rules, and the powers of the Chair and his or her deputy can be suspended. Where the Court does deem laws or decisions of lower courts to be unconstitutional, no restitution is available to those who have thereby suffered (*EECR* 3,4:84).

Constitutional rights will be difficult to embed in political and administrative practices so long as power struggles over property rights and the position of the former nomenklatura (evidenced in the conflict between the President and Congress of Deputies during 1992–3) remain unresolved. Gavriil Popov (former mayor of Moscow) argues that after the August 1991 attempted coup the apparat acted skilfully to preserve their power. The illusion of democratic transformation, he says, gave them new legitimacy on the basis of which the apparat and former nomenklatura (the '*demokratura*') reconstructed themselves without the CPSU, and placed advisers on powerful committees (*Izvestiya* 21 August 1992). Further, the vast scope of the Soviet military–industrial complex gives its former directors political influence that is unmatched in Central and Eastern European states. In the old Congress their interests were mobilized through the Civic Union group of factions, which included Arkady Volsky's Renewal League, Rutskoi's Free Russia Party and Travkin's Democratic Party (*Izvestiya* 21 August 1992), although doubts about the durability of this alliance proved to be valid (Lohr 1993). Nevertheless, if the military–industrial former nomenklatura are competing for hegemony in Russia's fluid political scene, they found a new spokesperson in Vladimir Polevanov who chaired the State Privatization Committee briefly between October 1994 and January 1995. Once he was appointed, Polevanov called for re-nationalization of the petro-chemical industry, claiming that privatization had undermined Russian national security by allowing foreign capital to penetrate strategic industries.[12] Although Polevanov was hastily removed by Yeltsin from the SPC, he continues to exercise influence in his new post as chairman of the President's Oversight Administration to tackle corruption (*Nezavisimaya gazeta* 26 January 1995).

Polevanov's appeal to national security as a legitimating strategy, and especially its deployment in relation to economic policy, was symptomatic of the growing influence of the Security Council in decision-making. The Security Council was established by presiden-tial decree as an advisory body in June 1992, to counterbalance the pro-Khasbulatov Congress, but began to formulate policy early in 1994.[13] In October 1994, immediately prior to Polevanov's appoint-ment to the SPC, the Security Council had claimed that the National Bank placed Russian national security at risk by allowing the value of the rouble to collapse. According to some accounts (e.g. *Segodnya* 12 January 1995) the Security Council ordered the invasion of Chechnya, rules as an unaccountable junta out of control of the Duma, threatening military authoritarianism throughout Russia, and signals that Yeltsin has broken with democratic allies and is seeking a new base in the security forces (*Rossiiskaya gazeta* 6 January 1995).

The tentative argument here, then, is that citizenship rights are dependent on how the state is embedded in the institutional orders of society, and the scope that this offers for social movement activity, which in turn can define the parameters of state power. Thus the rela-tive weakness of collective organization in Russia, combined with an unresolved power struggle over the relationship between state and

---

12 The re-nationalization proposal was widely regarded as a smokescreen for delaying privatization, giving the Duma time to introduce controls over the process (*Segodnya* 17 January 1995).

13 Chaired by Yeltsin, its permanent members as of mid-1995 were Viktor Cherno-myrdin (Prime Minister), Oleg. Lobov (Secretary), Vladimir Shumeiko (Chair of Council of the Federation), Ivan Rybkin (Chair of the State Duma). In addition there were eight temporary members: Sergei Shakhrai (Deputy Prime Minister), Pavel Grachev (Defence Minister), Viktor Yerin (Internal Affairs), Sergei Shoigu (Civil Defence), Andrei Kozyrev (Foreign Affairs), Sergei Stapashin (Counter-Intelligence), Andrei Nikolayev (Federal Border Service) and Yevgeny Primakov (Foreign Intelligence Service). It is widely reported, though, that the effective membership varies according to Yeltsin's whim.

economy, exacerbated the risk of authoritarianism. In terms of this schema, Bulgaria represents something of a hybrid case. Previously relatively immune from events elsewhere in Eastern Europe, the transformation began with a revolution from above, when Mladenov's intra-party coup ousted Zhivkov in December 1989. This, however, created the space for mass mobilization (at least among the Sofia intelligentsia) especially following the June 1990 elections that had resulted in the return of the Bulgarian Socialist Party, successor to the Communist Party, and defeat of the opposition Union of Democratic Forces (UDF – Sayuza na Demokratichnite Sili). Many in Sofia (where 26 of 28 constituencies had returned UDF candidates) did not accept the result as legitimate partly because of allegations of intimidation, control of the media by the BSP, and an incident in December 1989 when Mladenov had publicly threatened demonstrators with tanks. Public activism continued through the second half of 1990, beginning with the student-centred occupation of Sofia University in June–July, the continuous mass demonstration outside the Party head-quarters in Ploshtad 9 Septemvri, and symbolic actions such as the resignation of the Sociology professorial staff pending the government's resignation (*Demokratsiya* 6 July 1990). These protests were successful in gaining Mladenov's resignation, and were followed later that year by mass demonstrations combined with the threat of a general strike by the independent trade union, Podkrepa, which forced the resignation of Prime Minister Andrei Lukanov in November.

However, some suggest that traditions of authoritarian paternalism remain strong, while social movements and active concepts of citizenship are weak (Todorova 1993). A new Constitutional Court is exercising greater independence of judicial power from legislative and executive authorities than is the case in Russia, and there is a boundary across which exchanges between the judicial and political systems can occur, which was illustrated in recent disputes over the constitution. In September 1994, the Constitutional Court successfully declared unconstitutional four articles of the Act on the Judicial System and denied parliament's right to remove judges. However, a legal culture founded on the rule of law is not well developed (Melone and Hays 1994) and there were frequent allegations (mostly from the opposition UDF) of 're-communization' even prior to the December

1994 victory for the BSP.[14] These have related particularly to the government control of the media, the extension of the powers of the security services, and claims that active members of the UDF are subject to police harassment.[15] Whether well-founded or not, such allegations at least attest to a high level of polarization and low levels of impersonal trust in Bulgarian society, which will hinder further social differentiation by encouraging reliance on facework commitments. Moreover, as is the case in other post-communist societies, among the patrons of the ex-communist party are former members of the nomenklatura enriched in the privatization process (*Libération* 19 December 1994).

Risks associated with the transition are likely to be exacerbated, as elsewhere, by the high social costs and dislocation of the transformation. In 1991, 45.2 per cent of Bulgarians lived below subsistence level, which encourages widespread resistance to tax régimes and the widespread practice of taking second jobs in order to increase household income. Employers prefer to hire workers on second labour contracts, enabling them to evade social security payments which amount to 35–50 per cent of the wage bill (Chardanova 1993). Thus, as has been observed elsewhere, impoverishment of large sections of society generally reduces the credibility and legitimacy of the state, while the prevalence of consequent parallel systems of exchange erode formal–legal governance.

GENDER, CITIZENSHIP AND EXCLUSION

In relation to Marshall, Bottomore (1992:66) points out that the latter took formal membership of the state for granted, whereas migration in the later twentieth century has left large populations whose formal citizenship is in question, and a new politics of citizenship centres on the question of defining membership of the nation-state. All along, though, particularism has been central to the concept of citizenship

---

14 It should be noted that the leadership of the BSP is very different from that of the old BCP, since, despite being former Komsomol activists, the former are all under 35 years old and consequently deny any responsibility for the communist past (*Libération* 19 December 1994).

15 This observation is based on evidence from Bulgarian applications for refugee status in Australia, Germany and the UK.

which is a binary code expressing membership or non-membership of a political community. Citizenship is in many ways an ambiguous concept that reconciled universalism and particularity, since free and equal subjects were to pursue activities as private persons within civil society and a polity bounded by the nation-state. Hence in political theory there arose the double identity of 'man' and 'citizen', of abstract and particular concepts of rights (Habermas 1979:114–15). Both popular sovereignty (civil and political citizenship) and working-class empowerment (social citizenship) were limited by the particularistic criterion of membership of the nation-state.[16] Moreover, the sovereignty of individual states was always limited by the conflicting sovereignties of competing states and was thus ultimately dependent upon military force.

This double-sidednesss of citizenship (particularism and universalism) is further evident in its relationship to gender. Historically, the role of citizen within the nation has been linked to the capacity to bear arms which has been predominantly a masculine role (Fraser 1989; Walby 1994). This fusion of citizenship, militarism and masculinity reinforces the male occupation of the public sphere that is inscribed into the public–private dichotomy. The result is a civil contract among brothers combined with the feminization of the private sphere (Okin 1991; Pateman 1988). The template for citizenship is masculine and its benefits have accrued disproportionately to men – hence the social wage in capitalist countries tends to assume a male head of household with dependents, while social rights in state socialism presupposed the dual burden of women's paid employment and domestic work. The concept of citizenship is structured around roles of consumer, citizen, client and worker which, as Fraser (1989:121ff.) argues, obscures the dimension of gender. The role of 'worker' is male since women are generally in super-exploited locations in the workforce, and remain primarily wives and mothers who 'happen to be working', while the 'consumer' role is premised on the femininity of consumption. The 'citizen' is typically a male defender of the polity and protector of women, children and the elderly who supposedly cannot protect themselves. The masculine citizen–soldier–protector role links the state

---

16 Social democratic and, even more, communist internationalism were generally subordinated to the perceived interests of the national working class, which was evident in the concept of social imperialism in the German movement.

and the public sphere not only to each other but also to the family and to the paid workplace. The citizen–speaker role in turn links the state and the public sphere to the family and the official economy while the worker–breadwinner role integrates the family with the economy and the state, confirming women's dependent status in each.[17]

Thus women's emancipation to full citizenship is the unfulfilled potential of modernity, autonomy yet to be won, but in many places women's rights are being restricted in the post-communist world. It has been seen how the expansion of civic and political rights and freedoms has involved a considerable reduction in social citizenship entitlements, and significant in this are attacks on women's rights combined with the 'masculinization' of the public sphere (Watson 1993) and a re-privatization of childrearing (Williams 1994). As with socialism, the language of women's emancipation can be construed as a legacy of the *ancien régime*, while attacks on women's rights are often justified in terms of undoing the communists' disregard for the sacred role of motherhood and homemaking. Restrictions on abortion (see Figure 8.4) are often, in addition to regulating women's reproductive rights, a coded opposition to the 'godless régimes of state socialism' (Schepple 1995). It was noted in Chapter 5 that the rhetoric of emancipation under state socialism barely concealed women's substantive inequality. High participation in paid work was combined with a gendered occupational structure, the low wage cycle and perpetuation of women's domestic and second economy activity, which created the dual burden (Corrin (ed.) 1992; Deacon and Vidinova 1992; Panova et al. 1993; Heinen 1993).

However, Goven (1993) and Kiczková and Farašová (1993) argue that an explicitly anti-feminist discourse grew out of the anti-politics of the opposition, which, like Konrad's 'home and free time', celebrated privacy, the realm of women's subordination. As a consequence, feminist issues (such as rape, male violence, reproductive rights, equal opportunities) were generally not raised by opposition movements nor were women allowed full civic rights within them. In Solidarity, for example, women tended to occupy auxiliary posts, and

---

17 I argue elsewhere (Ray 1993:68–73) that Fraser's argument is based on typicality rather than systemic regulation, since not all consumers are women or all workers male, and she assumes that the traditional patriarchal family remains the dominant form, which thereby minimizes the influence of feminism itself on the restructuring of gender roles.

branches in which 90 per cent of the workers were women had all-male executives (Lasecka 1989). Further there has been a decline in women's participation in post-communist parliaments, falling from 25 to 13 per cent in the Sejm in 1989 to 9 per cent in 1991, rising to 13 per cent in 1993 (Heinen 1993).

Moreover, unemployment among women has risen faster than among men generally, and nowhere do laws prohibit sexual discrimination or harassment, two central ways in which women are excluded from full citizenship (Schepple 1995). Seventy per cent of Russia's unemployed are women and in Poland labour market participation by women fell from 53 to 40 per cent between 1990 and 1992 (Heinen 1993). With unemployment benefits at 33 per cent of average wages and few vocational training schemes in Poland, increased gender polarization around the public–private dichotomy is likely to increase. Indeed, this was explicitly acknowledged by a report from the Czech Association for Independent Social Analysis, which predicted, in view of the disproportionate increases expected in women's unemployment, that it would be necessary to change the way in which household incomes are composed. Here, it continues, emphasis should be placed on higher remuneration for higher work performance by the bread-winner (who is assumed to be male) and compensation for women through a revival of the tradition of social contacts based on hobby, civic, local and other associational activities (Boguszak et al. 1990: 16).

This brief discussion illustrates the general argument here, that rights are embedded in complex intersections of social movement activity, the mode of exit from state socialism, the form of state embeddedness in civil society and the relative balance of public and private spheres. The more cultural values tend towards the pole of privatized, familial ethics depicted at the end of Chapter 7, the more rights-based citizenship is likely to be hampered. In a consequently weakly differentiated society, a return to, or reinforcement of, patriarchal, ascriptive social relations can result, along with the privatization of the state into clientelistic networks rather than the development of a formal–legal mode of legitimation. Similarly, ascriptive criteria of membership of the societal community, such as gender and ethnicity, are likely to predominate over formal and achieved notions of citizenship. On the other hand, the more cultural values tend towards the poles of civil ethics, public spheres and collegial regulation, the greater are the chances for successful institutional regulation and plural values. This process is connected to the mode of privatization, in that frontier capitalism and nomenklatura privatization will be likely to engender a familial–patriarchal status society which maintains the culture of political capitalism of the *ancien régime*. The outcome of social transformation, then, depends upon the strategies of social actors, especially social movements, and the types of material and cultural resources available to be mobilized by them.

9. Globalization and Nationalism

The discussion in Chapter 8 focused on citizenship rights within the nation-state, which has traditionally been assumed by sociology to be the territorial site of 'society' (Giddens 1990:63–4). However, the notion of citizenship rights within nation-states did not successfully reconcile the problem of limiting inclusion and entitlements while adhering to values of bourgeois universalism. The tension within modernity between belonging and identity, *gemeinschaftlich* affectivity, as opposed to the atomized impersonality of the market and bureaucratic systems, remained unresolved. This is further complicated by claims that the nation-state is increasingly weakened by globalization, in which sovereignty is transferred upwards to the world system, and downwards to regions. It is claimed that global flows of finance, media images, risks, consumption patterns, populations and power destabilize established notions of national spatial boundaries. This process, however, appears paradoxically conjoined with a reassertion of particularistic ascriptive identity evidenced by nationalist revivals in the post-communist world. What is often called 'resurgent nationalism' in post-communism, especially in relation to Yugoslavia and the danger of wider Balkan and post-Soviet conflicts, was unexpected by many social scientists in that it appeared to run counter to modernist universalism. Classical sociologists such as Comte, Marx, Spencer and Durkheim tended to follow Kant in assuming that international commerce would 'reduce the dogmatism of nations'. Even more at the end of the twentieth century, with the spread of capitalism, international consumption styles and travel, and the electronic media, the world apparently becomes increasingly 'globalized' and homogeneous. Against this background, how might we make sense of the destructive force of national particularism?

GLOBALISM AND LOCALISM

According the Liah Greenfeld (1992:491) nationalism is essential to the transition to modernity, which it was largely responsible for accomplishing. Yet its relationship to modernity is profoundly ambiguous. The national idea was a product of modernity that reconstructed a new symbolic order in the face of the dislocation of traditional commitments and consequent *ressentiment* (1992:16). Anderson (1993) describes nations as 'imagined communities' which became possible only with 'print capitalism' when the mass circulation of printed media (novels and newspapers) made it conceivable to imagine oneself a member of a community of anonymous people who were united by common culture and language. This created a new relationship to time, as the pre-modern idea of simultaneity of past and present gave way to the movement of the national people through history. Imagined communities involved the construction of a mythical past, often lost from living culture, the 'memory' of which was created through communication media that disseminated national historical and literary scholarship.[1] National identity thus unified and replaced local communities with the identity of an abstract and anonymous collectivity, the cultural signs of which were no longer derived solely from the immediate locale but from cultural meanings sustained through mass media.[2]

This is not to say that national movements appeared spontaneously. On the contrary, the reconstruction of national identities first involved the formation of 'national' (as opposed to titular) intellectuals whose role was the reconstruction of lost history, literary language, myths and cultural traditions. Intellectuals, moreover, often expressed the frustrations of their particular social location, and the formation of national consciousness was a reaction to obstacles to social mobility created by titular authorities (Ben-David 1962–3). Independent

---

1 Nationalist iconography might include faked up glories of past greatness, but equally historic defeats, such as the defeat of the last Serbian Nemanjic prince at Kosovo in 1389 the ritualized memory of which fuels lasting animosity to Turks and Muslims (Kaplan 1993:36). The sense of loss and deprivation are important bases for national aspiration.

2 The opposite of this is exemplified by Hroch (1993) who reports that in the 1919 Polish census, people from the Polesie region, when asked their nationality, replied 'from here-abouts'.

national territories were established generally only through armed struggle which typically coincided with the implosion or defeat of empires and multinational states. Meanwhile the memory of nationhood was carried by 'half-forgotten poets and lonely philologists' among upwardly mobile cultural and business élites, among whom it functioned as part of a strategy of integration and social closure (Laitin 1991). This is the 'rising bourgeoisie' thesis of national movements.

The creation of national myths, however, suggest that nationalism was far from unambiguously modern, since it remained dependent on traditionalistic and ascriptive concepts of past and destiny. As Gellner says (1994:107), nationalism 'speaks of Gemeinschaft and is rooted in a semantically and often phonetically standardized Gesellschaft'; it is impersonal yet loathes 'cosmopolitanism' as a threat to its particular identity. This duality is captured in Tom Nairn's (1975) famous description of nationalism as 'Janus-faced': like the Roman god whose statue guarded gateways, he says 'thus does nationalism stand over the passage to modernity ... As humankind is forced through its straight doorway it must look desperately back into the past, to gather strength ... for the ordeal of "development"'.

Moreover, nationalism is an ambiguous phenomenon not least because it has taken two contrastive forms, political nationalism and ethno-cultural nationalism (e.g. Brubaker 1994; Gitelman 1992; Greenfeld 1992). Political nationalism invokes an abstract concept of citizenship and legal rights, irrespective of ethnicity, religion or other particular identity and presupposes the nation-state as the territorial entity within which rights pertain (Habermas 1992). It is associated with the radical republicanism in Figure 7.1, above, where state and individual are linked through constitutional rights which are achieved rather than ascribed. Ethno-cultural nationalism, however, is ascriptive, based on ethnic or religious criteria of membership, invoking notions of shared heritage, traditions and 'destiny'. Its aim is to create ethnically homogeneous citizenship, and the constituency of the movement is defined exclusively within territorial borders (e.g. to Serbs within Bosnia) but inclusively across borders, to a diasporic community, such as Hungarians in Romania and Slovakia, or Russians in the 'near abroad', or Albanians in Greece. Thus ethno-cultural nationalism is likely to be irredentist, reclaiming territory of the historic nation, and exclusive, withholding citizenship from 'non-national' minorities, as with Russian-speaking Estonians and Latvians (Stepan 1994).

Defining the external, geographic and internal boundaries of the state is the focus of a great deal of conflict in post-communist societies (Löwy 1993). To some extent, national identity concerns the exclusion of diffuse symbolic and material threats. What is often called the 'resurgence of nationalism' can be placed in the context of assessing and dealing with external environments and is thus importantly linked to the process of social differentiation. This, it was seen in Chapter 2, involves the transfer of risks through subsystems where time boundaries allow for auditing, processing and strategic responses to risks which are thereby de-dramatized and (potentially) available to public debate. Soviet societies, however, tended to keep from public scrutiny risks such as ecological damage, health and safety dangers and accidents, thus one of the greatest shocks of glasnost was the public visibility of risks and disasters, such as Chernobyl. This risk-aversion, though, was accompanied by the vanguard Party's claim to protect the populations of socialist countries from diffuse dangers, especially those arising from capitalist encirclement, imperialist agents and internal deviationists with foreign connections. Thus the idea of foreignness was closely associated with dangers that did not in the main lend themselves to calculation and public assessment.[3] Defining nations in post-communism is thus to some extent a response to externally-perceived danger, and ecological movements, such as Ekoglasnost in Bulgaria, the Hungarian Danube protest, the Green movement of Estonia, the Ukrainian Heritage (Spadschina) Club, each had a nationalist agenda and in some cases were the precursor of movements for national independence or self-assertion. Ecological movements were natural allies of national movements, both organized around reclaiming 'our land' and 'our environment' (Gitelman 1992:8).

The dominant form of nationalism in post-communist societies tends to be ethno-cultural rather than political, and is strongly secessionist and ascriptive (Kaldor 1993). Fragmentation is apparent, since

---

3 Whereas one can publicly debate the risks say, of siting nuclear power stations in particular locations, or of economic policies that will result in unemployment, the risks posed by deviationists failing to carry through the Party line do not lend themselves to calculation, but rather to dramatization.

as one layer of nationality is peeled away another deeper line of fracture appears. Beneath Moldova, for example, one finds the Russian-speaking minority of Transdniestria; after Ukraine, the separatists in the Crimea; after Kazakhstan, not only Russian settlers, but also Greeks and Meskhetian Turks. Ethno-cultural nationalism 'returns' to primal identities in an attempt to simplify complex social differentiation through myths of rootedness and the return to a lost body (Balibar and Wallerstein 1992). Further, ethno-national identity is inscribed in highly traditionalistic ways in programmes for social reconstruction, which circumscribe gender roles in the new heroic soldier-states. The Serbian Law on Social Care for Children (1990) restricted child care rights and emphasized women's nurturing role. Women are used in national symbolism both as sex objects and as mother of the nation figures, imagery that symbolizes a unified community in which women are subordinated as the property of the male state (Milic 1993). Similarly, the ruling Hrvatska Demokratska Zajednica (Croatian Democratic Union) project an image of the 'fruitful virgin mother' and insist on the 'sacred duty of every woman to stay at home and care for their family' (Drakulic 1993).

Some writers have suggested that this 'new nationalism' (Kaldor 1993) represents the reverse side of globalization. One consequence of globalization is that the nation-state, the traditional object of national aspiration, seems to be losing its pivotal role in international affairs, finding itself hollowed out, losing its established functions to regional authorities, intergovernmental and private international organizations. The ability of nation-states to regulate the activities within their territories is weakened by the combined drift towards global systems of exchange, conflict and co-operation at sub-national levels, such as regional economies and divisions of labour. Globalization entails both spatial differentiation and what Harvey (1994:240) calls time–space compression, as economic interdependencies appear to shrink the world to a 'global village'. However, this does not mean that globalization creates greater homogeneity. On the contrary, Appadurai (1990) emphasizes how the new global cultural economy is a complex, overlapping disjunctive order of increasing fluidity and irregularity. World systems theorists (e.g. Arrighi 1991), moreover, have argued that during the twentieth century the overall tendency has been towards global polarization of inequalities rather than towards homogeneity.

To be more specific, globalization refers to processes whereby:

- there is an interlacing of social events at a distance from locales, an intersection of presence and absence (Giddens 1991:21) such that the intersection of the local and global ('glocalization') become significant for social outcomes;
- economic organization becomes transnational, with global ownership and activities giving capital unprecedented mobility and flexibility such that the boundaries of the national economy become blurred (Jessop 1992);[4]
- there are flows of labour migration, refugees and exiles, such as those from Eastern Europe into the central 'buffer zone' of Poland, Hungary, Slovakia and the Czech Republic, or on to the EU (Wallace et al. 1995);
- global communications media (satellite TV, Internet, etc.) and international patterns of consumption create consciousness of living in a global culture (Featherstone 1990);
- risks escape the direct control of states, such as ecological damage, global pandemics and international crime (Beck 1992);
- some social movements address global issues (such as ecology, nuclear weapons and human rights) or global constituencies, such as diasporic nationalism or pan-Islamic revivalism, consciousness of which is facilitated by global media (Kaldor 1993; Ray 1993);
- nations are bound by conditions of membership of international organizations, such as the European Union, World Bank, IMF, GATT and NATO (Held 1991).

Thus in many ways globalization undermines the nation-state which encounters reduced ability to control what happens within its frontiers, and this weakens the idea of citizenship rights within a nationally defined space. The welfare state, for example, crucial to the idea of social citizenship, was tied to Fordist techniques of demand management and fiscal regulation that become less viable in a globalized economy. Jessop (1992) argues that there is a hollowing out of the post-war nation-state and differentiation of local, regional and national

---

4 In April 1989, foreign exchange trading averaged $650 billion a day, equivalent to twice the foreign reserves of the USA, Japan and the UK for a month, and 40 times the value of world trade per day (McGrew 1993:90).

modes of regulation in competition for locational advantage. This applies to the communist states' autarkic growth model which became unviable as planned economies were hollowed out through linkage with the global system via foreign debt and technological dependence. As we have seen, these exacerbated the crisis of the redistributive economy, with de-legitimating consequences which were in turn encouraged by cultural influences, such as the flow of media images from the West and increasing temporary labour migration to capitalist economies.

Some writers refer to a consequent 'crisis of governability', since the nation-state is now 'too small for the big problems of life and too big for small problems' (Bell 1987) which leads to a process of sub-national fragmentation.[5] Szelenyi (1990) argues that global economies of scale and regional specificity create a disjuncture between nation and state in which (often brutal) separatist movements re-define the boundaries of collectivities. This crisis of governability leads to sub-national fragmentation where the integration of locales in the global economy correspondingly weakens national cohesiveness. As the nation-state weakens, uneven development between regions within the state becomes a potent source of mobilization, illustrated, for example, in the Lombard League attempting to make moves to separate the more prosperous northern region of Italy from the less affluent south (Woods 1992). Here, Woods argues, state structures became an ideological tissue around which clientelistic linkages and ideological appeals could be made to the lost authority of regional constituencies. These had none the less remained crucial for the constitution of identities, despite their integration into a larger unit. The persistence and increasing intensity of global interconnections render national integration less important than in the past, and allow both wealthier and less developed regions to push for autonomy. For wealthier areas the aim of sub-nationalism is to off-load regions that they regard as economically dependent and less

5 This view is contested (e.g. by Panitch 1994) and a few caveats are in order. First, this process should not be exaggerated, and moves at a different tempo in particular locations. Thus Japan and South Korea, for example, are still national economies. Second, there is no necessary logic to globalization since it is driven politically rather than by economic or technical necessity. The deregulation of investment and trade is ultimately the consequence of decisions made by national governments in response to perceived demands of the environment. Third, the impact of the global system on locales will differ according to the latter's particular economic and cultural configurations and mode of integration into transnational networks.

culturally developed. For poorer regions, autonomy or independence offers emancipation from an exploiting metropolitan power (Bienefeld 1994). If citizenship as membership of a national community comes to be regarded as meaningless, then fragmentation along regional, clan and ethnic identities is likely to follow. Globalization undermines the nation-state and creates new regional and cultural linkages, while mass media in the vernacular make available new 'psycho-geographies' (Hroch 1993) of ethnic terrain, such as pan-Turkic identities in the former Soviet Central Asian republics.

Thus globalization only apparently or superficially creates a common culture of cosmopolitan identities but creates the conditions for sub-national fragmentation. How well does this explain post-communist nationalism? Most globalization literature addresses capitalist economies, where regions are formed by market forces creating global–regional interdependencies at the expense of national cohesion. However, the formation of regions differs in post-communist societies, where the process has been orchestrated from above through industrial location decisions without much regard for traditional local considerations (Jessop 1994). Where local networks emerged spontaneously, this was in response to the dysfunctions of central planning, deterioration of extended economic relations such as transport, crises of confidence in money and collapse in systemic trust. As we saw in Chapter 5, power shifted to some extent from a vertical axis between ministries and enterprises to reciprocal horizontal obligations between enterprises. The reciprocity and clientelism that this fostered could also be bases for intra-regional ties through traditionalistic ethnic and obligations (Willerton 1987).

As post-communist economies become increasingly market-oriented, though, regional fragmentation tends to be based in part on differential competitive advantage and divergent styles of privatization. In relation to Russia, Yegveny Yasin argues (*Rossiya* 16 December 1992) that a pattern of contradictions between regions and the centre is emerging, which could result in Russia's disintegration into smaller sovereign states. In any event, he says, Russia cannot be simultaneously unified and democratic, an observation that would seem to be borne out by the above discussion. Three styles of privatization can be identified that have different consequences for regional development. First, there is the open market model (e.g. Moscow and St. Petersburg provinces) where exports, small business growth and foreign investment are encouraged, which potentially increase global links at the expense of intra-Federal ones. Second, there is the 'Kuwait model' (e.g. Kaliningrad province) geared to the export of raw materials where the economy is regulated by the local authorities who exercise control over investment and exports. Third, there is the 'local autarky' model (e.g. Murmansk, Yaroslavl and, Ulyanovsk provinces) based on self-sufficiency, slow privatization, restrictions on exports, local taxes and coupons or local currencies. These models involve not only differing modes of economic adjustment but also distinct modes of political regulation and management of the tense relations between local and central authorities. This in turn places legitimation demands on the local authorities and appeals might be made to common ethnic, linguistic or religious identities.

However, this is not a straightforward matter because post-Soviet nationalities are territorially highly dispersed, the 1989 census showing that 73 million citizens (one-quarter of the total) lived outside their national territory (Brubaker 1994). Moreover, economically defined regions do not necessarily coincide with ethnic or cultural lines of fracture, and regions have the matreshka-like structure noted above, with sub-regions lying within larger units. Hughes (1994) describes the fate of the Siberia Agreement when Congress deputies attempted to act together to secure increased control over resources, claiming that Siberia produced 11 per cent of Russian GDP and 60 per cent of hard currency but was one of the least socially developed regions of the Federation. Deputies meeting in Krasnoyarsk in March 1993 spoke of 'decolonizing Siberia'. However, the Agreement was subsequently weakened by sub-regional polarization and autonomy movements in the Tyumen region, combined with the ability of the Federal government to play on inter-territorial conflicts.[6]

Globalization, then, may create conditions for the emergence of regional autonomy, but specific outcomes will depend upon particular

---

6 According to the Working Centre for Economic Reforms there are three distinct Siberian sub-regions defined by economic criteria: Western Siberia, with low density population, internal differentiation, petroleum and gas production, but dependent on food imports and quite unable to solve problems such as pollution; Eastern Siberia, able to exchange timber, copper and nickel for other commodities but dependent on the centre; the Far East, where food production exceeds the Russian average by 50 per cent and oriented towards Japanese and SEA markets (*Rossiya* 27 May 1992).

configurations of local forces. Autonomy initiatives may be abandoned, as with Belarus which is seeking admission into the Russian Federation, or crushed as in Chechnya. Regions may develop mutual co-operation and avoid internecine violence, as with the Czech Republic and Slovakia, now relinked economically through the Visegrad Agreement. However, where regions divide on ethno-cultural lines, given other conditions, they become shatter zones of conflicting identities, such as the former Yugoslavia. While a general theory of globalization may account for the tendency to fragmentation of the nation (and especially supranational) state, an adequate theory needs to offer a differentiated, comparative, explanation of why and where nationalist movements appear.

THE FORMATION OF NATIONAL MOVEMENTS

One influential approach stresses how national identity is a cultural and affective resource that becomes mobilized during periods of social strain, when people confine trust to their primordial associations (Olzak 1983:356). National identity provides a focus for channelling imagined wrongs and explanations of collective misfortunes (Žižek 1990). Here nationalism is understood as a pre-political unity of historic communities or 'ethnies', which were already rooted in folklore, customs, myths and symbols that stand opposed to the 'memoryless nature of any cosmopolitan culture created today' (A.D. Smith 1991). National movements are thus able to mobilize identifications transmitted through primary group socialization and sub-cultures (Johnston 1994). As with anomie theory, national movements result from a socio-psychological response of reaction-formation, as social strain leads to activation of memories of lost authenticity which find in nostalgia compensation for the experience of dislocation (e.g. Eder 1985:62; Hroch 1993; Miszlivetz 1991).

Another version of this approach I have called the 'Rip van Winkle thesis' (Ray 1993:103), according to which nationalism was put to sleep by communism to be reawoken with its fall. Illustrating this view, writing about the background to the civil wars in Yugoslavia, Misha Glenny (1993:13) argues that nationalism entered an artificial hibernation, since 'Tito threw hatred into deep freeze by enforcing communal life on the three communities' (Serbs, Croats and Muslims) but 'when the resentments were taken out of the historical deep freeze, the memory of hatred proved to be as fresh as ever after it thawed'. Michnik (1991) like Lane (1992) sees nationalism as creeping into an ideological vacuum with demons from bygone epochs. Kaplan (1993) understands most contemporary national conflicts in the Balkans in terms of deeply ingrained enmities whose origins lie in the division of the region between Ottoman and Austrian rulers, reawakened by the collapse of communism.

While not wanting to discount such explanations, neither reaction-formation nor awakening accounts are entirely adequate. The view that social strain leads to the activation of deeply ingrained cultural identities assumes that social change occurs via adaptation but can explain maladaptive responses only with reference to psychology. Yet meanings are created and sustained through cultural symbols, language, education, official events and media as well as through primary group values. People might have to *select* between conflicting national identities, such as 'Soviet' or 'Ukrainian', 'Yugoslav' or 'Croatian' and 'Bosnian' or 'Serb'. How identities are selected, fixed and combined is dependent on the relative power of social movements, campaigns and images provided by the media. For example, the question of whether Russian-speaking inhabitants of Estonia with over 20 years' residence should be enfranchised was subject to political struggle that culminated in the 1992 referendum (of Estonians) in which 52 per cent voted against granting any Russians citizenship rights (Stepan 1994).

Anyway, nationalism was not put to sleep during communism, but was nurtured both ideologically (under the banner of 'socialist patriot-ism') and by regional client networks. Brubaker (1994) argues that Soviet nationality policies tried to depoliticize nationalism by confining its expression to symbolic folk culture, but unintentionally created conditions for nationalist fragmentation. The Soviet Union created fifteen Union republics within which national intellectual and political cadres could become entrenched, while codifying national identity to an unprecedented extent by ascribing every citizen a putative home-land. In this way, long-ambiguous social identities were solidified by the Soviet 'ethnologizing culture' (Suny 1990). The formation of national identification among republic élites was further encouraged by the policy of 'nativization' (*korenizatsiya*). During the 1970s, this established channels for nationalism in the bureaucratic apparatus in which the local nomenklatura became increasingly important competing centres of patronage during the Brezhnev period (Kagarlitsky 1990:60). Thus, according to Rakowska-Harmstone (1977:29),

> rather than fostering national integration, the impact of modernization has given new impetus to the growth and crystallization of minority nationalisms, the rhetoric of 'proletarian internationalism' notwithstanding. All the national groups benefited from economic and social progress, but their relative position did not change and little integration resulted. Instead, an enhanced consciousness of separate identity and new foci of ethnic conflict appeared. ... [N]ew élites see themselves as permanently second best to the Russians and, legitimating their demands for their national heritage, seek competitive advantage in the assertion of cultural, economic and ... ultimately political nationalism.

Not only this, but also the communist authorities generated militaristic and compulsive attachment to the national cause (Žižek 1990) and often propagated the ideal of an ethnically homogeneous state. This was apparent in officially-orchestrated campaigns of anti-semitism, such as the Polish 'anti-Zionist' campaign in 1968–69, headed by General Mieczysław Moczar (Interior Minister) and supported by Gomułka and the Central Committee. Jewish politicians and academics were purged, formerly official Jewish publications (such as *Folks-Sztyme*) were disaffiliated from the Party, and Jewish Poles were invited to 'return to Israel' (Wieriorka 1984:64; Wistrich 1992:162ff.). The result of this campaign was that the post-Holocaust community of about 25,000 Polish Jews was reduced to about 8,000 (Rozenbaum 1977).

The process of mobilizing national resentments is exemplified by the way in which anti-semitism was again deployed in the post-communist transformation, for example in the anti-semitic rhetoric of Wałęsa and others in the 1990 presidential election (Gebert 1991) and more generally where the national tragedy of communism has been blamed on 'Jewish Stalinists'. An example of the latter was provided by the Solidarity newspaper, *Gazeta Wyborcza* (30 June 1990), commenting on a memorial being erected to victims of the Kielce pogrom in 1946, when 42 Jewish refugees in transit to Palestine were murdered by locals. *Gazeta Wyborcza* said, 'Fertile ground for anti-Jewish feelings had been created by the Soviets, who ... imposed on the country a regime experienced as alien by the population, among other reasons because both the party apparatus and the security police contained a disproportionately large number of Jews'. This tacit equation of Jews with foreignness permits the suggestion that Polish Communism was the result of a foreign occupation that recruited support among a local 'alien' population.

The durability of anti-semitism is of course a complex phenomenon (e.g. Wistrich 1992), but in this context it might be related to the meanings attributed to transformational risks since it offers a way of explaining, among other things, the discrepancy between market utopias and realities – inequalities of power, cartels, insider dealing, rigging markets and the reproduction of old élites. These can be attributed to a group that is culturally isolated from the 'true Christian nation' and can be represented as symbolizing cosmopolitan modernity (Bauman 1988). Anti-semitic propaganda projects the systemic imbalances of both state socialism and capitalism on to the intervention of Jews who remain eternal outsiders. Alleged Jewish 'cosmopolitanism' is combined with the belief that they are the 'original nation', with primary loyalties lying elsewhere. Thus Jews can be construed as a permanent threat to the authenticity of an imagined homogeneous community (Balibar and Wallerstein 1992:61). 'Cosmopolitan intellectual' is a code word for 'Jewish' in many parts of Eastern Europe and when *Sovetskaya Rossiya* (14 August 1991) claimed that 'the Soviet Union is being enlisted into world government', planned long ago by the 'cosmopolitan tendencies of monopoly capital', few readers would doubt who they were talking about. Thus risks of impersonal and functionally differentiated systems can be re-personalized through conspiracy theories that suggest, *inter alia* that the world is controlled by human agency after all.

Ethno-cultural ways of constructing identity and channelling anger, then, are available in prevailing frames of meaning and can be deployed by movements and politicians. However, this still does not explain why secessionist and exclusive national movements appear when and where they do. An important additional factor is the institutional way in which a systemic vacuum is filled by ethno-cultural movements. National movements and conflicts are likely where power has been lost from the centre to regional élites that are able to mobilize constituencies on the basis of ethnic identification. In the Soviet Union and Yugoslavia, the process of 'cadre nativization' during the 1970s increased the power of regional nomenklatura élites who became increasingly resistant to the centre. As with earlier national movements, the appearance of a rising stratum of intellectuals who develop national consciousness was important, and in Yugoslavia the 1974 Constitution gave extensive powers to republics, in which a local technocratic-managerial stratum began to challenge the position of the post-1945 élite (Vujacic and Zaslavsky 1991). Since the 1960s, figures such as Franjo Tudjman have played a key role in dissident movements, especially in Croatia where a nationalist resurgence provoked a purge in 1971 (MacKenzie 1977).[7] One motive suggested by a number of writers for the rise of ethnic nationalism in Yugoslav republics, consistent with the rising bourgeoisie thesis, was the frustration caused by graduate unemployment. Young humanities graduates turned their skills to reconstructing national culture, such as separating Croatian and Serbian as literary languages, codifying the 'Macedonian' language, 'discovering' the non-Slavic origins of Slovenian and so on. (Glenny 1993; Vujacic and Zaslavsky 1991; Shoup 1989; Nikolic 1989).

It has been noted, though, that despite similarities with earlier national movements, resurgent ethno-cultural nationalism, especially in Yugoslavia, is in some ways peculiar to the conditions of post-communism. Kaldor (1993) argues a kind of transposition thesis, that post-communist nationalism is the corollary of anomie and atomization experienced in communism. This view is shared by others who point out that since no political debate was allowed, the critical examination of identities within a pluralistic culture could not occur, and the public sphere was replaced by the violent politics of identity (e.g. Michnik 1991; Szacki 1991). Self-management in Yugoslavia addressed issues of economic power at a micro-level, but excluded macro-level political questions while encouraging latent integration based on particularism, in ways discussed above (Golubovic 1991). Moreover, the rhetoric of communism could be transposed into exclusive nationalism, as the 'socialist homeland' was converted into the ethnic homeland and class struggle into national struggle, which in the process sustains the vanguard ethic of pre-modern heroism, reducing social complexity to active will.

---

7 Tudjman's 1967 *Velike ideje i mali narodi* (Great Cause and Small Peoples) offered a historical justification for the fascist Croatian state of 1941–45.

A further significant factor is a crisis of legitimacy. Despite periods when the Yugoslavian idea was widely supported, the Federation, like the Soviet state, was ultimately unable to embed itself in social life sufficiently to prevent fragmentation. By the 1970s, the basis of legitimation in Soviet societies, it was argued in Chapter 4, was instrumental and linked to the redistribution of resources and welfare. When debt and economic crisis undermined the redistributive capacities of Soviet states, this was also a precondition for legitimation crisis and national fragmentation (Hroch 1993). Yugoslavian debt rose from $15 billion to $25 billion during 1979–88, and reforms in 1979 that were a condition of IMF debt restructuring involved price liberalization that led to hyperinflation by the later 1980s (Kraft 1991; Nikolic 1989; Shoup 1989). As debt servicing took 20 per cent of GDP, unemployment was about 33 per cent, and real wages fell by 40 per cent between 1978 and 1983, the authority of Prime Minister Ante Marković was seriously undermined. Meanwhile, the dispersal of power to local nomenklatura encouraged the fragmentation of social property in ways that occurred elsewhere (see Chapter 7), and weakened the sovereign power of the Party. Golubovic (1991) argues that the tacit 'agreement' between state and society which tolerated illegal and unofficial means for acquiring income, created a climate of moral nihilism and collapse of values, in which widespread informal privatization of state property occurred. This underlines the point made in Chapter 7, that systemic trust and the faceless co-ordination of action in socially differentiated orders are dependent on the regulatory authority of a legitimate state. A significant legacy of the Soviet period, then, was a legitimacy deficit combined with the rapid propertization of new élites, anarchic markets and potentially high levels of social disorder.

Finally, in addition to the above conditions for the emergence of national movements, Hroch (1993) argues that there must be a catalyst, namely that nationally relevant conflicts are mapped on to linguistic, religious or cultural divisions. An example of this might be where nineteenth-century Serbian peasants in Bosnia were working estates for Muslim landlords, and class conflict and resentments were articulated through national and religious sentiments (Andric 1977). Similarly, secessionist movements were able to mobilize resentment of perceived inequalities between regions. For example, Croatian nationalists in the 1970s claimed that while Croatia earned 40 per cent of Yugoslavian foreign currency, 90 per cent of investment went to Serbia and the southern states (Raditsa 1977). Indeed, Blackburn (1993) suggests that there was a high level of uneven development between the states. Taking the Yugoslavian average per capita social product as 100, Slovenia's was 208, Croatia's 128, Serbia's 101, Montenegro's 74, Macedonia's 74 and Kosovo's 27. However, since there were further regional disparities within Croatia, between the coast and the hinterland, unevenness is not a sufficient explanation for secessionist movements, but rather its combination with ethno-cultural divisions and the factors listed above.

Successful national movements, then, are able to mobilize ethno-cultural territorial grievances in such a way that national identity is selected as a master role, from other available role constellations (Johnston 1994). This enables us to present a tentative multi-causal model of post-communist nationalism, though many of these features will be present elsewhere in the world:

- There are important exogenous background conditions of globalization and sub-national regionalism, combined with the following endogenous factors.
- Social dislocation and reaction-formation draw on primary socialization, solidify ambiguous identities and activate a 'memory' of nationhood (Habermas 1992; Suny 1990; A.D. Smith 1991; Balibar and Wallerstein 1991; Žižek 1990).
- Cultural traditions of ethno-nationalism such as institutional anti-semitism are present (Žižek 1990; Wierorka 1984).
- National consciousness is asserted by intellectuals whose interest in social mobility separates them from titular bureaucracies (Anderson 1993; Hroch 1993; Laitin 1991; Suny 1990).
- Dense social networks transmit national culture (Hroch 1990) in combination with global media (Kaldor 1993).
- The nation-state is destabilized by legitimacy crisis (Hroch 1990; Kaldor 1993; Balibar and Wallerstein 1991).
- There is a catalyst in the form of and uneven development that is mapped on to ethnic–cultural divisions in a way that allows them to be articulated (Balibar 1991; Johnston 1994; Hroch 1993).

SOCIAL THEORY AND STATE SOCIALISM

The appearance of ethno-nationalism in many ways reflects the conditions for the crisis of Soviet societies, and this is an appropriate place to draw together some threads and to highlight central themes in the argument. In Chapter 2, I argued that mainstream sociological theory had focused on Western societies and concepts of differentiation, formal–legal legitimation, welfarism and post-modern consumption cultures, which did not necessarily encompass the repertoire of organizational forms in Soviet societies. One can, however, derive from current sociological theory a set of general propositions that guide analysis of Soviet societies:

- Modern societies differentiate self-steering systems (e.g. markets) where boundaries manage impersonal exchanges, thus avoiding overwhelming complexity, creating multi-level social organizations. Conflict and crisis, then, generally pertain to specific levels and rarely to the entire system.
- Impersonal communication takes place through the steering media of money and power, which are embedded in institutional orders of society, especially in norms, legitimacy and trust which are always conditional.
- The normative structure of modernity has no absolute foundations, following the disintegration of systematic worldviews, which releases the potential for reasoned deliberation on both cognitive and normative matters. Consequently the creation of procedural legitimacy and government by persuasion become central aspects of modern politics. These involve transferring risks back from the economy to the polity through welfare and intervention.
- Moreover, reasoned discourse potentially takes place in various social spaces of civil society – such as collegial associations, locales, action groups, social movements – but these are not separate from the state. On the contrary public spheres are dependent on procedural norms underwritten by citizenship rights.
- This, of course, is an ideal tendency and complex socially differentiated orders run high risks of dislocation, loss of meaning,

disembedding of steering (though this is always relative), social conflicts, de-differentiation through excessive dependence on markets or bureaucracy.

• Actual outcomes will depend upon social movement activity, the balance between public and private spheres, the historical constitution of citizenship rights, and the mode in which the state is embedded in civil society. The state's role as legitimate regulator of the economic subsystem is crucial to the maintenance of impersonal trust.

Soviet systems, however, represented a different form of social organization *sui generis*, a form of counter-modernity that combined complex agro-industrial production with a bureaucratic status system in which value and power accrued to an organizational élite largely via privileges. Their mode of functioning and eventual crisis, though, expands our understanding of both integration and crisis management and the processes and problems of macro-social transformation. Soviet societies, then, were:

• Complex but fused hierarchical systems in which the state was deeply embedded in social steering, and boundaries between subsystems, though present, were weak and permeable.

• The problem of impersonal co-ordination was solved initially through the organizational charisma of the vanguard Party and substantive rather than rational–legal norms.

• However, substantive norms (e.g. building communism) and organizational charisma were subject to routinization and exhaustion. After violent crises of the system (especially 1953–6), these gave way to political clientelism, instrumental social contracts (which had varying degrees of stability), and growing latent differentiation in the second society.

• Latent integration, increasingly symbiotic with official systems, created conditions for the hollowing out of the latter in which the mounting legitimacy deficit prompted a collapse of systemic trust and emphasis on privacy and informality.

• Meanwhile, the redistributive economy, the basis of social contracts, was under dual pressure from declining economic productivity (resulting from contradictions of the planning mechanisms and from the legitimation and motivation crises) combined with increasing global integration via debt, which itself had been a response to problems of social integration.

- The collapse of state socialism was a result of endogenous and exogenous crisis tendencies, combined with a crisis of self-legitimacy among the vanguard which coincided with opportunities for converting political capital in the status system into economic power in a class system. Thus the recomposition of the nomenklatura occurs within a context of increased flexibility and legitimacy since the social systems have undergone a shift towards self-steering, to different degrees in different places.

- Like other systemic transformations, though, this is not achieved without social conflict over ownership of productive property, which has occurred between the state, former nomenklatura and employees. Questions of co-ordination cannot be separated from those of ownership, since the stability of juridical regulation for example is affected by the covert nature of a great deal of asset conversion.

- Further, the evolution of a more socially differentiated system is dependent on the outcome of wider social conflicts over the parameters of 'society' itself, which becomes problematic in the context of globalization and new global–local and national–regional configurations. This is particularly apparent in nationalist conflicts which will influence whether post-communist societies develop in the direction of decentralized pluralism and rights-based state systems or de-differentiated authoritarian societal communities.

A central question raised by the post-communist transformations is whether the new societies will approximate to existing, especially 'Western', social orders. This bears on central sociological issues of convergence, universalism, modernity and post-modernity. I have argued that the anti-communist revolutions marked neither a return to the past nor a convergence with a (Western) present, but the emergence of novel structures in an unprecedented situation. Generalized cultural concepts grounded in the experience of Western capitalism, such as 'post-modernity', are thus singularly unhelpful for understanding these social changes. Issues raised here, such as nomenklatura privatization and consequent juridical ambiguities, the search for new sources of legitimation, and problems of institutionalizing constitutional regulation, all raise questions about what kinds of societal communities are emerging. A differentiation of the state, economy and civil society is dependent on the institutionalization of procedural rationality and citizenship rights. However, this analysis illustrates the dangers of a reversal towards authoritarianism and exclusive conceptions of citizenship that are in part legacies of the mode of integration of the Soviet system. Social outcomes will be a result of social struggles and movements that deploy and re-combine cultural values and resources, which in turn affect the stability of the process of social differentiation. Among these resources are the prevailing legitimating norms which in newly democratic orders create the potential – though not, of course, the necessity – for opening out more plural polities, collegial forms of association and universalistic societies.

Bibliography

Adam, J. (1987) 'The Hungarian Economic Reform of the 1980s', *Soviet Studies*, 39:610–27.

—— (1993) 'Transformation to a Market Economy in the Former Czechoslovakia', *Europe–Asia Studies*, 45,4:627–45.

Adamik, M. (1993) 'Feminism in Hungary' in Funk and Mueller (eds), *Gender Politics and Post-Communism*, pp. 207–12.

Adorno, T. and Horkheimer, M. (1973), *Dialectics of Enlightenment*, London: New Left Books; originally published in 1944.

Adriaansens, H.P. (1980) *Talcott Parsons and the Conceptual Dilemma*, London: Routledge.

Aganbegyan, A. (1988) *The Challenge: The Economics of Perestroika*, London: Hutchinson.

Albrow, M. (1994) 'Accounting for Organizational Feeling' in Ray and Reed (eds), *Organizing Modernity*, pp. 98–121.

Alexander, G. and Skapska G. (eds) (1994) *A Fourth Way? Privatization, Property and the Emergence of New Market Economies*, London: Routledge.

Alexander, J.C. (1978/1990) 'Formal and Substantive Voluntarism in the Work of Talcott Parsons: A Theoretical and Ideological Reinterpretation', *American Journal of Sociology* 43:177–98, reprinted in Colomy, P. (ed.), *Neo-Functionalist Sociology*, Aldershot: Edward Elgar.

—— (1984) 'Three Models of Culture and Society Relations: Toward an Analysis of Watergate', *Sociological Theory*, 3:290–314.

—— (1995) 'Modern, Anti, Post, Neo', *New Left Review*, 210:63–101.

—— and Colomy, P. (eds) (1990) *Differentiation Theory and Social Change: Comparative and Historical Perspectives*, New York: Columbia University Press.

Almond, G. (1987) 'The Development of Political Development', in Weiner, M and Huntington, S. (eds), *Understanding Political Development*, Boston: Little, Brown.

Anderson, B. (1993) *Imagined Communities*, London: Verso.

Andreff, W. (1992) 'Disappearing Soviet Empire: A Burdening Legacy of COMECON', Cracow: Freidrich Ebert Stiftung Seminar Papers no.18, pp. 7–49.

Andreski, S. (1970) 'Kleptocracy as a System of Government', in Heiden-heimer, A.J. (ed.), *Political Corruption: Readings in Comparative Analysis*, New York: Holt Rinehart & Winston, pp. 346–57.

Andrew, C. and Gordievsky, O. (1991) *The KGB*, London: Sceptre.

Andric, V. (1977) *Bosnian Story*, Belgrade: Angencija Jugoslavenska Autoska.

Anson, J., Todorova, E., Kressel, G., and Gevov, N. (eds) (1993) *Ethnicity and Politics in Bulgaria and Israel*, Aldershot: Avebury.

Antowska-Bartosiewicz, I. and Małecki, W. (1992) *Poland's External Debt Problem by the End of 1991*, Warsaw: Friedrich Ebert Stiftung.

Appadurai, A. (1990) 'Disjuncture and Difference in the Global Cultural Economy', in Featherstone (ed.), *Global Culture*, pp. 295–310.

Arato, A. (1981) 'Civil Society Against the State: Poland 1980–81', *Telos*, Spring 47:23–47.

―― (1982) 'Critical Sociology and Authoritarian State Socialism', in Thompson and Held, *Habermas: Critical Debates*, pp. 196–218.

―― (1991) 'Social Theory, Civil Society and the Transformation of Authoritarian Socialism', in Fehér and Arato (eds), *The Crisis in Eastern Europe*, pp. 1–26.

―― (1994) 'Revolution and Restoration: on the origins of right-wing radical ideology in Hungary', in Bryant and Mokrzycki (eds), *The New Great Transformation*, pp. 99–119.

Archer, M. (1990) 'Theory, Culture and Post-Industrial Society', in Featherstone (ed.), *Global Culture*, pp. 97–112.

Arendt, H. (1967) *Origins of Totalitarianism*, London: Allen & Unwin.

Arnason, J. (1991) 'Modernity as a Project and Field of Tensions', in Honneth and Joas (eds), *Communicative Action*, pp. 181–213.

―― (1993) *The Future that Failed: Origins and Destinies of the Soviet Model*, London: Routledge.

Arrighi, G. (1991) 'World Income Inequalities and the Future of Socialism', *New Left Review*, 189:28–63.

Ascherson, N. (1988) *Struggles for Poland*, London: Pan Books.

Ash, T.G. (1990) *We the People: The Revolutions of '89*, London: Granta Books.

Atta, D. van (1989–90) 'The USSR as a "Weak State": Agrarian Origins of Resistance to Perestroika', *World Politics*, 42:129–50.

Bahro, R. (1977) *The Alternative in Eastern Europe*, trans. D. Fernbach, London: New Left Books.

Bakos, G. (1994) 'The Hungarian Transition After Three Years', *Europe–Asia Studies*, 46,7:1189–214.

Balcerowicz, L. (1993) *Common Fallacies in the Debate on the Economic*

Transition in Central and Eastern Europe, London: EBRD working paper 11.

Balibar, E. (1991) '*Es gibt keinen Staat in Europa*: Racism and Poplitics in Europe Today', *New Left Review*, 186:5–20.

—— and Wallerstein, I. (1991) *Race, Nation and Class: Ambiguous Identities*, London: Verso.

Barker, R. (1990) *Political Legitimacy and the State*, Oxford: Clarendon Press.

Batt, J. (1991) *East Central Europe from Reform to Transition*, London: Pinter.

Battle, J. (1988) 'Uskorenie, Glasnost', and Perestroika: the Pattern of Reform under Gorbachev', *Soviet Studies*, 40:366–84.

Baudrillard, J. (1983) *For a Critique of the Political Economy of the Sign*, trans. C. Levin, St. Louis, MO: Telos Press.

Bauer, T. (1978) 'The Hungarian Alternative to Soviet-Type Planning', *Journal of Contemporary Economics*, 7,3:304–16.

Bauman, Z. (1979) 'Comment on Eastern Europe', *Studies in Comparative Communism*, XII 2–3:184–9.

—— (1984) in the 'Review Symposium on Soviet-type Societies', *Telos* 60:173–8.

—— (1988) 'Exit Visas and Entry Tickets: the Paradoxes of Jewish Assimilation', *Telos* 77:45–79.

—— (1989) 'Poland: on its own', *Telos*, Spring, 79:47–62.

—— (1992) *Intimations of Postmodernity*, London: Routledge.

—— (1994) 'After the patronage state: a model in search of class interests', in Bryant and Mokrzycki (eds), *The New Great Transformation*, pp. 14–35.

Bayard, C. (1992–3) 'The Changing Character of the Prague Intelligentsia', *Telos*, 94:131–44.

Beck, C. (1963) 'Bureaucracy and Political Development in Eastern Europe', in LaPalombara (ed.), *Bureaucracy and Political Development*, pp. 268–300.

Beck, U. (1992) *Risk Society: Towards a New Modernity*, trans. M. Ritter, London: Sage.

Beetham, D. (1992) *The Legitimation of Power*, London: Macmillan.

Bell, D. (1973) *The Coming of Post-Industrial Society*, New York: Basic Books.

—— (1987) 'The world and the US in 2013', *Daedalus*, 116,3:1–32.

Ben-David, J. (1962–3) 'Professions in the Class System of Present-Day Societies', *Current Sociology*, XII:247–330.

Benhabib, S. (1981) 'Modernity and the Aporias of Critical Theory', *Telos*, 49:38–61.

Berber, B. (1992) 'Neofunctionalism and the Theory of the Social System', in Colomy (ed.), *TheDynamics of Social Systems*, pp.36–55.

Berliner, J. (1952) 'The Informal Organization of the Soviet Firm', *Quarterly Journal of Economics*, 46:342–65.

Berman, M. (1985) *All That is Solid Melts into Air*, London: Verso.

Bessonova O.E. (1988) *Sovetskaya model' zhilishchnykh otnoshenii: Genezis sushchnnosti puti perestroika*, Novosibirsk: USSR Academy of Sciences, Siberian Branch, Institute of Economics and Socio-Political Processes.

Bienefeld, M. (1994) 'Capitalism and the Nation State in the Dog Days of the Twentieth Century', *Socialist Register*, London: Merlin Press, pp. 94–129.

Biernat, S. (1994) 'The Uneasy Breach with Socialized Ownership: Legal Aspects of Privatization of State-owned Enterprises in Poland', in Alexander and Skapska (eds), *A Fourth Way?*, pp. 19–32.

Birman, I. (1980) 'The Financial Crisis in the USSR', *Soviet Studies*, 32,1: 84–105.

—— (1988) 'The Imbalance of the Soviet Economy', *Soviet Studies*, 40,2: 210–21.

—— and Clarke R.A. (1985) 'Inflation and the Money Supply in the Soviet Economy', *Soviet Studies*, 37,4:494–504.

Black, M. (1961) 'Some Questions About Parsons' Theories', in Black (ed.), *The Social Theories of Talcott Parsons*, pp. 268–88.

—— (ed.) (1961) *The Social Theories of Talcott Parsons: a Critical Examination*, Englewood Cliffs, NJ: Prentice-Hall.

Blackburn, R. (1993) 'The Break-up of Yugoslavia and the Fate of Bosnia', *New Left Review*, 199:100–119.

Blanchard, O., Dornbusch R., Krugman P., Layard, R. and Summers, L. (1991) *Reform in Eastern Europe*, Cambridge, MA: MIT Press.

Blumenberg, H. (1985) *Work on Myth*, trans. R. Wallace, Cambridge, MA: MIT Press.

Boella, L. (1979) 'Eastern European Societies', *Telos*, 41:59–75.

Bogusak, M., Gabal, I. and Rak, V. (1990) *Czecho-Slovakia: Survey Report*, Prague: Association for Independent Social Analysis.

Bönker, F. (1993) 'External Determinants of the Patterns and Outcomes of East European Transitions', paper to conference on Transforming Post-Socialist Societies, Cracow Academy of Economics, October.

Böröcz, J. (1993) 'Simulating the Great Transformation: Property Change Under Prolonged Informality in Hungary', *Archives Européennes de Sociologie*, XXXIV, 1:81–107.

Borucha-Arctowa, M. (1994) 'Social Consciousness in Transition: Toward a New Economic and Political System', in Alexander and Skapska (eds), *A Fourth Way?*, pp. 150–62.

Bottomore, T.B. (1992) 'Citizenship and Social Class, Forty Years On', in

Marshall, T.H. and Bottomore, T.B., *Citizenship and Social Class*, London: Pluto Press, pp. 55–93.

Brand, A. (1990) *The Force of Reason, An Introduction to Habermas' Theory of Communicative Action*, London: Allen & Unwin.

Bratkowski, A. (1993) 'The Shock of Transformation or the Transformation of Shock? The Big Bang in Poland and Official Statistics', *Communist Economies and Economic Transformation*, 5,1:5–28.

Breslauer, G. (1976) 'Khrushchev Reconsidered', *Problems of Communism*, XXV,5:18–34.

Bromke, A. (1976) 'A New Juncture in Poland', *Problems of Communism*, XXV,5:1–18.

Brown, J.F. (1994) *Hopes and Shadows: Eastern Europe After Communism*, London: Duke University Press.

Brown P. and Crompton, R. (eds), (1994) *A New Europe? Economic Restructuring and Social Exclusion*, London: UCL Press.

Brubaker, R. (1994) 'Nationhood and the National Question in the Soviet Union and Post-Soviet Europe', *Theory and Society*, 23,1:47–78.

Brucan, S. (1986) *World Socialism at the Crossroads*, London: Praeger.

Brus, W. (1988) 'Enterprise and Socialism – are they compatible?, *Praxis International*, 8,1:99–108.

Bryant, C. (1994) 'Economic Utopianism and Sociological Realism: strategies for transformation in East–Central Europe', in Bryant and Mokrzycki (eds), *The New Great Transformation*, pp. 58–77.

—— and Mokrzycki, E. (eds) (1994) *The New Great Transformation, Change and Continuity in East–Central Europe*, London: Routledge.

Bugajski, J. and Pollack, M. (1989) *East European Fault Lines*, Boulder, CO: Westview.

Bunce, V. (1983) 'The Political Economy of the Brezhnev Era: The Rise and Fall of Corporatism', *British Journal of Political Science*, 13:129–58.

Burnham, J. (1964) *The Managerial Revolution*, Harmondsworth: Penguin.

Burrell, G. (1988) 'Modernism, Postmodernism and Organizational Analysis: The Contribution of Michel Foucault', *Organization Studies*, 9,2:221–35.

Callinicos, A. (1991) *The Revenge of History: Marxism and the Eastern European Revolutions*, Cambridge: Polity.

Campbell, J. (1992) 'The fiscal crisis of post-communist states', *Telos*, 93: 89–110.

Cancian, F. (1960) 'The Functional Analysis of Change', *American Sociological Review*, XXV, 6:818–26.

Carlo, A. (1989) 'Contradictions of Perestroika', *Telos*, Spring, 79:29–48.

Castells, E. (1989) *The Informational City*, Oxford: Basil Blackwell.

Castle-Kanerova, M. (1992) 'Social Policy in Czechoslovakia', in Deacon et al. (eds), *The New Eastern Europe*, pp. 91–117.

Castoriadis C. (1978/9) 'The Social Regime in Russia', *Telos*, 38:32–47.

Caute, D. (1988) *The Fellow-Travellers: Intellectual Friends of Communism*, London: Yale University Press.

Chalcraft, D. (1994) 'Bringing the Text Back In: On Ways of Reading the Two Editions of the Protestant Ethic', in Ray and Reed (eds), *Organizing Modernity*, pp. 16–45.

Chan, K. (1995) 'Poland at the Crossroads: The 1993 General Election', *Europe–Asia Studies*, 47, 1:123–46.

Chardanova, T. (1993) 'Irregular Economic Activity: The Case of Bulgarian Privatization', in Ringen and Wallace (eds), *Societies in Transition*, pp. 163–74.

Chirot, D. (1991) 'What Happened in Eastern Europe in 1989?', in Chirot (ed.), *The Crisis of Leninism and the Decline of the Left*, Seattle, WA: University of Washington Press.

Ciechocinska, M. (1987) 'Government interventions to balance housing supply and urban population growth: Warsaw', *International Journal of Urban and Regional Research*, 11,1:9–26.

Cirtautas, A.M. (1994) 'In pursuit of the democratic interest: the institutionalisation of parties and interests in Eastern Europe', in Bryant and Mokrzycki (eds), *The New Great Transformation*, pp. 36–57.

Clarke, S., Fairbrother, P., Borisov, V. and Bizukov, P. (1994) 'The Privatization of Industrial Enterprises in Russia: Four Case Studies', *Europe–Asia Studies*, 46, 2:179–215.

Clegg, S. (1975) *Power, Rule and Domination: A Critical and Empirical Understanding of Power in Sociological Theory and Organizational Life*, London: Routledge.

—— (1989) *Frameworks of Power*, London: Sage.

—— (1994) 'Max Weber and Contemporary Sociology of Organizations', in Ray and Reed (eds), *Organizing Modernity*, pp. 46–80.

Cliff, T. (1968) *Russia: A Marxist Analysis*, London: Pluto Press.

Cohen, J. and Arato, A. (1992) *Civil Society and Political Theory* Cambridge, MA: MIT Press.

Cohen, S.F. (1986) 'Stalin's Terror as Social History', *The Russian Review*, 45:375–84.

Colomy, P. (1990) 'The Neofunctionalist Movement', *Neofunctionalist Sociology*, Aldershot: Edward Elgar pp. xi–xli.

—— (ed.) (1992) *The Dynamics of Social Systems*, London: Sage.

Comisso, E. (1990) 'Crisis in Socialism or Crisis of Socialism?', *World Politics*, 42:563–96.

Connor, W.D. (1988) *Socialism's Dilemmas: State and Society in the Soviet Bloc*, New York: Columbia University Press.

—— (1991) *The Accidental Proletariat: Workers, Politics and Crisis in Gorbachev's Russia*, Princeton, NJ: Princeton University Press.

Conquest, R. (1990) *The Great Terror: A Reassessment*, London: Hutchinson.

Cook, L. (1992) 'Brezhnev's Social Contract and Gorbachev's Reforms', *Soviet Studies*, 44,1:37–56.

—— (1994) *The Soviet Social Contract and Why it Failed*, London: Harvester.

Cook P. and Kirkpatrick, C. (eds) (1988) *Privatization in Less Developed Countries*, London: Harvester.

Corrin C. (ed.) (1992) *Superwoman and the Double Burden: Women's experience of change in Central and Eastern Europe and the former Soviet Union*, London: Scarlet Press.

—— (1993) 'Gendered Identities: Women's Experience of Change in Hungary', in Rai et al. (eds), *Women in the Face of Change*, pp. 167–85.

Crook, S., Pakulski. J. and Waters, M. (1992) *Postmodernization: Change in Advanced Societies*, London: Sage.

Crozier, E. and Friedberg. E. (1977) *L'Acteur et le système*, Paris: Editions du seuil.

Csaba, L. (ed.) (1991) *Systemic Change and Stabilization in Eastern Europe*, Aldershot: Dartmouth.

Csaszi, L. and Kullberg, P. (1985) 'Reforming health care in Hungary', *Social Science and Medicine*, 21,8:849–55.

Dąbrowski, M. (ed.) (1993) *The Gaidar Programme: Lessons for Eastern Europe*, Warsaw: Friedrich Ebert Stiftung.

Dahrendorf, R. (1990) *Reflections on the Revolution in Europe*, London: Chatto & Windus.

Dallago, B. (1990) *The Irregular Economy*, Aldershot: Dartmouth.

Danecki, J. (1993) 'Social Costs of System Transformation in Poland', in Ringen and Wallace (eds), *Societies in Transition*, pp. 47–60.

Dangschat, J. (1987) 'Social Disparities in a "Socialist City": Warsaw', *International Journal for Urban and Regional Research*, 11:37–60.

Daniels, R. (1993) *The End of the Communist Revolution*, London: Rout ledge.

Davies, T. (1988) 'A Framework for Relating Social Welfare Policy to Economic Change: Evidence from Hungarcity', in Millard, F. (ed.), *Social Welfare and the Market*, London: London School of Economics.

Davis, H. and Scase, R. (1985) *Western Capitalism and State Socialism* Oxford: Blackwell.

Deacon, B. (1992) 'East European Welfare: Past, Present and Future in Comparative Context', in Deacon, B. et al. (eds), *The New Eastern Europe*, pp. 1–30.

——, Castle-Kanerova, M., Manning, N., Millard, F., Orosz, E., Szalai, J. and

Vidinova, A. (eds) (1992) *The New Eastern Europe: Social Policy Past, Present and Future*, London: Sage.

—— and Vidinova, A. (1992) 'Social Policy in Bulgaria', in Deacon et al. (eds), *The New Eastern Europe*, pp. 67–90.

Delorme, R. (1992) 'Challenges for Economic Policy-making in Central and Eastern European Countries with a Special Reference to Poland', *Transformation Processes in Eastern Europe*, Warsaw: Friedrich Ebert Foundation Seminar Papers no. 15.

Deutscher, I. (1990) *Stalin*, Harmondsworth: Penguin.

Devereux, E.C. (1961) 'Parsons', Sociological Theory', in Black (ed.), *The Social Theories of Talcott Parsons*, pp. 1–63.

DiMaggio, P., and Powell, W. (1983) 'The Iron Cage Revisited', *American Sociological Review*, 48,1:147–60.

Disco, C. (1987) 'Intellectuals in Advanced Capitalism: capital, closure, and the new-class thesis', in Eyerman, R., Svensson, L. and Söderqvist, T. (eds), *Intellectuals, Universities, and the State in Western Modern Societies*, Berkeley, CA: University of California Press, pp. 50–77.

Djilas, M. (1957) *The New Class: An Analysis of the Communist System*, London: Thames & Hudson.

Drakulic, S. (1993) 'Women and the New Democracy in the Former Yugoslavia', in Funk and Mueller (eds), *Gender Politics and Post-Communism*, pp. 123–30.

Du Gay, P. and Salaman, G. (1992) 'The Cult[ure] of the Customer', *Journal of Management Studies*, 29:5: 615–33.

Dunham, V. (1976) *In Stalin's Time*, Cambridge: Cambridge University Press.

Durkheim, E. (1984) *Division of Labour in Society*, New York: Free Press.

Dux, G. (1991) 'Communicative Reason and Interest', in Honneth and Joas (eds), *Communicative Action*, pp. 74–96.

EBRD (1994) *Transition Report: Economic Transition in Eastern Europe and the Former Soviet Union*, London: EBRD.

Eccles, R. and Crane, D. (1988) *Doing Deals: Investment Banks at Work*, Boston, MA: Harvard Business School.

Eder, K. (1985) *Geschichte als Lernprozess?*, Frankfurt: Suhrkamp.

Eisenstadt, S.N. (1990) 'Modes of Structural Differentiation, Elite Structure and Cultural Visions', in Alexander and Colomy (eds), *Differentiation Theory and Social Change*, pp. 17–51.

—— (1992), 'The Breakdown of Communist Regimes and the Vicissitudes of Modernity', *Daedalus*, Spring, 121,2:21–41.

Eldridge, J. (1994) 'Work and Authority. Some Weberian Perspectives', in Ray and Reed (eds), *Organizing Modernity*, pp. 81–97.

Eley, G. (1986) 'History With the Politics Left Out – Again?', *The Russian Review*, 45:385–94.

Ellman, M. (1975) 'Did the Agricultural Surplus Provide Resources for the Increase in Investment in the USSR?', *Economic Journal*, 85:844–64.

Elson, D. (1988) 'Market Socialism or Socialization of the Market?', *New Left Review*, 172:3–44.

Ely, J. (1992) 'The Politics of "Civil Society"', *Telos*, 93:173–91.

Ernste, H. and Meier, V. (eds) (1992) *Regional Development and Contemporary Industrial Response*, London: Belhaven.

Evans, A. (1986) 'The Decline of Developed Socialism? Some Trends in Recent Soviet Ideology', *Soviet Studies*, 38,1:1–23.

Fainsod, M. (1963) 'Bureaucracy and Modernization: The Russian and Soviet Case', in LaPalombara (ed.), *Bureaucracy and Political Development*, pp. 233–67.

Featherstone, M. (1988) 'In Pursuit of the Postmodern', *Theory, Culture and Society*, 5,2/3:195–216.

—— (1990) (ed.) *Global Culture: Nationalism, Globalization and Modernity*, London: Sage.

Federowicz, M. (1994) *Poland's Economic Order: Persistence and Transformation*, Warsaw: Friedrich Ebert Stiftung.

Fehér, F. (1979) 'Kádárism as the Model State of Khrushchevism', *Telos*, 40:19–31.

—— (1982) 'Paternalism as a Mode of Legitimation in Soviet-type Societies', in Rigby and Fehér (eds), *Political Legitimation in Communist Societies*, pp. 64–81.

—— (1986) 'In the Bestarium: A Contribution to the Cultural Anthropology of "Real Socialism"', in Fehér and Heller (eds), *Eastern Left – Western Left*, pp. 260–78.

—— and Arato A. (eds) (1989) *Gorbachev: The Debate*, New York: Humanities Press.

—— and Arato A. (eds) (1991) *The Crisis in Eastern Europe*, New Brunswick, NJ: Transaction Books.

—— and Heller, A. (1986) *Eastern Left–Western Left*, Cambridge: Polity.

—— , Heller, A. and Márkus, G. (1984) *Dictatorship Over Needs: An Analysis of Soviet Societies*, Oxford: Basil Blackwell.

Fields, G. (1991) 'The Road from Gdansk: How Solidarity Found a Haven in the Marketplace', *Monthly Review*, 43:95–121.

Filatotchev, I., Buck, T. and Wright, M. (1992a) 'Privatization and Buy-Outs in the USSR', *Soviet Studies*, 4,2:265–82.

—— (1992b) 'Privatization and Entrepreneurship in the Break-up of the USSR', *World Economy*, 15,4:505–24.

Filtzer, D. (1991) 'Contradictions of a Marketless Market: Self-financing in the Soviet Industrial Enterprise, 1986–90', *Soviet Studies*, 43,6:989–1009.

—— (1992a) 'Economic Reform and Production Relations in Soviet Indus try, 1986–90', in Smith and Thompson (eds), *Labour in Transition*, pp. 110–48.

—— (1992b) *Soviet Workers and De-Stalinization*, Cambridge: Cambridge University Press.

Fischer, S., Summers, L. and Nordhaus, W. (1992) 'Stabilization and economic reform in Russia', *Brookings Papers on Economic Activity*, 1:77–126.

Fitzpatrick S. (1978) 'Cultural Revolution as Class War', in Fitzpatrick (ed.), *Cultural Revolution in Russia, 1928–1931*, pp. 8–40.

—— (ed.) (1978) *Cultural Revolution in Russia, 1928–1931*, London: Indiana University Press.

—— (1979a) *Education and Social Mobility in the Soviet Union 1921–1934*, Cambridge: Cambridge University Press.(

—— 1979b) 'Stalin and the Making of a New Elite', *Slavonic Review*, 38:377–402.

—— (1986) 'New Perspectives on Stalinism', *The Russian Review*, 45:357–73.

Flaherty, P. (1988) 'Restructuring the Soviet State: Organizational Politics in the Gorbachev Era', *Socialist Review*, London: Merlin Press, pp. 90–131.

—— (1992) 'Cycles and Crises in Statist Economies', *Review of Radical Political Economics*, 24:111–53.

Flakierski, H. (1979) *Economic Reform and Income Distribution: A Case Study in Hungary and Poland*, White Plains, NY: M.E. Sharpe.

Foucault, M. (1979) *Discipline and Punish: The Birth of the Prison*, Harmondsworth: Penguin.

—— (1980) *Power/Knowledge*, Brighton: Harvester.

Fox, A. (1974) *Beyond Contract: Work, Power and Trust Relations*, London: Faber & Faber.

Fraenkel, E. (1941) *The Dual State*, New York: Oxford University Press.

Frank, G. (1991) 'No Escape from the Laws of World Economics', *Review of African Political Economy*, 50:21–32.

Fraser, N. (1989) *Unruly Practices: Power, Discourse and Gender in Contemporary Social Theory*, Cambridge: Polity.

Friedgut, T. and Siegelbaum, L. (1990) 'Perestroika from Below: the Soviet Miners' Strike and its Aftermath', *New Left Review*, 181:5–32.

Friedrich, C.J. and Brzezinski, Z.K. (1964) *Totalitarian Dictatorship and Autocracy*, New York: Praeger.

Fukuyama, F. (1992) *The End of History and the Last Man*, New York: Free Press.

Funk, N. and Mueller, M. (eds) (1993) *Gender Politics and Post-Communism: Reflections from Eastern Europe and the Former Soviet Union*, London: Routledge.

Fuszara, M. (1993) 'Abortion and the Formation of the Public Sphere in

Poland', in Funk and Mueller (eds), *Gender Politics and Post-Communism*, pp. 241–52.

Galbraith, J.K. (1972) *The New Industrial State*, London: Deutsch.

Gebert, K. (1991) 'Anti-Semitism in the 1990 Polish Presidential Election', *Social Research*, 58,4:723–55.

Gelb, M. (1993) '"Karelian Fever": The Finnish Immigrant Community during Stalin's Purges', *Europe–Asia Studies*, 45,6:1091–1116.

Gellner, E. (1994) *Conditions of Liberty: Civil Society and its Rivals*, Harmondsworth: Penguin.

Gerner, K. and Hedlund, S. (1989) *Ideology and Rationality in the Soviet Model: A Legacy for Gorbachev*, London: Routledge.

Getty, J.A. (1985) *Origins of the Great Purges: The Soviet Communist Party Reconsidered, 1933–38*, Cambridge: Cambridge University Press.

Giddens, A. (1979) *Central Problems in Sociological Theory*, London: Macmillan.

—— (1982) *Profiles and Critiques in Social Theory*, London: Macmillan.

—— (1984) *The Constitution of Society*, Cambridge: Polity.

—— (1990) *The Consequences of Modernity*, Cambridge: Polity.

—— (1991) *Modernity and Self-Identity*, Cambridge: Polity.

Ginzburg, E. (1981) *Within the Whirlwind*, London: Collins-Harvill.

Gitelman, Z. (1992) 'Ethnopolitics and the Future of the Former Soviet Union', in Gitelman (ed.), *The Politics of Nationality in the Erosion of the USSR*, London: Macmillan.

Glasman, M. (1994) 'The Great Deformation: Polanyi, Poland and the Terrors of Planned Spontaneity', *New Left Review*, 204:59–86.

Glaziev, S. (1991) 'Transformation of the Soviet Economy: Economic Reforms and Structural Crisis', *National Economic Review*, 138:97–108.

Glenny, M. (1990) *The Rebirth of History: Eastern Europe in the Age of Democracy*, London: Penguin.

—— (1993) *The Fall of Yugoslavia*, Harmondsworth: Penguin.

Goldman, M. (1991) *What Went Wrong with Perestroika*, London: Norton.

Goldmann, J. and Kouba, K. (1969) *Economic Growth in Czechoslovakia*, Prague: Academia.

Golubovic, Z. (1991) 'Yugoslav Society and "Socialism": the Present-Day Crisis and the Possibilities for Evolution', in Fehér and Arato (eds), *The Crisis in Eastern Europe*, pp.393–454.

Gomulka, S. (1986) *Growth, Innovation and Reform in Eastern Europe*, Brighton: Harvester.

Gooding, J. (1990) 'Gorbachev and Democracy', *Soviet Studies*, 42,2:195–231.

Gorbachev, M. (1986) 'Politicheskii doklad Tsentralnogo Komiteta KPSS XXVII s"yezdu Kommunisticheskoi partii Sovetskogo Soyuza' [Political

Report of the CPSU Central Committee to the 27th Congress of the CPSU], *Pravda*, 25 February, pp. 2–10.

Gorlice, J. (1986) 'Introduction to the Hungarian Democratic Opposition', *Berkeley Journal of Sociology*, 31:111–65.

Gouldner, A. (1976) *The Dialectic of Ideology and Technology*, London: Macmillan.

Goven, J. (1993) 'Gender Politics in Hungary: Autonomy and Antifeminism', in Funk and Mueller (eds), *Gender Politics and Post-Communism*, pp. 224–40.

Granovetter, M. (1992) 'Economic Action and Social Structure: The Problem of Embeddedness', in Granovetter, M. and Swedberg, R. (eds), *The Sociology of Economic Life*, Boulder, CO: Westview, pp. 53–84.

Greenfeld, L. (1977) 'The Second Economy of the USSR', *Problems of Communism*, 26,5:25–40.

—— (1992) *Nationalism: Five Roads to Modernity*, Cambridge, MA: Harvard University Press.

Grossman, G. (ed.) (1960) *Value and Plan: Economic Calculation and Organization in Eastern Europe* Berkeley, CA: University of California Press.

Grzegorz, T. and Jedzjczak, G. (1991) 'Privatization and the Private Sector', in Blazyca, G. and Rapacki, R. (eds), *Poland into the 1990s: Economy in Transition*, New York: St. Martin's.

Guber, A. (1985) *Intensified Economy and Programmes in Science and Technology*, Moscow: Novosti.

Habermas, J. (1976) *Legitimation Crisis*, London: Heinemann,

—— (1979) *Communication and Evolution of Society*, London: Heinemann.

—— (1982) 'Reply to My Critics', in Thompson and Held (eds), *Habermas: Critical Debates*, pp. 219–83.

—— (1984) *The Theory of Communicative Action: Reason and the Rationalization of Society*, vol.1, London: Heinemann.

—— (1989) *The Theory of Communicative Action, Lifeworld and System: A Critique of Functionalist Reason*, vol.2, Cambridge: Polity.

—— (1990) 'What Does Socialism Mean Today? The Rectifying Revolution and the Need for New Thinking on the Left', *New Left Review*, 183:3–22.

—— (1991) 'A Reply', in Honneth and Joas (eds), *Communicative Action*, pp. 214–64.

—— (1992) 'Citizenship and National Identity: Some Reflections on the Future of Europe', *Praxis International*, 12,1:1–19.

—— (1994) *The Past As Future*, Cambridge: Polity.

Hacker, A. (1961) 'Sociology and Ideology', in Black (ed.), *The Social Theories of Talcott Parsons*, pp. 289–310.

Hall, S. (1993) 'The Question of Cultural Identity', in Hall, S., Held D. and

McGrew, T. (eds), *Modernity and its Futures*, Cambridge: Polity, pp. 274–316.

Hankiss, E. (1990) *East European Alternatives: Are there any?* Oxford: Clarendon Press.

—— (1991) 'The "Second Society": Is There an Alternative Social Model Emerging in Contemporary Hungary?', in Fehér and Arato (eds), *The Crisis in Eastern Europe*, pp. 303–34.

Harrison, M. (1993) 'Soviet Economic Growth Since 1928: The Alternative Statistics of G I Khanin', *Europe–Asia Studies* 45,1: 141–68.

Harvey, D. (1994) *The Condition of Post-Modernity*, Oxford: Basil Blackwell.

Hauslohner, P. (1989) 'Gorbachev's Social Contract', in Fehér and Arato (eds), *Gorbachev: the Debate*, pp. 83–123.

Hausner J. (1992) *Populist Threat in Transformation of Socialist Society*, Warsaw: Friedrich-Ebert Foundation.

—— and Mosur, G. (eds) (1993) *Transformation Processes in Eastern Europe: Western Perspectives and the Polish Experience*, Cracow: Institute of Political Studies.

—— and Nielsen, K. (1992) 'The Post-Socialist Transformation Process: Systemic Vacuum, Search Processes, Implementation Problems and Social Struggle', presented at the Conference on Post-Socialism: Problems and Prospects, Charlotte Mason College, Cumbria, UK, July.

—— and Wojtyna, A. (1991) 'Trends and Perspectives in the development of a System of Interest Representation in Post-Socialist Society', in J. Hausner (ed.), *System of Interest Representation in Poland*, Cracow: Cracow Academy of Economics.

Havel, V. (1988) 'Anti-Political Politics', in Keane (ed.), *Civil Society*, pp. 381–98.

Hay, C. (1993) 'The Political Economy of State Failure in Britain's Post-War Reconstruction', Paper to the ECPR Conference on the Political Economy of Post-War Reconstruction, Leiden, Netherlands, April.

—— (1994) 'The Structural and Ideological Contradictions of Britain's Post-War Reconstruction', *Capital and Class*, 54:25–66.

—— (1995) 'Rethinking Crisis: Narratives of the New Right and Constructions of Crisis', *Rethinking Marxism*, vol. 8.

Hegedüs, J. (1987) 'Reconsidering the Roles of State and Market in Socialist Housing Systems', *International Journal of Urban and Regional Research*, 11:79–97.

—— and Tosics, I. (1990) 'Disintegration of the Eastern European Housing Model', in Andrusz, G., Harloe, H. and Szelenyi, I. (eds), *Restructuring Socialist Cities*, Oxford: Basil Blackwell.

Heinen, J. (1993) 'Employment Policy and the Female Workforce in Poland', in Ringen and Wallace (eds), *Societies in Transition: East–Central Europe Today*, pp. 61–70.

Held, D. (1991) 'Democracy, the Nation-State and the Global System', in Held (ed.), *Political Theory Today*, pp. 197–235.

—— (ed.) (1991), *Political Theory Today*, Cambridge: Polity.

Heller, A. (1982) 'Phases of Legitimation in Soviet-Type Societies', in Rigby and Fehér (eds), *Political Legitimation*, pp. 45–63.

—— (1988) 'On Formal Democracy', in Keane (ed.), *Civil Society and the State*, pp. 129–46.

Hewett, E.A. (1988) *Reforming the Soviet Economy: Equality vs Efficiency*, Washington, DC: Brookings.

Hill, R.J. (1988) 'The *Apparatchiki* in Soviet Political Development', in Potichnyj, P. (ed.), *The Soviet Union: Party and Society*, Cambridge: Cambridge University Press, pp. 3–25.

—— (1992) 'Communist Politics: An Evolutionary Approach', *Journal of Communist Studies*, 8:3–22.

—— and Zielonka, J. (eds) (1990) *Restructuring Eastern Europe: Towards a New European Order*, Aldershot: Edward Elgar.

Hirszowicz, M. (1986) *Coercion and Control in Communist Society: The Visible Hand of Bureaucracy*, Brighton: Harvester.

Holmes, L. (1993) *The End of Communist Power*, Cambridge: Polity.

Holmes, S. (1994) 'The End of Decommunization', *Eastern European Constitutional Review*, 3,3/4:33–6.

Holton, R.J. (1986) 'Talcott Parsons and the theory of economy and society', in Holton and Turner (eds), *Talcott Parsons on Economy and Society*, pp. 25–106.

—— (1990) 'Problems of crisis and normalcy in the contemporary world', in Alexander, J. and Sztompka, P. (eds), *Rethinking Progress*, Boston, MA: Unwin Hyman, pp. 39–52.

—— and Turner, B. (1986) 'Against Nostalgia: Talcott Parsons and a sociology for the modern world', in Holton and Turner (eds), *Talcott Parsons on Ecomony and Society*, pp. 207–34.

—— and Turner, B. (eds) (1986) *Talcott Parsons on Economy and Society*, London: Routledge .

Holub, R.C. (1991) *Jürgen Habermas: Critic in the Public Sphere*, London: Routledge.

Honneth, A. and Joas, H. (eds) (1991) *Communicative Action: Essays on Jürgen Habermas's "The Theory of Communicative Action"*, trans. J. Gaines and D. L. Jones, Oxford: Polity.

Hoós, J. (1993) 'Social Welfare Policy in Hungary during transition in political and economic structures', ms, Budapest University of Economic Sciences.

Horkheimer, M. (1973) 'The Authoritarian State', *Telos*, 115:3–20 (first published 1940).

Horvat, B. (1976) *The Yugolsavian Economic System*, White Plains, NY: International Arts and Sciences Publishers.

Horváth, A. and Szakolczai, A. (1992) *The Dissolution of Communist Power: The Case of Hungary*, London: Routledge.

Hosking, G.A. (1992) *A History of the Soviet Union 1917–91*, London: Fontana.

——, Aves, J. and Duncan, P. (1992) *The Road to Post-Commmunism: Independent Social Movements in the Soviet Union, 1985–1991*, London: Pinter.

Hough, J. (1969) *Soviet Prefects: The Local Party Organs in Industrial Decision-Making*, Cambridge, MA: Harvard University Press.

—— (1976) 'The Brezhnev Era', *Problems of Communism*, XXV,2:1–17.

—— (1978) 'The Cultural Revolution and Western Understandings of the Soviet System', in Fitzpatrick (ed.), *Cultural Revolution in Russia*, pp. 241–53.

Hroch, M. (1993) 'From National Movement to the Fully-formed Nation', *New Left Review*, 198:1–20.

Hughes, J. (1994) 'Regionalism in Russia: The Rise and Fall of Siberian Agreement', *Europe–Asia Studies*, 46,7:1133–63.

Hughes, S. (1994) 'Of Monoliths and Magicians: Economic Transition and Industrial Relations in Hungary', *Work, Employment & Society*, 8,1:69–86.

Jackson, M. (1991) 'Constraints on Systemic Transformation and their Policy Implications', *Oxford Review of Economic Policy*, 7,4:16–25.

Jakóbik, W. (1993) *Restructuring Poland's Industry at the Time of Transformation*, Warsaw: Friedrich Ebert Stiftung.

Janos, A.C. (1991) 'Social Science, Communism and the Dynamics of Political Change', *World Politics*, 44:81–112.

Jarosz, M. (1993) 'Privatization: Its Chances and Threats', in Hausner and Mosur (eds), *Transformation Processes in Eastern Europe*, pp. 91–106.

Jessop, B. (1990) *State Theory: Putting Capitalist States in their Place*, Oxford: Polity.

—— (1992) *From the Keynesian Welfare to the Schumpeterian Workfare State*, Lancaster Regionalism Group: Working Paper 45.

—— (1994) *Regional Economic Development and its Strategies in Post-Socialist Societies: Contexts, Constraints and Conjectures*, Lancaster Working Papers in Political Economy 48.

——, Nielson, K. and Hausner, J. (1993) 'The Protracted Failure of State Socialism and the Incipient Failure of Neo-Liberalism: Reflections on Systemic and Strategic Vacuums', paper to conference on Transfoming Post-Socialist Societies, Cracow Academy of Economics, October 21–23.

Johnston, H. (1994) 'New Social Movements and Old Regional Nationalisms', in Laraña, Johnston and Gusfield (eds), *New Social Movements*, pp. 267–86.

Jowitt, K. (1978) *The Leninist Response to National Dependence*, Berkeley, CA: Institute of International Relations.

—— (1983) 'Soviet Neotraditionalism: The Political Corruption of a Leninist Regime', *Soviet Studies*, XXXV, 3:275–97.

—— (1991) 'Weber, Trotsky and Holmes on the Study of Leninist Regimes', *Journal of International Affairs*, 45,1:31–49.

Kagarlitsky, B. (1988) 'The Dialectic of Reform', *New Left Review*, 169:63–84.

—— (1990) *Farewell Perestroika: A Soviet Chronicle*, trans. R. Simon, London: Verso.

Kaldor, M. (1993) 'Yugoslavia and the New Nationalism', *New Left Review*, 197:96–112.

Kaminski, B. (1991) *The Collapse of State Socialism: The Case of Poland*, Princeton, NJ: Princeton University Press.

Kaplan, R. (1993) *Balkan Ghosts, A Journey Through History* London: Macmillan.

—— (1994) 'The Coming Anarchy', *Atlantic Quarterly*, 273 (February), 44–76.

Karklins, R. (1994) 'Explaining the regime change in the Soviet Union', *Europe–Asia Studies*, 46,1:29–46.

Katsenelinboigen, A. (1977) 'Coloured Markets in the Soviet Union', *Soviet Studies*, 29,1:62–85.

Kazimierz, L. (1993) 'Transition from the Command to the Market System: what went wrong and what to do now?', Vienna: Vienna Institute for Comparative Economic Studies.

Keane, J. (ed.) (1988) *Civil Society: New European Perspectives*, London: Verso.

Kecskemeti, (1969) *The Unexpected Revolution*, Stanford, CA: Stanford University Press.

Kellner, D. (1988) 'Postmodernism as Social Theory', *Theory, Culture and Society*, pp. 239–70.

Kelly, D.R. (1991) 'Gorbachev's Reforms and the Factionalization of Soviet Politics: Can the New System Cope with Pluralism?', in Huber, R. and Kelly, D.R. (eds), *Perestroika-Era Politics*, Armonk, NY: M.E. Sharpe, pp. 79–104.

Kenez, P. (1986) *The Birth of the Propaganda State, 1917–29*, Cambridge: Cambridge University Press.

Kerr, C. (1983) *The Future of Industrial Societies: Convergence or Continuing Diversity?*, Cambridge, MA: Harvard University Press.

Bibliography

—, Dunlop, F.H. and Meyers, C.A. (1960) *Industrialism and Industrial Man*, Cambridge, MA: Harvard University Press.

Kharkhordin, O. (1993) 'De-traditionalization in Russia: The Bolshevik Reformation and the Non-Confessing Self', paper to the Conference on De-Traditionalization: Authority and Self in an Age of Cultural Uncertainty, Lancaster University, 8–10 July.

—— and Gerber, T. (1994) 'Russian Directors' Business Ethic: A Study of Industrial Enterprises in St. Petersburg', *Europe–Asia Studies*, 46,7:1075–1109.

Kiczková, A. and Farkašova, E. (1993), 'The Emancipation of Women: A Concept that Failed', in Funk and Mueller (eds), *Gender Politics and Post-Communism*, pp. 84–94.

Kolakowski, L. (1987) *Main Currents in Marxism*, vol. 3, Oxford: Oxford University Press.

Kolodko, G.W. (1992) 'From Output Collapse to Sustainable Growth in Transition Economies: the Fiscal Implications', *Report to the Fiscal Affairs Department*, Washington, DC: International Monetary Fund.

Konrad, G. (1984) *Antipolitics*, London: Harcourt Brace Jovanovich.

—— and Szelenyi, I. (1979) *Intellectuals on the Road to Class Power*, Brighton: Harvester.

Konstantinova, V. (1992) 'The women's movement in the USSR: a myth or a real challenge?', in Rai et al. (eds), *Women in the Face of Change*, pp. 200–217.

Kopacsi, S. (1986) *In the Name of the Working Class*, London: Fontana.

Kopstein, J. (1994) 'Ulbricht Embattled: the Quest for Socialist Modernity in the Light of New Sources', *Europe–Asia Studies*, 46,4:597–615.

Kornai, J. (1980) *The Economics of Shortage*, Amsterdam: North-Holland.

—— (1986) 'The Hungarian Reform Process: visions, hopes, and reality', *Journal of Economic Literature*, 24:1687–2037.

—— (1990a) *The Road to a Free Economy*, New York: Norton.

—— (1990b) 'The Affinity Between Ownership Forms and Coordination Mechanisms: The Common Experience', *Journal of Economic Perspectives*, 4,3:131–47.

Koronski, A. (1989) 'The Politics of Economic reform in Eastern Europe: The Last 30 years', *Soviet Studies*, XLI,1:1–19.

Körösényi, A. (1991) 'Revival of the Past or a New Beginning? The Nature of Post-Communist Politics', *Political Quarterly*, 62,19: 52–74.

Korosić, M. (1988) *Jugoslavenska kriza* (Yugoslav Crisis), Zagreb: Naprijed.

Korvacs, J.M. (1990) 'Reform Economics: The Classification Gap', *Daedalus*, (Winter) 119,1:215–48.

Kostov, G.R. (1993) 'Changing the Political System in Bulgaria', in Anson et al. (eds), *Ethnicity and Politics*, pp. 224–7.

Kowalik, T. (1991) 'Marketization and Privatization: The Polish Case', *Socialist Register*, pp. 259–77.

—— (1994) 'A Reply to Maurice Glasman', *New Left Review*, 206:133–44.

Kraft, E. (1991) 'Yugoslavia 1986–88: Transition to Crisis', in Fehér and Arato (eds), *Crisis in Eastern Europe*, pp. 455–80.

Krejci, J. (1976) 'Classes and Elites in Socialist Czechoslovakia', in Faber, B.L. (ed.), *The Socialist Structure of Eastern Europe*, New York: Praeger.

Krizan, M. (1987) '"Civil Society" and the Modernization of Soviet-Type Societies', *Praxis International*, 8,1:90–110.

Kumar, K. (1988) *The Rise of Modern Society: Aspects of the Social and Political Development of the West*, Oxford: Basil Blackwell.

Kwasnicki W. (1992) 'Notes on Neoclassical and Evolutionary Perspectives in Economics', *Transformation Processes in Eastern Europe*, Warsaw: Friedrich Ebert Foundation Seminar Papers no. 15 .

Kymlicka, W. and Norman, W. (1994) 'Return of the Citizen', *Ethics*, 104,2:352–81.

Kyn, O., Schrettl, W. and Slamam J. (1979) 'Growth Cycles in Centrally Planned Economies', in Kyn and Schrettl (eds), *On the Stability of Contemporary Economic Systems*, Göttingen: Vandenhock & Ruprechht, pp. 109–32.

Laclau, E. and Mouffe, C. (1985) *Hegemony and Socialist Strategy*, London: Verso.

Laitin, D. (1991) 'The National Uprisings in the Soviet Union', *World Politics*, 44,1:139–77.

Landes, J. (1988) *Women and the Public Sphere in the Age of the French Revolution*, Ithaca, NY: Cornell University Press.

Lane, D. (1979) 'Soviet Industrial Workers: The Lack of a Legitimation Crisis?', in Denitch, B. (ed.), *Legitimation of Regimes*, London: Sage, pp. 177–94.

—— (1988) *Elites and Political Power in the USSR*, Aldershot: Edward Elgar.

—— (1992) *Soviet Society Under Perestroika*, London: Routledge.

LaPalombara, J. (ed.) (1963) *Bureaucracy and Political Development*, Princeton, NJ: Princeton University Press.

Laraña, E., Johnston, H. and Gusfield J.R. (eds) (1994) *New Social Movements: From Ideology to Identity*, Philadelphia, PA: Temple University Press.

Lasecka, J.(1989)'To be a woman in Poland',*The Bloc*, 159/160:21–2.

Lash, S. (1988) 'Discourse or Figure? Postmodernism as a Regime of Signification', *Theory, Culture & Society*, 5,2/3:311–36.

—— and Urry J. (1994) *Economies of Signs and Space*, London: Sage.

Laue, T. von (1971) *Why Lenin? Why Stalin?*, New York: Lippincott.

Lehman, E.W. (1988) 'The Theory of the State vs the State of the Theory', *American Sociological Review*, 53:807–23.

Lemke, C. and Marks, G. (eds) (1992) *The Crisis of Socialism in Europe*, Durham, NC, and London: Duke University Press.

Lenin, V.I. (1969) *What is to be Done?* Moscow: Progress.

Lessig, L. (1994) 'Introduction to Roundtable on the Russian Court', *East European Constitutional Review*, 3,3–4:72–4.

Levitas, A. and Strzalkowski, P. (1990) 'What does "Uwłaszczenie Nomenklatury" (Propertization of the Nomenklatura) really mean'? *Communist Economies*, 2:413–16.

Lewin, M. (1978) 'Society, State and Ideology during the First Five Year Plan', in Fitzpatrick (ed.), *Cultural Revolution in Russia*, pp. 41–77.

—— (1988) *The Gorbachev Phenomenon*, Berkeley, CA: University of California Press.

Lewis, P. (1994) *Central Europe Since 1945*, London: Longman.

Lohr, E. (1993) 'Arkadii Volsky's Political Base', *Europe–Asia Studies*, 45,5: 811–30.

Long, T. (1981) 'On the Class Nature of Soviet-Type Societies: Two Perspectives From Eastern Europe', *Berkeley Journal of Sociology*, 26:167–88.

Lovas, I. and Anderson, K. (1982) 'State Terrorism in Hungary: the Case of Friendly Repression', *Telos*, 54:77–86.

Lovenduski, J. and Woodall, J. (1987) *Politics and Society in Eastern Europe*, London: Macmillan.

Löwy, M. (1979) *Marxisme et Romantisme révolutionnaire*, Paris: Le Sycamore.

—— (1993) 'Why Nationalism?', *Socialist Register*, London: Merlin, pp. 125–38.

Luhmann, N. (1982) *The Differentiation of Society*, New York: Columbia University Press.

—— (1990) *Essays on Self-Reference*, New York: Columbia University Press.

—— (1992) *Risk: A Sociological Theory*, Berlin: de Gruyter.

Luke, T. (1988) 'The Dreams of Deep Ecology', *Telos*, 76:65–92.

Lyotard, J.-F. (1990) *The Postmodern Condition*, Manchester: Manchester University Press.

Mackenzie, D. (1977) 'The Background: Yugoslavia Since 1964', in Simmonds (ed.), *Nationalism in the USSR*, pp. 446–57.

Magas, B. (1992) 'The Destruction of Bosnia-Hertzegovina', *New Left Review*, 196:102–12.

Majkowski, W. (1985) *People's Poland: Patterns of Social Inequality and Conflict*, London: Greenwood.

Malkov, L. (1992) 'How Rational is the Behaviour of Economic Agents in Russia?', *Comparative Economic Studies*, XXXIV, 1:26–40.

Manchin, R. (1988) 'Individual Strategies and Social Conscious- ness', *Social Research*, 55,1–2:77–95.

Mandel, D. (1988) 'Economic Reform and Democracy in the Soviet Union', *Socialist Register*, pp. 132–53.

—— (1991) 'The Struggle for Power in the Soviet Economy', *Socialist Register*, pp. 95–127.

Mandel, E. (1977) *Marxist Economic Theory*, London: Merlin.

—— (1991) *Beyond Perestroika, the Future of Gorbachev's USSR*, London: Verso.

—— (1992) *Power and Money: A Marxist Theory of Bureaucracy* London: Verso.

Marcuse, H. (1971) *Soviet Marxism: A Critical Analysis*, Harmondsworth: Penguin.

Mares, P., Musil, L., and Rausic L. (1994) 'Values and the Welfare State in Czechoslovakia', in Bryant and Mokrzycki (eds), *The New Great Transformation?*, pp. 78–98.

Márkus, M. (1982) 'Overt and Covert Modes of Legitimation', in Rigby and Fehér (eds), *Political Legitimation in Communist Regimes*, pp. 82–93.

Marody, M. (1991) 'On Polish Political Attitudes', *Telos*, 89:109–13.

Marrese, M. (1981) 'The Bureaucratic Response to Economic Fluctuations: An Economic Investigation of Hungarian Investment Policies', *Journal of Policy Modeling*, 3,2:221–43.

Marshall, T.H. (1950/1992) 'Citizenship and Social Class', in Marshall, T.H. and Bottomore, T.B., *Citizenship and Social Class*, London: Pluto Press, pp. 3–54.

Martin, B. and Szelényi, I. (1987) 'Beyond Cultural Capital: Toward a Theory of Symbolic Domination', in Eyerman, R., Svensson, L. and Söderqvist, T. (eds), *Intellectuals, Universities, and the State in Western Modern Societies*, Berkeley, CA: University of California Press, pp. 16–49.

Marx, K. (1973) *Grundrisse*, Harmondsworth: Penguin.

—— (1978) *Karl Marx: Selected Writings*, ed. D. McLellan, Oxford: Oxford University Press.

Matthews, M. (1978) *Privilege in the Soviet Union*, London: Allen & Unwin.

Mayhew, L.H. (1984) 'In Defense of Modernity: Talcott Parsons and the Utilitarian Tradition', *American Journal of Sociology*, 89:1273–305.

McCarthy, T. (1978) *The Critical Theory of Jürgen Habermas*, London: Hutchinson.

McGrew, A. (1993), 'A Global Society?', in Hall et al. (eds), *Modernity and its Futures*, pp.61–116.

McIntyre, R.J. (1988) *Bulgaria: Politics, Economics and Society*, London: Pinter.

Medvedev, R. (1991) 'Politics After the Coup', *New Left Review*, 189:91–110.

Melone, A. and Hays, C. (1994) 'The judicial role in Bulgaria's struggle for human rights', *Judicature*, 77,5:248–53.

Mesjasz, C. (1992) 'Metaphors and Analogies of Stability and Chaos, and Current Changes in Socioeconomic Systems', in *Transformation Processes in Eastern Europe*, Warsaw: Friedrich Ebert Foundation Seminar Papers no. 15, pp. 41–54.

Meyer, A. (1986) 'Coming to Terms with the Past – and with One's Older Colleagues', *The Russian Review*, 46:401–8.

Michnik, A. (1986) *Letters from Prison*, London: University of California Press.

—— (1991) 'Nationalism', *Social Research*, 58,4:758–63.

Milic, A. (1993) 'Women and Nationalism in the Former Yugoslavia', in Funk and Mueller (eds), *Gender Politics and Post-Communism*, pp. 131–7.

Minassian, G. (1994) 'The Bulgarian Economy in Transition: Is There Anything Wrong With Macroeconomic Policy?', *Europe–Asia Studies*, 46,2: 337–52.

Mintzberg, F. (1989) *Mintzberg on Management: Inside our Strange World of Organizations*, New York: Free Press.

Miszlivetz, F. (1991) 'The Unfinished Revolutions of 1989: the Decline of the Nation State?', *Social Research*, 58, 4:781–804.

Misztal, B. (1993), 'Understanding Political Change in Eastern Europe: A Sociological Perspective, *Sociology*, 27,3:451–70.

Mizsei, K. (1992) 'Privatization in Eastern Europe: A Comparative Study of Poland and Hungary', *Soviet Studies*, 44,2:283–96.

Mokrzycki, E. (1983) 'Socialism after Socialism: Continuity in the East European Transition', *Archives Européennes de Sociologie*, XXXIV,1: 108–15.

Mokrzycki, E. (n.d.) 'Class Interests, Redistribution and Corporatism', Polish Academy of Sciences, unpublished.

Moore, B. (1969) *Origins of Dictatorship and Democracy*, London: Penguin.

Morawski, W. (1993) 'Beyond Industrial Democracy: the Coming of Corporatism', in Hausner and Mosur (eds), *Transformation Processes in Eastern Europe*, pp. 243–54.

Morse, C. (1961) 'The Functional Imperatives', in Black (ed.), *The Social Theories of Talcott Parsons*, pp. 100–154.

Mozny, I. (1991) *Proc tak snadno* [Why so Easy?], Prague: SLON.

Mujzel, J. (1993) 'Privatization: The Polish Experience', in Hausner and Mosur (eds), *Transformation Processes in Eastern Europe*, pp. 77–90.

Münch, R. (1990) 'Differentiation, Rationalization, Interpretation: The Emergence of Modern Society', in Alexander and Colomy (eds), *Differentiation Theory and Social Change*, pp. 441–64.

Murray, R. (1992) 'Flexible specialization and development strategy: the relevance for Eastern Europe', in Ernste and Meier (eds), *Regional Development*, pp. 197–218.

Musil, J. (1987) 'Housing Policy and the Sociospatial Structure of Cities in a Socialist Country', *International Journal of Urban and Regional Research*, 11:27–36.

Nagels, J. (1993) *La tiers-mondisation de l'ex-URSS?*, Brussels: Editions de l'Université de Bruxelles.

Nairn, T. (1975) 'Marxism and the Modern Janus', *New Left Review*, 94:3–30.

Naishul, V. (1993) 'Liberalism, Customary Rights and Economic Reforms', *Communist Economies and Economic Transformation*, 5,1:29–44.

Neumann, L. (1992) 'Decentralization and Privatization in Hungary: Opportunities for Flexible Specialization', in Ernste and Meier (eds), *Regional Development*, pp. 233–46.

Nielson, K. (1993) 'Pluralism, Corporatism and the Negotiated Economy: Persepctives for Post-Communism', in Hausner and Mosur (eds), *Transformation Processes in Eastern Europe*, pp. 199–242.

Nikolic, M. (1989) 'Yugoslavia's Failed *Perestroika*', *Telos*, 79:119–28.

Nikolov, S.E. (1993) 'Depoliticization of an over-politicized society', in Anson, J. et al. (eds)., *Ethnicity and Politics in Bulgaria and Israel*, Aldershot: Avebury, pp. 138–48.

Nove, A. (1975) 'Is there a Ruling Class in the USSR?', *Soviet Studies*, XXVII:615–38.

—— (1988) 'Introduction', to Aganbegyan, *The Challenge: The Economics of Perestroika*, pp. xvi–xxvii.

—— (1991) *The Economics of Feasible Socialism Revisited*, London: Harper Collins Academic.

O'Connor, J. (1973) *The Fiscal Crisis of the State*, London: Macmillan.

Offe, C. (1976) 'Crisis of Crisis Management', *International Journal of Politics*, 6:29–67.

—— (1984) *Contradictions of the Welfare State*, Cambridge, MA: MIT Press.

—— (1991) 'Capitalism by Democratic Design? Democratic Theory Facing the Triple Transition in East Central Europe', *Social Research*, 58, 4: 865–92.

—— and Preuss, U. (1991) 'Democratic Institutions and Moral Resources', in Held (ed.), *Political Theory Today*, pp. 143–72.

Okin, S.M. (1991) 'Gender, the Public and the Private', in Held (ed.), *Political Theory Today*, pp. 67–90.

Okun, A. (1981) *Prices and Qualities*, Washington, DC: Brookings.

Olzak, S. (1983) 'Contemporary Ethnic Mobilization', *Annual Review of Sociology*, 9:355–74.

Ost, D. (1989) 'The Transformation of Solidarity and the Future of Central Europe', *Telos*, Spring 79.

—— (1990) *Solidarity and the Politics of Antipolitics: Opposition and Reform in Poland since 1968*, Philadelphia, PA: Temple University Press.

—— (1995) 'Labor, Class and Democracy: Shaping Political Antagonisms in Post-Communist Society', in Crawford, B. (ed.), *Markets, States, Democracy: The Political Economy of Post-Communist Transfromation*, Boulder, CO: Westview, pp. 177–203.

Outhwaite, W. (1994), *Habermas*, Cambridge: Polity.

Pakulski, J. (1986) 'Legitimacy and Mass Compliance: Reflections on Max Weber and Soviet-Type Societies', *British Journal of Political Science*, 16,1:35–56.

Panitch, L. (1994) 'Citizenship, Nationalism and Globalization', *Socialist Register*, pp. 60–93.

Panków, W. (1993) *Work Institutions in Transformation: The Case of Poland 1990–2*, Warsaw: Friedrich Ebert Stiftung .

Panova, R., Gavrilova, R., and Merdzanska, C. (1993) 'Thinking Gender: Bulgarian Women's Im/possibilities', in Funk and Mueller (eds), *Gender Politics and Post-Communism*, pp. 15–23.

Parsons, T. (1961) 'The Point of View of the Author', in Black (ed.), *The Social Theories of Talcott Parsons*, pp. 311–63.

—— (1970) *The Social System*, New York: Free Press.

—— (1971) *The System of Modern Societies*, Englewood Cliffs, NJ: Prentice-Hall.

—— (1986) 'Power and the Social System', in Lukes, S. (ed.), *Power*, Oxford: Basil Blackwell, pp. 94–143.

—— and Smelser N. (1966) *Economy and Society: A Study in the Integration of Economic and Social Theory*, London: Routledge & Kegan Paul.

Pashkin, S. (1994) 'Second Edition of the Constitutional Court', *East European Constitutional Review*, 3,3/4:82–5.

Pateman, C. (1988) *The Sexual Contract*, Cambridge: Polity.

Patkay P. (1993) 'Unions' Role in Privatization and Prospects for Workers to Become Owners in Hungary', *Proceedings of a Conference on Privatization and Transformation in Eastern Europe*, Warsaw: Friedrich Ebert Stiftung, pp. 78–81.

Pedersen, O. (1993) 'Selling the State or Building a Society: Private Property Reforms in West and East', in Hausner and Mosur (eds), *Transformation Processes in Eastern Europe*, pp. 37–76.

Pelczynski, Z.A. (1988) 'Solidarity and the Rebirth of Civil Society in Poland 1976–81', in Keane (ed.), *Civil Society*, pp. 361–80.

Pellicani, L. (1989) 'The Cultural War Between East and West', *Telos*, 89:127–31.

Pestoff, V.A., Hoós, J. and Roxin, V. (1993) *Institutional Changes in Basic Social Services in Central and East Europe During Transition*, Cracow: Academy of Economics.

Petrova, D. (1993) 'The Winding Road to Emancipation in Bulgaria', in Funk and Mueller (eds), *Gender Politics and Post-Communism*, pp. 22–30.

Phelps, E., Frydman, R., Rapaczynski A. and Shleifer, A. (1993) 'Needed mechanisms of corporate governance and finance in Eastern Europe', EBRD Working Paper 1.

Piaget, J. (1965) *Moral Judgement of the Child*, trans. M. Cook, Harmondsworth: Penguin.

Piccone, P. (1989) 'Introduction to the Special Issue on Eastern Europe', *Telos*, 79:2–8.

—— (1990) 'Paradoxes of Perestroika', *Telos*, 84:3–33.

Pickvance C.G. (1988) 'Employers, Labour Markets and Redistribution in Hungary', *Sociology*, 22, 2:193–214.

Pilkington, H. (1992) 'Whose space is it anyway? Youth, gender and civil society in the Soviet Union', in Rai et al. (eds), *Women in the Face of Change*, pp. 105–29.

Pine, F. (1992) 'Uneven burdens, women in rural Poland', in Rai et al. (eds), *Women in the face of Change*, pp. 57–78.

Piore M., and Sabel, C. (1984) *The Second Industrial Divide: Possibilities for Prosperity*, New York: Basic Books.

Podgorecki, A. (1991) 'A Concise Theory of Post-Totalitarianism (Poland 1989/1990)', *Polish Sociological Bulletin*, 2:89–100.

Polanyi, K. (1944) *The Great Transformation*, Boston: Beacon Press.

Pollock, F. (1978) 'State Capitalism: its Possibilities and Limitations', in Arato, A. and Genhardt, E. (eds), *The Essential Frankfurt School Reader*, Oxford: Basil Blackwell, pp. 71–94.

Poulantzas, N. (1968) *Political Power and Social Classes*, London: New Left Books.

Prins, G. (ed) (1990) *Spring in Winter: The 1989 Revolutions*, Manchester: Manchester University Press.

Prpic, G.J. (1977) 'Bogdan Raditsa's "Nationalism in Croatia Since 1964": A Commentary', in Simmonds (ed.), *Nationalism in the USSR*, pp. 470–73.

Pryor, F. (1973) *Property and Industrial Organization in Communist and Capitalist Nations*, Bloomington, IN: Indiana University Press.

Przeworski, A. (1993) *Democracy and the Market: Political and Economic Reforms in Eastern Europe and Latin America*, Cambridge: Cambridge University Press.

Racz, B. and Kukorelli, I. (1995) 'The "Second-generation" Post-Communist Elections in Hungary in 1994', *Europe–Asia Studies*, 47,2:251–80.

Raditsa, B. (1977) 'Nationalism in Croatia Since 1964', in Simmonds (ed.), *Nationalism in the USSR*, pp. 458–69.

Rai, S., Pilkington, H. and Phizacklea A. (eds) (1993) *Women in the Face of Change: The Soviet Union, Eastern Europe and China*, London: Routledge.

Raiklin, E. (1992) 'On Some Aspects of the Soviet-Type Development', *International Journal of Social Economics*, 19/6:42–54.

Rakovski, M. (Janos Kis) (1978) *Towards an East European Marxism*, London: Allison & Busby.

Rakowska-Harmstone, T. (1977) 'The Study of Ethnic Politics in the USSR', in Simmonds (ed.), *Nationalism in the USSR*, pp. 20–36.

Ray, L.J. (1990) 'A Thatcher Export Phenomenon? The Enterprise Culture in Eastern Europe', in Abercrombie, N. and Keat, R. (eds), *Enterprise Culture*, London: Routledge, pp. 114–35.

—— (1993) *Rethinking Critical Theory: Emancipation in an age of global social movements*, London: Sage.

—— (1994) 'The Collapse of Soviet Socialism: Legitimation, Regulation and the New Class', in Brown, P. and Crompton, R. (eds), *A New Europe? Economic Restructuring and Social Exclusion*, London: UCL Press, pp. 196–221.

—— and Reed, M. (1994) 'Max Weber and the dilemmas of modernity', in *Organizing Modernity*, pp. 198–204.

—— (eds) (1994) *Organizing Modernity: New Weberian Perspectives on Work, Organization and Society*, London: Routledge.

Reed, M. (1991) 'The End of Organized Society: A Theme in Search of a Theory', in Blyton, P. and Morris, J. (eds), *A Flexible Future? Prospects for Employment and Organization*, New York: Walter de Gruyter.

Rigby, T.H. (1982) 'Introduction: Political Legitimation, Weber, and Communist Mono-organizational Systems', in Rigby and Fehér (eds), *Political Legitimation in Communist Societies*, pp.1–26.

—— (1986) 'Was Stalin a Disloyal Patron?', *Soviet Studies*, 38:311–24.

—— (1988) 'Staffing the USSR Incorporated: The Origins of the Nomenklatura System', *Soviet Studies*, 40:523–37.

—— (1990a) *The Changing Soviet System*, Aldershot, Edward Elgar.

—— (1990b) *Political Elites in the USSR*, Aldershot, Edward Elgar.

—— and Fehér, F. (eds) (1982) *Political Legitimation in Communist Societies*, London: Macmillan. .

Ringen, S. and Wallace, C. (eds) (1993) *Societies in Transition: East–Central Europe Today*, Prague Papers on Social Responses to Transformation, vol. 1, Prague: Central European University.

Rittersporn, G. (1979) 'The State Against Itself: Socialist Tensions and Political Conflict in the USSR 1936–38', *Telos*, 41:87–104.

—— (1989) 'Reforming the Soviet Union', *Telos*, 79:9–28.

Rizzi, B. (1985) *Bureaucratization of the World* (first published 1939), trans. A. Westoby, New York: Free Press.

Rödel, U., Frankenberg, G. and Dubiel H. (1989) *Die demokratische Frage*, Frankfurt: Suhrkamp Verlag.

Roesler, J. (1994) 'Privatization in East Germany: Experience with the Treuhand', *Europe–Asia Studies*, 46,3:505–17.

Rostowski, J. (1993) 'Mutual Debt of Enterprises', in Dąbrowski (ed.), *The Gaidar Programme*, pp. 183–96.

Rozenbaum, W. (1977) 'The Jewish Question in Poland since 1964', in Simmonds (ed.), *Nationalism in the USSR*, pp. 335–43.

Rueschemeyer, D. (1986) *Power and the Division of Labour*, Cambridge: Polity.

Rumer, B. (1991) 'New Capitalists in the USSR', *Challenge*, 34,3:19–22.

Runciman, W.G. (1995) 'The "Triumph" of Capitalism as a Topic in the Theory of Social Selection', *New Left Review*, 210:33–47.

Rupnik, J. (1988) 'Totalitarianism Revisited', in Keane (ed.), *Civil Society: New European Perspectives*, pp. 263–89.

Rutland, P. (1992–3) 'Thatcherism Czech-style: Transition to Capitalism in the Czech Republic', *Telos*, 94:103–130.

—— (1994) 'Privatization in Russia: One Step Forward: Two Steps Back', *Europe–Asia Studies*, 46,7:1109–33.

Sajo, A. (1994) 'Has State Ownership Truly Abandoned Socialism? The Survival of Socialist Economy and Law in Post-Communist Hungary', in Alexander and Skapska (eds), *A Fourth Way?*, pp. 198–214.

Sakwa, R. (1990) *Gorbachev and His Reforms 1985–1990*, London: Philip Allen.

Sampson, S. (1985–86) 'The Informal Sector in Eastern Europe', *Telos*, 66: 44–67.

Sayer, A. (1995) *Radical Political Economy: A Critique*, Oxford: Basil Blackwell.

Scarborough, H. and Corbett, M.J. (1992) *Technology and Organization*, London: Routledge.

Schepple, K. (1995) 'Women's Rights in Eastern Europe', *East European Constitutional Review*, 4,1:66–70.

Schierup, C.-U. (1992) 'Quasi-proletarians and a Patriarchal Bureaucracy: Aspects of Yugoslavia's Re-peripheralisation', *Soviet Studies*, 44,1:79–99.

Schmitter, P. (1979) 'Modes of Interest Intermediation and Models of Societal Change in Western Europe', in Lehmbruch G. and Schmitter, P. (eds), *Trends Towards Corporatist Intermediation*, London: Sage.

Schoepflin, G. (Schöpflin) (1990) 'The Political Traditions in Eastern Europe', *Daedalus*, Winter, 119,1:55–90.

—— (1991) 'Conservations and Hungary's Transition', *Problems of Communism*, January–April:60–68.

Schuluchter, W. (1985) *The Rise of Western Rationalism: Max Weber's*

Developmental History, Berkeley, CA: University of California Press.

Schumpeter, J.A. (1976) *Capitalism, Socialism and Democracy,* London: Allen & Unwin; originally published 1928.

Sciulli, D. (1992) *Theory of Societal Constitutionalism: Foundations of a non-Marxian critical theory,* New York: Cambridge University Press.

—— and Bould, S. (1992) 'Neocorporatism, Social Integration, and the Limits of Comparative Political Sociology', in Colomy (ed.), *The Dynamics of Social Systems,* pp. 238–68.

Seldon, M. (1983) 'Imposed Collectivization and the Crisis of Agrarian Development in the Socialist States', in Berseson, A. (ed.), *Crisis in the World System,* London: Sage.

Seton, F. (1961) 'The Soviet Economy in Transition', *Problems of Communism,* 10/1:34–41.

Shanin, T. (1983), *The Late Marx,* London: Routledge.

Sharlet, R. (1978) 'Pashukanis and the Withering Away of Law in the USSR', in Fitzpatrick (ed.), *Cultural Revolution in Russia,* pp. 169–88.

Shlapentokh, V. (1988) 'The XXVII Congress: A Case Study of the Shaping of a New Party Ideology', *Soviet Studies,* 40/1:1–20.

Shoup, P. (1989) 'Crisis and Reform in Yugoslavia', *Telos,* 79:129–47.

Sik, E. (1988) 'Reciprocal Exchange of Labour in Hungary', in Pahl, R.E. (ed.), *On Work: Historical, Comparative and Theoretical Approaches,* Oxford: Basil Blackwell, pp. 527–47.

Šik, O. (1976) *The Third Way: Marxist Leninist Theory and Modern Industrial Society,* trans. M. Sling, London: Wildwood House.

Simmel, G. (1990) *The Philosophy of Money,* ed. and trans. D. Frisby and T. Bottomore, London: Routledge.

Simmonds, G.W. (ed.) (1977) *Nationalism in the USSR in the Era of Brezhnev and Kosygin,* Detroit, MI: University of Detroit Press.

Simoneti, M. (1993) 'A Comparative Review of Privatization Strategies in Four Former Socialist Countries', *Europe–Asia Studies,* 45,1:79–102.

Skapska, G. (1994) 'Beyond Constructionism and Rationality of Discovery: Economic Transformation and Institution-Building Processes', in Alexander and Skapska (eds), *A Fourth Way?,* pp. 150–62.

Skilling, G.H. (1966) 'Interest Groups in Communist Politics', *World Politics,* 18:435–51.

Slepyan, K.D. (1993) 'The Limits of Mobilization: Party, State, and the 1927 Civil Defence Campaign', *Europe–Asia Studies,* 45,5:851–868.

Slider, D. (1986) 'More Power to the Soviets? Reform and Local Government in the Soviet Union', *British Journal of Political Science,* 16,4: 495–511.

Smart, B. (1992) *Modern Conditions, Postmodern Controversies,* London: Routledge.

Smith, Adam (1966) *Theory of Moral Sentiments,* reprinted New York: Kelley.

Smith, Alan (1993) *Russia and the World Economy: Problems of Integration,* London: Routledge.

Smith, A.D. (1991) 'National identity and the idea of European unity', *International Affairs,* 68,1:55–76.

Smith, C. and Thompson, P. (eds) (1992) *Labour in Transition: the Labour Process in Eastern Europe and China,* London: Routledge.

Smith, G. (1991) 'The State, Nationalism and the Nationalities Question in the Soviet Republics', in Merridale, C. and Ward, C.(eds), *Perestroika: The Historical Perspective* (London: Edward Arnold), pp. 202–16.

Solomon, S. (ed.) (1983) *Pluralism in the USSR,* London: Macmillan.

Staniszkis, J. (1989) 'The Obsolescence of Solidarity', *Telos,* Summer, 80: 37–50.

—— (1991) 'Political capitalism in Poland', *Eastern European Politics and Societies,* 5,1:127–41.

—— (1992) *The Ontology of Socialism,* Oxford: Clarendon Press.

Stark, D. (1990) 'Privatization in Hungary: From Plan to Market or from plan to Clan?', *Eastern European Politics and Societies,* 4,3:351–92.

—— (1992a) 'Path Dependency and Privatization Strategies in East–Central Europe', *Eastern European Politics and Societies,* 6, 1:17–51.

—— (1992b) 'Bending the Bars of the Iron Cage', in Smith and Thompson (eds), *Labour in Transition,* pp. 41–72.

—— (1993) 'Not By Design: Recombinant Property in Eastern European Capitalism', paper to the conference on Transforming Post-Socialist Societies, Cracow, October 1993.

Starr, S.F. (1978) 'Visionary Town Planning During the Cultural Revolution', in Fitzpatrick (ed.), *Cultural Revolution in Russia,* pp. 207–40.

—— (1988) 'Soviet Union: A Civil Society', *Foreign Policy,* Spring:26–41.

Stepan, A. (1994) 'When Democracy and the Nation-State are Competing Logics: Reflections on Estonia', *Archives Eurpoéennes de Sociologie,* XXXV,1:127–41.

Stillman, E.O. and Bass, R.H. (1955) 'Bulgaria: A Study in Satellite Non-Conformity', *Problems of Communism,* 4:26–33.

Suhij, I. and Lepekhin, V. (1993) 'Evolution of interest representation and the development of labour relations in Russia', Moscow unpublished.

Suny, R. (1990) 'The Revenge of the Past: Socialism and the Ethnic Conflict in Transcaucasia', *New Left Review,* 184:5–36.

Sutela, P. (1994) 'Insider Privatization in Russia: Speculations on Systemic Change', *Europe–Asia Studies,* 46,3:417–37.

Svitak, I. (1982) 'Lessons from Poland', *Telos* 52:194–199.

Swain, N. (1987) 'Hungarian Agriculture in the Early 1980s: Retrenchment Followed by Reform', *Soviet Studies,* 39:24–39.

—— (1992) *Hungary: The Rise and Fall of Feasible Socialism*, London: Verso.

Szabó, M. (1994) 'Greens, Cabbies, and Anti-Communists: Collective Action during Regime Transition in Hungary', in Laraña, Johnston and Gus field (eds), *New Social Movements: From Ideology to Identity*, pp. 287–303.

Szacki, J. (1991) 'Polish Democacy: Dreams and Reality', *Social Research*, 58,4:711–22.

Szalai, E. (1991) 'Integration of Special Interests in the Hungarian Economy: The Struggle Between Large Companies, the Party and State Bureaucracy', *Journal of Comparative Economics*, 15:304–24.

—— (1994) 'The power structure in Hungary after the political transition', in Bryant and Mokrzycki (eds), *The New Great Transformation*, pp. 120–43.

Szalai, J. (1986) 'Inequalities in access to health care in Hungary', *Social Sceience and Medicine*, vol.22, 2:135–140.

—— (1989) 'The Dominance of the Economic Approach in Reform Propos als in Hungary and Some of the Implications of the Crisis of the 80s', in Gathy, V. (ed.), *State and Civil Society: Relationships in Flux*, Budapest: Institute of Sociology.

—— (1992) 'Social participation in Hungary in the context of restructuring and liberalization', in Deacon, B. (ed.), *Social Policy, Social Justice and Citizenship in Eastern Europe*, Aldershot: Gower, pp. 37–55.

Szamuely, T. (1988) *The Russian Tradition*, London: Fontana.

Szelenyi, I. (1979) 'Social Inequalities in State Socialist Redistributive Economies', *International Journal of Comparative Sociology*, XIX,1/2: 63–87.

—— (1983) *Urban Inequalities under State Socialism*, Oxford: Oxford University Press.

—— (1984) in the 'Review Symposium', *Telos*, 60:166–73.

—— (1988) *Socialist Entrepreneurs: Embourgeoisement in Rural Hungary*, London: Polity.

—— (1990) 'Alternative Futures for Eastern Europe: The Case of Hungary', *Eastern European Politics and Societies*, 4,2:231–54.

—— and Mankin, R. (1987) 'Social Policy under State Socialism', in Rein, M. et al., *Stagnation and Renewal in Social Policy*, Armonk, NY: M.E. Sharpe, pp. 81–92.

—— and Szelenyi, S. (1991) 'The Vacuum in Hungarian Politics: Classes and Parties', *New Left Review*, 187:121–38.

Sztompka, P. (1993) *The Sociology of Social Change*, Oxford: Basil Blackwell.

Tardos, M. (1989) 'Economic Organizations and Ownership', *Acta Oeconomica*, 40,1–2:17–37.

Tarkowska, E. and Tarkowski, J. (1991) 'Civil Society or Amoral Familism?', *Telos*, 89:103–6.

Tarkowski J. (1981) 'Political Clientelism in Poland', in Eisenstadt, S.N. and Lemarchand, R. (eds), *Political Clientelism, Patronage and Development*, London: Sage, pp. 173–90.

—— (1989) 'Old and New Patterns of Corruption in Poland and the USSR', *Telos*, 80:51–62.

—— (1990) 'Endowment of the nomenklatura', *Innovation*, 4:89.

Thompson E.P. (1991) *Customs in Common*, London: Merlin.

Thompson, J.B. and Held, D. (eds) (1982) *Habermas: Critical Debates*, London: Macmillan.

Thurston, R.W. (1986) 'Fear and Belief in the USSR's "Great Terror"', *Slavonic Review*, 45:213–34.

Ticktin, H.H. (1976) 'The Class Structure of the USSR and the Elite', *Critique*, Spring, 9:37–61.

—— (1987) 'The Political Economy of Class in the Transitional Epoch', *Critique*, 20/21:7–26.

—— (1992) *Origins of the Crisis in the USSR*, Armonk, NY, and London: M.E. Sharpe.

Timofeev, L. (1985) *Soviet Peasants (or the Peasants' Art of Starving)*, Washington, DC: Telos Press.

Tinbergen, J. (1959), *Selected Papers*, edited by Klassen, L.H., Koyck, L.M. and Witteren, H.J., Amsterdam: North Holland.

Tittenbrun, J. (1993) *The Collapse of 'Real Socialism' in Poland*, London: Janus.

Todorova, E. (1993) 'Survival and Adjustment: The main ideology of contemporary Bulgarians', in Anson et al. (eds), *Ethnicity and Politics in Bulgaria and Israel*, pp. 173–80.

Torfing, J. (1991) 'A Hegemony approach to capitalist regulation', in Bertramsen, R., Peter, J., Thomsen F. and Torfing J.(eds), *State Economy and Society*, London: Unwin Hyman, pp. 35–93.

Tosics, I. (1988) 'Inequalities in East European Cities: Can Redistribution ever be Equalising...?', *International Journal for Urban and Regional Research*, 12:133–6.

Touraine, A. (1990) 'The Idea of Revolution', in Featherstone (ed.), *Global Culture*, pp. 121–42.

Turner, B.S. (1986) 'Parsons and his critics', in Holton and Turner (eds), *Talcott Parsons on Economy and Society*, pp. 179–206.

—— (1990) 'Outline of a theory of citizenship', *Sociology*, 24,2:189–217.

—— (1992) 'Citizenship, Social Change and the Neofunctionalist Paradigm', in Colomy (ed.),*The Dynamics of Social Systems*,pp.214–37.

—— (1994) 'Max Weber on Individualism, Bureaucracy and Despotism: On

Political Authoritarianism and Contemporary Politics', in Ray and Reed (eds), *Organizing Modernity*, pp. 122–40.

Unger, A.L. (1969) 'Stalin's Removal of the Leading Stratum', *Soviet Studies*, 20:321–30.

Vajda, M. (1988) 'East–Central European Perspectives', in Keane (ed.), *Civil Society and the State*, pp. 333–60.

Varese, F. (1994) 'Is Sicily the Future of Russia? Private Protection and the Rise of the Russian Mafia', *Archives Européennes de Sociologie*, 35,2:224–58.

Voskamp, U. and Wittke, V. (1991) 'Industrial Restructuring in the Former GDR', *Politics and Society*, 19,3:341–71.

Voslensky, M. (1984) *Nomenklatura: Anatomy of the Soviet Ruling Class*, London: Bodley Head.

Vujacic, V. and Zaslavsky, V. (1991) 'The Causes of Disintegration in the USSR and Yugoslavia', *Telos*, 88:120–40.

Walby, S. (1994) 'Is Citizenship Gendered?', *Sociology*, 28,2:379–95.

Wałęsa, L. (1988) *A Path of Hope: An Autobiography*, London: Pan.

Walicki, A. (1991a) 'From Stalinism to Post-Communist Pluralism: the Case of Poland', *New Left Review*, 185:92–121.

—— (1991b) 'Notes on Jaruzelski's Poland', in Fehér and Arato (eds), *The Crisis in Eastern Europe*, pp. 335–91.

Walker, M. (1988) *The Waking Giant: The Soviet Union Under Gorbachev*, London: Sphere.

Wallace, C., Chmuliar, O. and Sidorenko, E. (1995) 'The Eastern Frontier of Western Europe: Mobility in the Buffer Zone', Prague: Central European University, unpublished ms.

Waller, M. (1992) 'Groups, Interests and Political Aggregation in East Central Europe', *Journal of Communist Studies* 8,1:128–47.

Watson, P. (1993) 'Eastern Europe's Silent Revolution: Gender', *Sociology*, 27,3:471–88.

Webb, B. and Webb, S. (1936) *Soviet Communism: A New Civilization?*, 2 vols, London: Longman.

Weber, M. (1976) *The Protestant Ethic and the Spirit of Capitalism*, London: Unwin Hyman.

—— (1978) *Economy and Society*, 2 vols, London: University of California Press.

Webster, L. and Charap, J. (1993) *A Survey of Private Manufacturers in St. Petersburg*, London: EBRD Working Paper 5.

Weick, K.E. (1979) *The Social Psychology of Organizing*, Reading, MA: Addison-Wesley.

Weitman, S. (1992) 'Thinking the Revolutions of 1989', *British Journal of Sociology*, 43:11–24.

Wellmer, A. (1971) *Critical Theory of Society*, London: Herder & Herder.

—— (1983) 'Reason, Utopia and the Dialectic of Enlightenment', *Praxis International* 3:83–107.

Whetten, L.L. (1989) *Interaction of Political and Economic Reforms within the Eastern Bloc*, London: Crane Russak.

White, S. (1990) 'Democratization in the USSR', *Soviet Studies*, 42,1:3–25.

—— (1992a) 'The Soviet Union: Gorbachev, *Perestroika* and Socialism', *Journal of Communist Studies*, 8:23–49.

—— (1992b) *Gorbachev and After*, Cambridge: Cambridge University Press.

——, Gill, G. and Slider, D. (1993) *The Politics of Transition: Shaping a Post-Soviet Future*, Cambridge: Cambridge University Press.

Wieriorka, M. (1984) *Les Juifs, la Pologne, et Solidarnosc*, Paris: Denoel.

Wildt, A. (1979), 'Totalitarian State Capitalism', *Telos*, 41:33–58.

Wiles, P. (1960) 'Rationality, the Market, Decentralization and the Territorial Principle', in Grossman (ed.), *Value and Plan*, pp. 184–203.

—— (1974) *The Distribution of Income East and West*, Amsterdam: North Holland.

Willerton, J.P. (1987) 'Patronage Networks and Coalition-Building in the Brezhnev Era', *Soviet Studies*, 39:175–204.

Williams, J. (1994) 'Privatization as a Gender Issue', in Alexander and Skapska (eds), *A Fourth Way?*, pp. 215–50.

Williamson, P.G. (1989) *Corporatism in Perspective*, London: Sage.

Winiecki, J. (1986a) 'Are Soviet-type Economies Entering an Era of Long-Term Decline', *Soviet Studies*, 38:325–48.

—— (1986b) 'Soviet-type Economies: Considerations for the Future', *Soviet Studies*, 38:543–61.

—— (1994) 'East–Central Europe: A Regional Survey – The Czech Repub lic, Hungary, Poland, and Slovakia', *Europe–Asia Studies*, 46,5:709–35.

Wistrich, R. (1992) *Antisemitism: The Longest Hatred*, London: Thames Mandarin.

Wittfogel, K. (1959) *Oriental Despotism: A Comparative Study of Total Power*, New Haven, CT: Yale University Press.

Wojtyna, A. (1993) 'Privatization and Industrial Policy in Transforming the Economy', in Musil J. (ed.), *Privatization and Transformation in Eastern Europe: A Trade Union Perspective*, Warsaw: Friedrich Ebert Stiftung, pp. 82–108.

Wolnicki, M. (1989) 'Self-Government and Ownership in Poland', *Telos*, 80:63–78.

Woods, D. (1992) 'The Crisis of the Italian Party–State and the Rise of the Lombard League', *Telos*, 93:111–26.

World Bank (1990) *Bulgaria Reconnaissance Mission*, Aide-memoire.

Yakovlev, A. (1993) *The Fate of Marxism in Russia*, trans. C.A. Fitzpatrick, London: Yale University Press.

Yasin, Y. (ed.) (1992) *Reforms in Russia: Stage Two*, Moscow: The Experts' Institute, Russian Union of Industrialists and Entrepreneurs.

Yuval-Davis N. (1991) 'The Citizenship Debate: Women, Ethnic Processes and the State', *Feminist Review*, 39:58–68.

Zaslavskaya, T. (1984) 'The Novosibirsk Report', *Survey*, 28,1:88–108.

Zaslavsky, V. (1982) *The Neo-Stalinist State: Class, Ethnicity and Consensus in Soviet Society*, Armonk, NY: M.E. Sharpe.

—— (1985) 'The Soviet World System: Origins, Evolution, Prospects for Reform', *Telos*, 65:3–22.

Zeleny, M. (1985) 'Spontaneous Social Orders', *International Journal of General Systems*, 11,2:117–31.

Zemtsov, I. (1976) *Partiya ili mafiya? Razvorannaya respublika* [Party or Mafia? The Republic of Plunder] Paris: Les Editeurs réunis.

—— (1985) *Policy Dilemmas and the Struggle for Power in the Kremlin: The Andropov Period*, Virginia: Hero Books.

Ziółkowski, J (1990) 'The Roots, Branches and Blossoms of Solidarnosc', in Prins (ed.), *Spring in Winter*, pp. 40–62.

Žižek, S. (1989) *The Sublime Object of Ideology*, London: Verso.

—— (1990) 'East Europe's Republics of Gilead', *New Left Review*, 183: 50–62.

Zloch-Christy, I. (1987) *Debt Problems of Eastern Europe*, Cambridge: Cambridge University Press.

Zolo, D. (1990–91) 'Autopoiesis: Critique of a Postmodern Paradigm', *Telos*, 86:61–80.

Zon, H. van (1992) *Alternative Senarios for Central Europe*, Brussels: FAST Commission of the European Communities, Science Research and Development.

—— (1993) 'Problems of Transitology: Towards a New Research Agenda and New Research Practice', paper to the Conference on Transforming Post-Socialist Societies, Cracow Academy of Economics, October 1993.

Zuboff, S. (1988) *In the Age of the Smart Machine: The Future of Work and Power*, London: Heinemann.

Index